Turning Up the Flame

Turning Up the Flame

Philip Roth's Later Novels

Edited by
Jay L. Halio and Ben Siegel

DELAWARE

Newark: University of Delaware Press

Associated University Presses
2010 Eastpark Boulevard
Cranbury, NJ 08512

The paper used in this publication meets the requirements of the American National Standard for Permanence of Paper for Printed Library Materials Z39.48-1984.

Library of Congress Cataloging-in-Publication Data

Turning up the flame : Philip Roth's later novels / edited by Jay L. Halio and Ben Siegel.
    p.   cm.
    Includes bibliographical references and index.
    ISBN 0-87413-902-3 (alk. paper)
    1. Roth, Philip—Criticism and interpretation.   I. Halio, Jay L. II. Siegel, Ben, 1925–
PS3568.O855Z94   2005
813'.54—dc22   2004021038

PRINTED IN THE UNITED STATES OF AMERICA

Contents

Preface

PHILIP ROTH IS THAT LITERARY RARITY—AN AMERICAN NOVELIST WHO gets better with age. In recent years he has astounded critics with both the quality and the quantity of his literary output. Roth has been publishing fiction for over four decades. He has never been satisfied merely to repeat himself, to keep mining the same themes and material. Some critics did feel that he was doing just that in his Zuckerman novels. Apparently stung by such criticism, Roth set out to explore new territory, to make each new novel an experimental, challenging, even outrageous effort. He has succeeded beyond all critical expectations—in terms of quantity, quality, and dramatic effect. The time would appear ripe then to take a closer look at Roth's more recent or "later" fiction—that is, his writings of the last two decades or so. That is the intent of this modest gathering of critical essays. We are unaware of any other essay collection devoted primarily to Roth's fiction of the last two decades. To gather these essays, we organized panels at meetings of the American Literature Association and the Modern Language Association, and otherwise requested, pleaded, and cajoled some of the leading Roth specialists to contribute essays to this volume. We are proud of what we are here able to offer to those readers who have an interest in the fiction of one of America's premier active novelists.

Co-editor Ben Siegel starts us off with a discussion of Roth's primary attitudes and approaches to writing fiction. In "Reading Philip Roth: Facts and Fancy, Fiction and Autobiography," he offers a brief overview of Roth's interplay of the real and the nonreal, especially his mix of the personal or autobiographical and the fictional or imaginative. Siegel discusses some of the parallels between Roth's writing and that of Saul Bellow and E. L. Doctorow, who use some of the same techniques. All three tease their readers with protagonists who often strongly resemble themselves in terms of age and circumstance, time and place. But when questioned by interviewers about the similarities, each novelist will insist that, while he may have borrowed certain details from his own life, he should not be confused with his hero or his hero with him. What these writers are doing, Siegel suggests, "is underscoring the interplay between fact and fiction, history and literature, the real and imaginative, and often between the present and past. And because they are Jewish, they frequently will draw from the general Jewish experience in America." In recent years this has meant that they "have turned increasingly to Israel's triumphs and tensions and to what is undoubtedly for Jews the most traumatic experience of the twentieth century, if not of all time: the Holocaust."

We are fully aware, of course, that Roth's earlier novels cannot be totally ignored, and our contributors have seen to it that they are not. Comparisons with what Roth did earlier in his career and what he is doing now are very relevant. Most of our essayists, therefore, refer usefully to the earlier fiction, showing how the later novels compare or contrast with them, or at times build on them. For example, Debra Shostak does just that in her "Philip Roth's Fictions of Self-Exposure." A salient feature of Roth's recent writing, as already mentioned, is his ongoing need to experiment. He appears to approach each new book as a challenge not merely to explore but also to extend the boundaries of fiction by finding new and different ways of depicting modern human relationships by means of biography and autobiography, contemporary history and politics, humor and dialogue, and varied other narrative modes.

One major theme that runs through Roth's fiction and takes many forms is the nature of the self and the problems of self-worth or self-identity. This theme is by no means unique to modern fiction, much less to Roth's later works. Certainly Neil Klugman in *Goodbye, Columbus* (1959) and Gabe Wallach in *Letting Go* (1962) were not the first modern young men to set out in quest of self-discovery. But at those early points and increasingly in his later fiction, Roth gives the theme some interesting twists as he introduces elements of his own life into his novels. In *Zuckerman Unbound* (1985), he presents the novelist Nathan Zuckerman, whom he had introduced in *My Life as a Man* (1974) and in *The Ghost Writer* (1984), as a kind of facsimile of himself. Zuckerman is the author of a notorious novel called *Carnovsky* that seems very much in substance and reputation like Roth's own *Portnoy's Complaint.* But as Debra Shostak argues, Roth is here playing with autobiography, making the most of anticipated reader inclinations to interpret factually what is presented fictionally. Roth's tendency to mingle fiction and fact reaches its culmination in *Deception* (1990) and *Operation Shylock* (1993), wherein a character named "Philip" and another called "Philip Roth" appear as the chief protagonists. The "peculiar tensions" in these novels, as Shostak refers to them, are among the most intriguing in contemporary fiction. Indeed, her analysis of the later fiction is both trenchant and illuminating.

In her "Autobiography: False Confession?" Margaret Smith focuses also on Roth's ways of introducing autobiography or certain "facts" into his fiction and transforming them imaginatively into narrative. She argues "that Roth does not write autobiography as such and that his fiction is not a mere rendition of facts colored by his imagination. On the contrary, Roth contrives to blur the boundaries of both fiction and autobiography as a narrative strategy." Consequently, she rejects the supposition of those critics and readers who view Nathan Zuckerman (or any of Roth's other protagonists) "as Roth's hidden, or second, self." Instead, Smith accepts Roth's claim that Zuckerman is merely a narrative construct whose task is merely "to show the power harnessed by fiction to 'illuminate life.'" Roth explains, and Smith agrees, that "Zuckerman is an act," an example of "the art of impersonation," one that "prohibits narrator-figures such as Zuckerman and his fellow protagonists from relaying any aspect of 'truth' due to their singular fictional capacity within the text."

The international appeal of Roth's fiction is underscored here by the appearance of a noted Indian specialist in American literature. G. Neelakantan pursues further this topic of self-exposure and the interplay of autobiography and fiction in his "Textualizing the Self: Adultery, Blatant Fictions, and Jewishness in Philip Roth's *Deception*." Not only is this novel significant for the first appearance of "Philip" as a character in his own right, but also for its unusual narrative style. Written mostly in dialogue, unlike any of his previous novels, it shows Roth's continuing interest in experimentation and contains the famous indictment by "Philip" of critics who repeatedly misinterpret his work. "I write fiction and I'm told it's autobiography, I write autobiography and I'm told it's fiction, so if I'm so dim and they're so smart, let *them* decide what it is or it isn't." But of course that is precisely the confusion Roth has worked so diligently to create.

Alexis Kate Wilson, like our other authors, is interested in Roth's treatment of the complex questions of Jewish identity. In "The Travels of the American *Talush*," she centers on Roth's use of the modernist trope of the artist, in the person of a Jew who stands outside his culture to function as an observer or commentator. She is intrigued by the ways Roth both echoes and alters this modernist trope so that "the modernist themes of marginality and alterity" inevitably surface for him, even in Israel. For even in that Jewish homeland, Roth's American Jews find themselves "insiders and outsiders at the same time." Roth explores this Jewish American relationship with Israel most notably in *The Counterlife*. Here he devotes five chapters to "overlapping and contradicting stories about Nathan Zuckerman and his brother, Henry." Writing in this postmodern spirit, Wilson states, Roth has in essence "created an antinovel."

In "Texts, Lives, and Bellybuttons: Philip Roth's *Operation Shylock* and the Renegotiation of Subjectivity," Derek Parker Royal continues the discussion of self-awareness and self-identity. He does so with an in-depth examination of subjectivity, specifically ethnic subjectivity. "Ever since *My Life as a Man*," notes Royal, Roth "has engaged in a relentless negotiation between life and art, a metafictional no-man's land where narrative is an uncertain combination of creator and creation." As does Shostak, Royal rejects the contention of some critics that the "autobiographical" novels are merely narcissistic, and he argues instead that Roth is engaged in a more philosophical investigation of reality, truth, and identity. Like Kafka, a writer he much admires, Roth deliberately ponders the written world and the unwritten world, the world of fiction and the world of fact—or what we think of as fact.

Roth presents this issue most pointedly in *The Facts: A Novelist's Autobiography* (1988). He wrote this personal account when he was emerging from a Halcion-induced depression and needed to find his way back to fiction—a situation both Shostak and Royal treat in their essays. Even here, Roth involves his primary alter ego, Nathan Zuckerman, by starting his little book with a letter to him asking for his opinion of this venture into life writing. He ends his memoir with Zuckerman's reply—a long argument summed up in two words: "Don't publish." Zuckerman insists that Roth is an impersonator, not an autobiographer; that he needs Zuckerman as much as Zuckerman needs him. Roth appears to agree. He admits that *The Facts* begs more questions than it answers, and that "Memories of the past are not memories of facts but memories of your imaginings of the facts." English critic Frank Kermode also seems to agree. In his memoir *Not Entitled* (1995), Kermode, too, speaks perceptively of the inevitable mixture of fact and fiction, or what he calls fantasy, when one tries to write autobiography and also write well at the same time.

These comments on the inevitable mingling of fact and fiction would seem then to characterize most autobiography—including, ironically enough, Claire Bloom's *Leaving a Doll's House* (1996), her no-holds-barred attack on Roth, their marriage, and their life together. Roth wrote *The Facts* well before Bloom's book appeared and well before she and Roth were married and divorced, though they had been living together for many years. Royal calls her account a countertext to Roth's own, notwithstanding that *The Facts* does not extend into Roth's life as far as his liaison with Bloom. Whether *I Married a Communist* (1998) is a countertext to that countertext, Royal does not say, nor does Shostak. Instead, Shostak and Royal concentrate on *Operation Shylock*, subtitled *A Confession*, which is not a confession in the usual sense of the term, though it is intended to read like one.

But in "Death, Mourning, and Besse's Ghost: From Philip Roth's *The Facts* to *Sabbath's Theater*," James Mellard returns our attention to Roth's memoir writing proper and that mode's implications for his later fiction. He shows how *The Facts* and *Patrimony*, Roth's account of his father's last years and death, are closely related. Mellard points up a happening easily overlooked in *Patrimony* and certainly not immediately apparent in *The Facts*. He notes that Besse Roth's death in 1981 underlay much of what Philip wrote in both books and also motivated *The Facts* "subterraneanly." These two autobiographical works, then, are thus connected by the deaths of his parents—unconsciously in the first, overtly in the second.

Mellard's Lacanian analysis of these two books is marked by other useful and penetrating insights. The same can be said of his discussion of Roth's symbolic dream of Herman Roth as a silent, disabled warship drifting toward the shore, or of the 1937 photograph of Roth, his father, and his brother appearing on the dust jacket and as the frontispiece of *Patrimony*. Skipping over the intervening fiction, Mellard then goes directly to *Sabbath's Theater*, which he also associates with Roth's biographical work. He views this novel as the legacy of the mother, and describes it as "a history of unresolved mourning that drives Mickey Sabbath away from the family and into a lifelong search for satisfaction of desire that comes with a successful resolution of the Oedipus complex." Is Mickey Sabbath yet another Roth surrogate? Mellard does not say so, nor does he hint at any such suggestion (but see Shostak on her representation of the "transgressive features of the 'Roth' persona"). Mellard also does not mention the novel's epigraph, but it, too, connects this book with the other two.

It comes from Shakespeare's *The Tempest*: "Every third thought shall be my grave." In fact, so drenched in death is *Sabbath's Theater* that some readers were moved to wonder about the state of Roth's physical and metal health. His three subsequent and very different novels provided a ready answer.

Andrew Gordon shifts our attention from Roth's obsession with death to his fascination with the pastoral. In his "The Critique of Utopia in Philip Roth's *The Counterlife* and *American Pastoral*," Gordon argues that, in these two novels, Roth is "deconstructing some contemporary versions of the pastoral." Roth's satiric, subversive bent moves him to reject "utopian longings" and to validate "perpetual struggle, complexity, and uncertainty in both life and art." This is especially true in *The Counterlife*. For in *American Pastoral*, "despite his demolition of the American dream," Roth still clings to "certain pastoral ideals"—that is, he contrasts "the wonderful lost America of his Newark childhood in the 1940s to the fallen America of the 1960s and 1970s." As does Nathan Zuckerman, Roth has to keep fighting his own attraction to "pastoral illusions." Part of his struggle is directed at "the persistent appeal of pastoral fantasies of innocence; defeat one and another emerges in its place." In *The Counterlife*, Roth sees all individuals "as fiction makers." Thus he "forces us to reconsider the nature of the utopias we all script, the counterlives we would prefer to live." Each novel section "constitutes a critique of a utopia which is constructed only to be deconstructed." These utopias include "the myths of romantic love, of Zionism, and of 'Christendom.' He rejects all these as fantasies of innocence, retreats to the womb." The single utopia "Roth will allow is that of fiction making itself: the power of the human mind endlessly to imagine and to re-imagine our lives."

The next four essays also treat *American Pastoral* from various perspectives. For Bonnie Lyons, the novel is an American tragedy. In her "Philip Roth's American Tragedies," she argues that *American Pastoral*, *I Married a Communist*, and *The Human Stain* "establish Roth "as our most important author of significant American tragedies." She is "not using the word 'tragedy' to indicate a type of drama," she explains, "but to assert that these are novels which share a deeply tragic vision or tragic version of reality." All three novels "depict heroes whose fates are intricately enmeshed in their specifically American settings and times." Thus they are for her truly "*American* tragedies" that depict "man at the limits of his sovereignty." In addition, all three center "on the hero's will to 'fight against his destiny

. . . and state his case before God or his fellows.' Each embodies then the crux of the tragic vision."

In "Newark Maid Feminism in Philip Roth's *American Pastoral,*" Marshall Bruce Gentry focuses on feminist aspects of the novel, an approach that may surprise readers who have hitherto, rightly or wrongly, regarded Roth as a misogynist. Alluding to M. M. Bakhtin's theory of how, on occasion, characters win battles with their authors, Gentry argues that Roth experiments with ways that give women "room to show him up." If he sometimes tries too hard to do this, as in *Deception,* Roth succeeds better in *American Pastoral* where, according to Gentry, the women "seem to win a battle over the dominant male voices of its main character, Swede Levov, the narrator Nathan Zuckerman, and even, to some extent, Philip Roth himself." Gentry makes a strong case for his point of view, but he is acutely aware that not all readers will agree with him. Indeed, he cites a number of reviewers who do not. Gentry reveals how Roth leads the reader early on to believe that he sides with Zuckerman, who is both the narrator and in a way the "inventor" of the story, as well as with Swede, the principal character. But then, as the female characters start responding to Swede, the reader notices how much more aware Roth is than Zuckerman of the limits of Swede's world. Most reviewers have seen the novel as chiefly a critique of the 1960s culture of permissiveness. However, Gentry adds a new dimension to that perception. He argues that Swede and all he represents are at least indirectly responsible for the nightmarish experiences that followed. And this point, Gentry insists, is made mainly through the women in the novel.

Timothy Parrish, in focusing on "the end of identity" in *American Pastoral,* develops further the theme that the earlier contributors have emphasized. He begins by maintaining that Roth's definition of the self, which Parrish calls "postmodern," makes it hard to see how his books endorse a particular point of view, "Jewish" or any other. On the other hand, as in *Patrimony,* where Roth buries his father in the traditional burial shroud, and *Operation Shylock,* in which Roth confronts his double in Israel, his books of the 1990s seem to point to the author accepting his identity as a "Jewish writer." This is especially true in *American Pastoral,* which Parrish views as a kind of tribal narrative. For Zuckerman identifies with Swede Levov as a member of our "tribe," and the narrative becomes an "elegy" for the sort of Jewish identity that Roth's earlier novels tended to undermine.

Another element that has always fascinated Roth's readers is his use of the erotic. In "Eros and Death in Roth's Later Fiction," co-editor Jay Halio offers a brief but fresh look at Roth's recent linking of the erotic and death, most notably in *Sabbath's Theater* and *The Dying Animal.* "Whether these preoccupations result from Roth's own advancing age and past serious illnesses," notes Halio, "I cannot say, though it would hardly surprise me if that were true. We have learned, however, not to make too close a connection between fiction and autobiography. Roth has always been emphatic on that point."

In the same vein, Ellen Gerstle meets head-on the oft-repeated charges of obscenity, misogyny, and sexual perversion leveled at Roth through the years. In "*The Dying Animal:* The Art of Obsessing or Obsessing about Art?" she points out that this novel "does call up questions about obscenity and art, subjects that often have drawn him into conflict with his readers." Such complaints, she states, have a "disturbingly familiar ring, echoing earlier rebukes of misogyny and sexual perversion." Other critics claim Roth here is "overworking past themes." Gerstle concedes that Roth "was looking at an old theme: the nature of obsession." But she feels "he was doing so in a way that created a rich subtext to the obvious plot line of a May-December love affair." In addition, the "novel is as much about dying," she states, as it is about sexual desire, individual freedom, and artistic expression. These are all "signature Rothian themes," she concludes, so that it is difficult to be certain "whether *The Dying Animal* represents Roth's discourse on the art of obsessing or Roth obsessing about art."

It is clear, then, that we have assembled here a group of strong-minded critics with fresh and distinctive ways of reading Roth's later novels. Of course, each reader will add his or her own interpretations to the mix.

Jay Halio
Ben Siegel

NOTE: The essays by Debra Shostak, G. Neelakantan, Derek Parker Royal, James Mellard, Marshall Bruce Gentry, and Timothy L. Parrish originally appeared in *Shofar* 19 (Fall 2000), and are reprinted here with permission. Philip Roth's novel, *The Plot Against America* (2004), a satirical political fantasy involving the Roth family, appeared after this volume was in production.

Turning Up the Flame

Introduction: Reading Philip Roth: Facts and Fancy, Fiction and Autobiography— A Brief Overview

Ben Siegel

Serious students of literature are keenly aware that all writing that passes for fiction contains a good deal of history. They also know that novelists and short-story writers draw upon both past and present authors and events. Writers read the newspapers and news magazines and watch television and internet news reports, in search of ideas and characters they can filter through their creative imaginations and present anew in their own long and short narratives. Perhaps most importantly, they draw upon their own lives and the lives of family members and friends. We also know that those who write history do some of the same things as they sift through the archives, manuscripts, chronicles, and artifacts of the past. If they are good historians, they, too, filter their findings through their own creative imaginations to produce those writings they and we call "history." Often enough, it is difficult to tell the difference between a compelling work of history and a moving work of fiction. This is especially true of that form of history we call autobiography.

These familiar observations can be described as truisms, but they apply very strongly to much of the fiction being published by contemporary American writers, especially Jewish American fiction writers. Of the latter group, three of the most prominent are Saul Bellow, E. L. Doctorow, and Philip Roth. These three novelists like to tease their readers by presenting protagonists who often strongly resemble themselves in terms of time and place, age and circumstance. In other words, the basic details of their protagonists' lives strongly parallel their own. But when questioned by interviewers about the similarities, each novelist will reply that while he may have borrowed certain details from his own life, he should not be confused with his hero or his hero with him. What these writers are doing then is underscoring the interplay between fact and fiction, history and literature, the real and imaginative, and often between the present and past. And because they are Jewish, they frequently will draw from the general Jewish experience in America. In earlier years, Jewish writers relied upon the immigrant experience of their grandparents, parents, or their own. The next generation then tended to focus on America's Depression years of the 1930s, and then on the years following World War II—with their Cold War politics, civil rights struggles, and feminist movement. But in recent years America's Jewish writers have turned increasingly to Israel's triumphs and tensions and to what is undoubtedly for Jews the most traumatic experience of the twentieth century, if not of all time: the Holocaust.

For them to do so, however, has not been easy, and it has taken them time. In the immediate postwar years, many American writers felt they had no right to deal with that cataclysmic event, because they were so geographically distant from it. In fact, Saul Bellow has expressed in print his regret at having taken so long to confront the Holocaust in his fiction. Reviewers had criticized him in the early 1950s when he published *The Adventures of Augie March* (1953)[1] and failed to mention the destruction of Jews in Europe. He now admits that he was too focused on other matters—that is, on his own life and career in America. But in more recent years he has opted to "remember" this Jewish trauma in his fiction.

Only with the passing of time have American novelists grown to feel the Holocaust a suitable subject for their fiction. Bellow's first attempt at dealing with that painful subject was *Mr. Sammler's Planet* (1970).[2] Artur Sammler, all Bellow readers will recall, was a survivor of the death camps. He had lost his wife there, as well as his vision in one eye. Bellow returned to the theme of the Holocaust in his short novel, *The Bellarosa Connection* (1989).[3] He has several times referred to himself as a chronicler, who is better able to present a clear picture of a time and place than most so-called historians. He feels that most competent novelists can do the same. Bellow is, like Philip Roth, a strongly "autobiographical" fictionist. His monologists, whether or not they speak in the first person, generally share many of his views, traits, and personal experiences. His essays and interviews make this clear. In *The Bellarosa Connection*, Bellow again allows his narrator to speak in the first person. Indeed, to render his storyteller's identity more suggestive, Bellow does not even give him a name. Yet he proves the least disguised of Bellow heroes and, characteristically, resembles strongly several predecessors. But unlike earlier Bellow figures, this narrator has had no political, economic, or cultural wisdom to impart. His field is neither politics nor economics; nor is it history or literature. It is memory. A retired expert in memory training, this elderly entrepreneur is, therefore, a collector of old images, impressions, and ideas. He is not that different then from Artur Sammler, who also was a Zammler or "collector" of memories of an eventful life—or from such great remembrancers as Saul Bellow, Philip Roth, and E. L. Doctorow, among others. This individual has made his fortune merely by teaching his clients tricks of memory. Indeed, critics have made much of the parallels between *The Bellarosa Connection* and *Mr. Sammler's Planet.*

It is worth noting that the controlling metaphor of the earlier novel is vision or seeing—as it is so often in Bellow's fiction. However, in *The Bellarosa Connection*, Bellow has shifted his central metaphor from seeing to remembering and his narrative perspective from that of a European Jewish survivor to that of two American Jews: the famous impresario Billy Rose and the memory-expert narrator. Both feel removed from the Holocaust by being native-born Americans. Neither wishes to give much thought to the trauma of their fellow Jews. Indeed, the unnamed narrator again strongly resembles the young Saul Bellow, who also did not want to think of the painful events in Europe, much less write about them. He also parallels, if in different ways, such earlier Bellow figures as Moses Herzog, Charlie Citrine, Willis Mosby, Ijah Brodsky, and Samuel Braun. They are all, when last seen, busy reflecting on their past relationships with families and friends and on their own moral characters as they prepare for the Great Inevitable that is death. Saul Bellow appears to be doing the same. Much of the narrative irony in his fiction, as in American-Jewish fiction generally, stems from repeated reminders that Jews in America quickly developed a selective memory. Many blocked out much of their own ancestral heritage. Such forgetfulness, the Holocaust aside, has never been really true of Bellow; he has spent his entire professional life writing about what he remembers. In fact, to critics who may wonder when he will stop writing, he makes his position clear: "[I]f you have worked in memory, which is life itself," his narrator explains, "there is no retirement except in death."[4]

With Bellow, then, we have touched on those elements mentioned at the outset: the interplay of fact and fancy, past and present, his-

tory or autobiography and fiction—as well as the subject that has
grown more, rather than less, persistent in recent American-Jewish
fiction, the Holocaust—with which Bellow deals rather extensively
in his latest novel, *Ravelstein* (2000).[5] These same elements, if in understandably different forms, are to be found in the fiction of Philip
Roth and E. L. Doctorow. The latter is another very talented writer
who happens to be Jewish and who also likes to blur the lines between fiction and history, the creative imagination and biography or
autobiography. Doctorow's most directly autobiographical novel is
World's Fair (1985),[6] which was characterized by one reviewer as "a
peculiar hybrid of novel and memoir."[7] It is a nostalgic view of life
in New York during the Depression, as experienced by a young boy
who recounts his first nine years and ends his account with his 1939
visit to the World's Fair in Flushing Meadow. The boy's first name is
Edgar (as is Doctorow's), and he grows up in the Bronx in the 1930s.
His parents, like those of Doctorow, are named Rose and Dave. His
brother's name—like that of the author's brother—is Donald. The
family name, however, has been changed. Other details of the family's life are to be found in Doctorow's short story "The Writer in the
Family," which appears as the first tale in Doctorow's story collection *Lives of the Poets: A Novella and Six Stories* (1984).[8] But the Doctorow novel best known to readers is *Ragtime* (1975),[9] which has
taken on new life as a motion picture and a highly successful stage
musical. In it Doctorow returns to the nation-changing time span
between the twentieth century's start and World War I. Those years
saw the creation of the auto assembly line and the Model T. Ford,
moving pictures and ragtime music. They witnessed also the constant arrivals of "rag ships" laden with immigrants. But what is significant here is that to tell his story, Doctorow intermingles a cluster
of historical figures of that era with three fictional families. Working
from what pop history and biographies relate about such celebrities
as J. P. Morgan and Henry Ford, Emma Goldman and Evelyn Nesbit,
Harry K. Thaw and Stanford White, Harry Houdini and Archduke
Franz Ferdinand, Sigmund Freud and Carl Jung, Theodore Dreiser
and Arctic explorer Robert E. Peary, Doctorow rearranges events in
their lives to interweave them with those of his three fictional families. Thus does he blend fact and fiction to create what some critics
termed "faction." For instance, he has J. P. Morgan and Henry Ford
meeting and discussing their common interest in reincarnation.
When interviewers asked Doctorow if Morgan and Ford had ever
met in real life, he answered, "Well, they have now." In other words,

the true reality is that of the imagination rather than of history. There is also a Jewish component in *Ragtime*, in that one of the families is that of the poor Jewish immigrant peddler who is identified only as "Tateh" (the Yiddish word for "father"). He is an ardent socialist who rises from New York's Lower East side to become the powerful movie mogul Baron Ashkenazi, who creates the "Our Gang" comedies. Doctorow, then, like Bellow and Roth, is also attempting to point up the difficulty of separating fact from fancy or history from fiction—that is, of finding, grasping, and conveying reality, through the imagination, amid the world's cultural confusions and political tensions.

Doctorow has structured several of his books as a writer's working papers. His *Lives of the Poets*, for example, is presented, the book jacket blurb informs the reader, as "six tense, poignant, and mysterious stories . . . followed by a novella in which the writer emerges from his work to reveal his own mind. Here the images and the themes of the earlier stories become part of the narrator's unsparing confessions about his own life . . . and in this brilliant, funny, and painful story about the story, the writer's mind in all its aspects—its formal compositions, its naked secrets—emerges as a rare look at the creative process and its connection to the heart." In an interview in the *New York Times Book Review*, Doctorow offered his own thoughts on this work. "I write to find out what I'm writing," he explained. "In *The Book of Daniel* (1971), I had to find the voice before I could tell the story. In *Lives of the Poets*, I was lucky. The voice came to me." He considered the book's short stories and novella to be unified. "I found myself writing them in sequence as they appear in the book. As I read the stories over, I discovered a connection, like a mind looking for its own geography. I found that I was creating the character of the person creating them. So I wrote the novella to give him a voice. I saw the possibility of presenting a writer's mind in both formal stories and then in a confessional mode. The novella is the story of the stories."[10] In Doctorow's more recent novel *City of God* (2000), the reader is again instructed how to read the narrative. "In his workbook," the reader is informed, "a New York City novelist records the contents of his teeming brain—sketches for stories, accounts of his love affairs, riffs on the meanings of popular songs, ideas for movies, obsessions with cosmic processes. He is a virtual repository of the predominant ideas and historical disasters of the age."[11] One of those "historical disasters," not surprisingly, is the

Holocaust, which Doctorow here treats with dramatic passion and historical insight.

Philip Roth, like his two esteemed colleagues, has also devoted—and to a much greater degree—a good deal of his fiction in recent years to this postmodernist habit of writing about writing. His protagonists or heroes almost always seem to resemble their author in age and appearance, time and place, and in personal circumstances. But after having teased his readers with such strong parallels, especially in the recurring figure of Nathan Zuckerman, Roth likes to dismiss the autobiographical elements in his work as products of his creative imagination. "Like any writer," says Roth, "I have only the floor under my feet to stand on. I get my facts from what I see of life and of myself. Then I have to make another world out of them, a world of words that is more interesting than what exists."[12] On another occasion, he stated: "I think the autobiographical connection in fiction is looser than it appears, even in mine. . . . The level of invention rises and sinks, in each paragraph."[13] That is undoubtedly true. His point is that the autobiographical element is almost always present in both his fiction and nonfiction. "Give me a mask and I'll tell you the truth," William Butler Yeats once remarked. Roth appears to have taken this thought to heart.[14] Like Bellow, whom he has long admired, Roth places a good deal of importance on memory. In *Patrimony* (1991), his nonfiction account of his father's painful last months and death, Roth writes: "'I must remember accurately,' I told myself, 'remember everything accurately so that when he is gone I can re-create the father who created me.' *You must not forget anything.*"[15]

In other words, Philip Roth, like Bellow and Doctorow, has also entertained, bemused, and confused critics and readers with his elusive interplay of fiction and autobiography, the creative and "factual," the invented and real, or what he himself terms "the relationship between the written and the unwritten world." He has tried to explain to his readership that we are not to read his fiction as autobiography or his alleged autobiography as literal fact. He makes this especially clear in *The Facts: The Autobiography of a Novelist* (1988),[16] most of which is presented as a straightforward account of his life, and much of which *appears* to be just that. Yet the very subtitle, "The Autobiography of a Novelist," suggests a note of caution. Most experienced readers have learned that no novelist or fiction writer is to be entirely believed when discussing his or her own life. Indeed, when has *any* autobiography been entirely devoid of creative selection and convenient arrangement of personal details? *Granta* editor Ian Jack put the matter into perspective when speaking of a recently published confessional essay that had drawn considerable public attention: "Honesty, of course, can be a literary device like any other. One can appear to be honest without really being honest."[17] From Captain John Smith and Benjamin Franklin to the present, autobiographers have tended to create the persona and "truth" they wished to present to the world.

However, Roth is something of an exception in that, as Paul Gray has pointed out, he "has tirelessly insisted on the distinction between the raw material of life and the transforming power of fiction."[18] Interviewer David Lida has noted several of Roth's explanations. One example: "Roth does acknowledge similarities between his own fury at writer Irving Howe's diatribes against his fiction and a climactic moment in *The Anatomy Lesson* (1983) "when an outraged Zuckerman makes a ranting phone call to the critic Milton Appel—but he neatly sums up the differences. 'The rage is absolutely real,' Roth concedes, 'but the situation in which it's embedded is invented. Did I ever call Irving Howe? Of course not. I'm not quite the *schmuck* Zuckerman is,' he says with a laugh."[19] Roth has also made this point in print. "In *The Facts,* Roth claims that the most directly factual passages in his work are the scenes in *My Life as a Man* (1974) in which Peter Tarnopol's wife belatedly confesses to having duped him into marriage by obtaining a urine sample from a pregnant woman and claiming it as her own. 'I say I couldn't improve on that,' says Roth, 'but if we took that passage I could show you, "This is distortion, this is shading, this is total invention, this is a lie.' It's all grounded in the autobiographical, but it's also all invented.' "[20]

Whether it is his intention here or not, Roth is making the point that *all* fiction is "grounded in the autobiographical." Wallace Stegner, a highly gifted writer and teacher of writing, has summarized clearly the relationship of the writer to his life and the people in it: "Because he writes fiction in order to reflect or illuminate life, his materials obviously must come out of life," Stegner noted. "These materials are people, places, things—especially people. If fiction isn't people it is nothing. . . . The people of his stories and novels will be, inevitably but in altered shapes, the people he himself has known." Lest anyone miss his point, Stegner then adds: "The flimsy little protestations that mark the front gate of every novel, the solemn statements that any resemblance to real persons living or dead is entirely coincidental, are fraudulent every time. A writer has no other material to make his people from than the people of his experience. If there is no resemblance to any real person, living or dead, the character is going to be pretty unconvincing. The only thing the writer can do is to recombine parts, suppress some characteristics and emphasize others, put two or three people into one fictional character, and pray the real-life prototypes won't sue."[21]

Very likely, Stegner was not thinking particularly of Roth when penning these comments, but they serve as an accurate gloss on the latter's writing methods. From the start, Roth has shrewdly manipulated his readership into wondering how much of his fiction is fact and how much fiction. His has wished, and generally succeeded, in piquing the interest of his readers. For example, he has done so by swearing at the beginning of a novel like *Operation Shylock* (1993)[22] that every word is true and then at the end declaring the entire narrative to be false. In effect, he is having it both ways. Roth even has the chutzpah to pretend outrage at the gullibility, if not the mendacity, of readers who want to believe he is exposing his own life. But then, where would Philip Roth be today as a writer if readers had not responded willingly to his teasing, suggestiveness, and trickiness? Conversely, what would be his current literary situation if he had claimed without qualification that in all these years everything he has written about his heroes is essentially true about *his* life? How many would believe him then? He would have been accused of being a poseur, a phony, as was, for example, Jerzi Kosinski, who apparently had added imaginative or creative flourishes to what he insisted had been his own experiences during the Holocaust. Roth, shrewd student of human nature that he is, has been walking a tenuous but carefully constructed tightrope of credibility. It would be difficult to point to a more artful literary dodger at work today. How many readers now think that everything Roth has revealed in his narratives about Neil Klugman, Gabe Wallach, Alexander Portnoy, David Kepesh, Peter Tarnopol, and Nathan Zuckerman is an accurate chronicle of the life of Philip Roth? Undoubtedly such readers are few in number. On the other hand, could not a convinced or "believing" reader argue that *all* the accounts are true—even if they never happened? Is there only one kind of truth—the literal, actual, factual? What if this bemused reader were to argue that every word Roth has made up about his protagonists is psychologically or emotionally or internally "true" of Philip Roth? What if his novels are read as a basically valid composite psychological profile of Philip-Roth-as-human-being, warts and all?

At the same time, every writer must recognize that, despite his or her best intentions and despite ardent strivings to be original, certain underlying themes—whether conscious or intuitive—will be embodied in his or her writings. Peter Cooper has succinctly pinpointed Roth's basic artistic and psychological concerns. He points most specifically to Roth's "fiction from the mid 1970s on." Beginning with *My Life as a Man*, Cooper notes that Roth has been examining "how the 'unwritten world' of life experiences becomes transformed in literature and how the 'written world' of literature can affect courses of action taken in life." In doing so, "Roth has assiduously mined his life and background for ore-bearing material, but, he admits, he has 'looked only for what could be transformed' by 'turning the flame up under my life and smelting stories out of all I've known.'" The events that Roth most typically recalls, says Cooper, "document the struggle of the self to realize autonomy in some restrictive environment, often by trying to frame an account of its own history and development." Generally, Roth's protagonist, often a writer himself, will "attempt to compose himself through the act of writing—to exorcise demons from his life, or to impart some sense to it, by putting it into literary form. In these works especially, strategies for narrative expression become strategies for self-discovery and self-definition. Since the characters' strivings parallel the author's, Roth produces a literature that is both psychologically and aesthetically self-conscious." Roth and his central figures, especially "his writer-characters, face the dilemma of choosing between two antithetical styles of personality and narrative expression: that of the polished, high-minded, restrained, and responsible intellectual, whom he calls 'the nice Jewish boy,' and that of the brash, crude, and rebellious iconoclast, whom he dubs 'the Jewboy.'"[23]

As have Bellow and Doctorow, Roth, too, has several times introduced the Holocaust as an important theme into his fiction. He has done so most extensively in *Operation Shylock*, a darkly bitter and intentionally provocative book. The story line has two Philip Roths, a "real" one and an imposter, and a series of highly implausible events and figures. Roth litters his novel with mistaken identities, plots that double back on themselves, references to earlier Roth novels, and allusions to actual Jewish events. All these things are meant to demonstrate Roth's ability to integrate into his art the world in which he lives. In *Operation Shylock*, Roth uses these events to introduce almost all the issues and elements then confronting the State of Israel. We should keep in mind that Roth, throughout his career, has made a game of mixing in both his fiction and nonfiction what is real and what is not. He feels the resulting uncertainty adds to the literary pleasure of both reader and writer. For example, he titles this novel *Operation Shylock: A Confession.* This would seem to imply that the novel deals with actual events. But then Roth mischievously includes in the book itself a concluding "Note to the Reader." It states: "This book is a work of fiction. . . . This confession is false." Any alert reader is likely to think: "Of course it is; after all, the book is a *novel.*" Yet in numerous follow-up interviews, Roth insisted that *Operation Shylock* is nonfiction—that it is a record of real events. Such contradictory declarations have greatly upset reviewers. But no thoughtful reader should be upset or even surprised by such behavior on Roth's part. He is merely doing what he has been doing for years. In other words, if his particular story seems too absurd to be true, and his explanations are too contradictory to be credible, Roth is merely reminding us once again that the "facts" of history and life, especially Jewish history and life, are indeed stranger than fiction.

He is also doing what so many of his Jewish literary contemporaries are doing: He is wrestling metaphorically with the lessons of Jewish history and the issues besetting the Jewish people today, especially as these issues are embodied by the horrors of the Holocaust and in the hopes engendered by the beleaguered State of Israel. Here Roth is again seeking some answers to the question of what it means to be a Jew so late in the twentieth century—and, of course, so early in the twenty-first. It is also worth noting that here, as in *Patrimony,* and as had Bellow in *The Bellarosa Connection,* Roth urges his readers not to forget—not to forget their patrimony, their heritage, their debt to the past.

Roth has been as good as his word. He himself, in midcareer, felt the need to take stock of himself as writer and as person, and the result was *The Facts.* Roth bookends his narrative with two letters. The first is a nine-page note from the author to his major literary alter ego, Nathan Zuckerman. The book concludes with a thirty-five-page response from Zuckerman to his creator, Philip Roth. The first letter serves as the book's introduction, and in it Roth explains that he was moved to writing about himself rather than another fictional alter ego by his lingering thoughts of his mother's death in 1981 and his growing realization of his father's failing health at age eighty-six.

He hoped that writing this "life" would enable him to recapture that moment in time when the Family Roth—his mother, father, brother, and he—were still together and all seemed well in their small Newark, New Jersey world. He also offers a second reason. Following minor surgery in 1987, he experienced an emotional breakdown and, to alleviate the resulting depression, he began searching for the vigorous, clear-minded, youthful idealist he had been before he fragmented himself into his various literary alter egos. "If the breakdown itself was partly caused by the strain of remaking himself as myth in the Nathan Zuckerman books," suggests David Denby, "part of the cure was a return to his own identity, to the core self that was beginning to elude him."[24] Roth adds his own rationale: "If this manuscript conveys anything," he reasons, "it's my exhaustion with masks, disguises, distortions, and lies."[25]

True to his word, Roth presents himself and his life, in the 150-page personal chronicle between the two letters, in a low-key, nondramatic fashion very different from the manic lives of his fictional heroes. Some years earlier, Roth tried to put both his work and life into proper perspective. Asked by an interviewer if his books should be read "as confession, as autobiography barely disguised," Roth seized the occasion. "You should read my books as fiction, demanding the pleasures that fiction can yield," he responded. "I have nothing to confess and no one I want to confess to. Nor has anyone asked me to make a confession or promised forgiveness if I do so." He then added: "As for my autobiography, I can't begin to tell you how dull it would be. My autobiography would consist almost entirely of chapters about me sitting alone in a room looking at a typewriter. The uneventfulness of my autobiography would make Beckett's *The Unnamable* read like Dickens."[26]

Roth was, as usual, being disingenuous and employing his familiar literary license, as subsequent media accounts of his troubled divorce from actress Claire Bloom revealed. But his claim is in line with the low-key self-portrait he presents in *The Facts*. As David Lida points out, Roth offers himself "as a nice Jewish boy who, after an almost suffocatingly rosy childhood, grew up into a nice Jewish man who 'writes books and wants to be left alone.'" But, adds Lida rather shrewdly, "because the book is written with such politesse and filial respect, one is bound to wonder about the unexplained sources of rage that inform so many of Roth's novels. Any autobiography is bound to leave questions unanswered: but in the last chapter of *The Facts*, they are almost all asked—by none other than Nathan Zucker-

man." Lida seems somewhat surprised by this literary ploy. He need
not have been. Roth is simply up to one of his oldest tricks: He has
often attempted to disarm his critics by asking and answering their
questions before they can ask them. Roth even concedes as much:
"It's not just a story," he explains, "it's a story that is challenged.
That's part of 'a novelist's autobiography.'"[27]

Not only is autobiography an important element in Roth's fiction
but so also is a sense of *place*. Roth has himself discerned this shaping
pattern in his writing. "Ever since *Goodbye, Columbus*," he has noted,
"I've been drawn to depicting the impact of place on American
lives. *Portnoy's Complaint* is very much the raw response to a way of
life that was specific to his American place during his childhood in
the 1930s and '40s. The link between the individual and his historic
moment may be more focused in the recent trilogy, but the interest
was there from the start."[28] It is, therefore, instructive to recall that
Roth was an English major at Bucknell who went on to take graduate
work, albeit briefly, in English at the University of Chicago. In those
years, the 1950s, the New Criticism held sway in graduate English
departments, and the University of Chicago was the home of the
self-designated Aristotelian school of the New Critics. In *The Facts*,
Roth is doing what then was expected of every literature student
there and elsewhere: he is "explicating the text"—extracting every
linguistic, semantic, psychological, or tonal nuance from each word
and image. In short, the text was to be explored from every possible
point of view. That is, simply put, the task Roth here assigns to his
"student," Nathan Zuckerman.

But in recent years Roth has moved far beyond mere narrative ex-
plication of his characters and plots. As early as *The Counterlife*
(1987), for instance, Roth—as David Denby astutely explains—
"abandoned narrative solidity altogether, reviving characters supposedly dead, allowing characters to review their fictional representation, folding fictions within fictions, becoming, in fact, an earnest writer of 'metafiction.'" Denby is right: these, too, are some of
the things Roth does in his fiction. But the related question here
then would seem to be "why?" Why does Roth write as he does?
Many critics and reviewers have offered explanations. But that suggested by Denby seems close to the mark. "Roth's formal games,"
he reasons, "emerged as the inevitable result of his dialectical habits
of mind, habits that have grown obsessive in recent years. He loves
to argue, often with himself. By creating a character who 'dies' and

is then reborn—forging a new ego out of the unfulfilled longings of the old—he was carrying out the ultimate argument with himself."[29]

Clearly then, Philip Roth is both similar to and different from most of his literary colleagues, both professionally and personally. One notable difference meriting mention is his editing of the "Voices from the Other Europe" series for Penguin. This one-time "bad boy of American literature" thereby brought to the attention of the English-reading world the works of besieged and under-appreciated Eastern bloc writers. Also unlike many of his literary contemporaries, Roth keeps a relatively low profile between novels. Hence those readers curious to know what is up with this most intriguing of writers must generally await his next novel. And that in itself is, obviously, not a bad thing.

NOTES

1. Saul Bellow, *The Adventures of Augie March* (New York: Viking, 1953).

2. Saul Bellow, *Mr. Sammler's Planet* (New York: Viking, 1970).

3. Saul Bellow, *The Bellarosa Connection* (New York: Penguin Books, 1989). Hereafter referred to as *BC*.

4. Ibid., 2.

5. Saul Bellow, *Ravelstein* (New York: Viking, 2000).

6. E. L. Doctorow, *World's Fair* (New York: Random House, 1985).

7. David Leavitt, "Looking Back on the World of Tomorrow," a review of *World's Fair*, by E. L. Doctorow, *New York Times Book Review*, November 10, 1985, 3.

8. E. L. Doctorow, *Lives of the Poets: Six Stories and a Novella* (New York: Random House, 1984).

9. E. L. Doctorow, *Ragtime* (New York: Random House, 1975).

10. Herbert Mitgang, "Finding the Right Voice," a review of *Lives of the Poets: Six Stories and a Novella*, by E. L. Doctorow, *New York Times Book Review*, November 11, 1984, 36. See also Ben Siegel, "Introduction," in *Critical Essays on E. L. Doctorow*, ed. Ben Siegel (New York: G. K. Hall, 2000), 30.

11. E. L. Doctorow, *City of God* (New York: Random House, 2000).

12. Andrea Chambers, "Philip Roth: Portnoy's Creator Would Like It Known: His Books Are Novels not Confessionals," *People Weekly* (December 19, 1983): 98.

13. David Lida, "Philip Roth Talks—a Little: 'I'm not Quite the Schmuck Zuckerman Is,'" *Vogue* (September 1988): 434.

14. See Edmund White, "The Hearts of Men: Who Knows What Shadows Lurk . . . ," *Vogue* (January 1987): 94.

15. Philip Roth, *Patrimony* (New York: Simon and Schuster, 1991), 177.

16. Philip Roth, *The Facts: The Autobiography of a Novelist* (New York: Penguin Books, 1988). Hereafter referred to as *Facts*.

17. Jack was referring to Kathryn Chetkovich's essay "Envy," dealing with her relationship with Jonathan Franzen, author of the award-winning novel *The Corrections*. Jack published the essay, concluding, "but she was really honest." See Tim

Rutten, "A Novel End to a Love Affair," *Los Angeles Times Calendar*, July 19, 2003, E1, E23.

18. Paul Gray, "Philip Roth: Novelist," *Time* (July 9, 2001): 50.

19. Lida, "Philip Roth Talks," 434.

20. Ibid. For Roth's detailed chronicling of this incident, see *Facts*, 102–12.

21. Wallace Stegner, *On Teaching and Writing Fiction*, ed. Lynn Stegner (New York: Penguin Books, 2000), 4–5.

22. Philip Roth, *Operation Shylock* (New York: Simon & Schuster, 1993). Hereafter referred to as *OS*.

23. Peter Cooper, *Philip Roth*, Scribner's Writers Series (New York: Charles Scribner's Sons, 1991), 3, 2, 1–2.

24. David Denby, "The Gripes of Roth," a review of *The Facts: A Novelist's Autobiography*, by Philip Roth, *The New Republic* (November 21, 1988): 37.

25. *Facts*, 6.

26. Alan Finkielkraut, "The Ghosts of Roth," *Esquire* (September 1981): 94.

27. Lida, "Philip Roth Talks," 434, 444.

28. Gray, "Philip Roth Novelist," 50.

29. Denby, "The Gripes of Roth," 37–38.

Philip Roth's Fictions of Self-Exposure

Debra Shostak

Among Philip Roth's most startling gestures in a career that has not lacked for surprises is his decision in *Deception* (1990) and *Operation Shylock* (1993) to refer to his main character as "Philip" in the former and "Philip Roth" in the latter, breaking decorum about the illusion of an invented persona who directs and dominates the narratives.[1] Each novel advertises itself as a life history, offering its "I" as both ubiquitous eye and actor, and I think we are to retain awareness of the speaker as simultaneously a conventional narrative mask and the historical Philip Roth. Few writers dare to name themselves at the center of their inventions, which is why it is so arresting to find a work of fiction that pronounces its author's name within the text. Because readers are frequently tempted, from either prurient interest or more impartial motives, to discern autobiography in a fictional narrative, most writers of fiction seem to labor out of modesty, a sense of privacy, or a display of imaginative capacities to erase the traces of their own lives from their work.

Not so Philip Roth. Especially since his invention of Nathan Zuckerman, Roth has encouraged readers to interpret the narrating voice of his fiction as a self-revealing "I," a Roth surrogate who, by the time of *Deception* and *Operation Shylock*, is no longer a surrogate but is "Roth" himself. Roth is preoccupied with self-performance, with projections of the self's voice into the other—with, for example, the figure of impersonation that appears in *The Counterlife* (1986) or of ventriloquism that appears in *Sabbath's Theater* (1995).[2] What I argue here is not that Roth is, strictly, writing autobiographically, but rather that he makes capital out of his readers' inclinations toward biographical interpretations of his work. The "Roth" in the text must always be read in quotation marks, even when seemingly most unmediated, in order to underscore the indeterminacy of the "Roth" who appears in each narrative and to distinguish this narrativized "Roth" from the man who writes the books and lives in Con-

31

necticut—a distinction the texts labor to obscure. I would argue further that there is a recognizable arc to Roth's career in regard to what I call here his fictions of self-exposure. His interest in the place of the autobiographical in fiction can be traced with some precision to show how he arrives at naming himself in the novels of the late 1980s and early 1990s and then exhausts the need for self-reference to return to the guises of the overtly fictive.[3] Along the way, Roth's gestures of self-exposure create peculiar tensions within the novels as well as within the reader-text relationship, allowing inquiry not only into the meaning of "autobiography" but also more broadly into the relationship between fiction and fact and into the process by which readers interpret evidence.

Roth's interest in exploiting autobiographical references—in offering "Roth" to varying degrees within narrative contexts—seems largely to have emerged from his entanglement with his readers during his first years of publication. Some early readers accused him of mining untransformed material from his life, of writing autobiography every time he wrote a novel; he was castigated for doing what in fact his readers mistakenly took him to be doing—for exposing himself and those nearest him. Roth was charged with anti-Semitism and self-hatred after the appearance of *Goodbye, Columbus* (1959), and the essay "Writing About Jews" (1963) attests to the sensitive nerve that his readers hit.[4] His outrage seemed to bubble to the surface with *Portnoy's Complaint* (1969)[5] in ways that made the metaphor of self-exposure all too literal for some readers. Any reader of Roth who sees his name in the same sentence as "self-exposure" is likely to think first of *Portnoy's Complaint,* where Roth broke taboos with the notorious descriptions of Alex Portnoy's compulsive masturbation and the unflattering portraits of Portnoy's Jewish family. The confessional mode of Roth's narration caused some readers naïvely to take the book as thinly disguised autobiography, causing him to complain that "a novel in the guise of a confession was received and judged by any number of readers as a confession in the guise of a novel."[6] Roth's exposure of both sex and Jewishness in the novel breached the ordinary contract between writer and reader, because both matters seemed too intimately represented to have been dreamed up. What is most taboo is accordingly most unrepresentable; to narrate the unspeakable is to suggest peculiar access to its facts. Roth's transgressions against cultural prohibitions seemed to produce a corollary transgression against narrative convention: the novel eroded the assumption, in place since the realists dominated the nineteenth century, that a first-person narrator is necessarily a fiction, no matter how compellingly "real."

Given Roth's protestations at being faulted for making the translation from life to art credible, the apparent autobiographical turn in his fiction by the mid-1970s is surprising. It is as if, following the reception of *Goodbye, Columbus* and *Portnoy's Complaint*, he said, "All right, you want 'Roth,' I'll give you 'Roth.'" The writer has given us "Roth" in the work of the last two decades mainly in two related ways: through the adoption of narrators who seem only minimally displaced from Roth's own voice; and through thinly disguised references to details from his biography. *Portnoy* provides an example of the former strategy. The latter is exemplified by *My Life as a Man* (1974), which offers a "Roth" in disguise, in fact doubly disguised.[7] "Roth" exists in the young writer Peter Tarnopol who invents his own fictional alter ego, Nathan Zuckerman, who, in turn, narrates "Salad Days" and "Courting Disaster," the two stories that constitute the "Useful Fictions" of the book's first section. The Zuckerman persona allows Tarnopol to project into narrative form his anger and angst over "a career in which being married and then trying to get unmarried would become my predominant activity and obsession."[8] That Tarnopol's marital career hews in significant ways to the marriage that Roth himself suffered in the early 1960s and recounts at length in *The Facts* (1988)[9] might well cause readers to believe that Roth, like Tarnopol, was using the autobiographical form of fiction as a way to master the traumatic events of his life.[10]

After Tarnopol avails himself of Zuckerman's voice, he becomes dissatisfied with this mode of autobiographical displacement, at which point Roth cautiously sets up a tension between the efficacy of fiction and of untransformed "facts" to represent the deepest truths. Tarnopol shifts to "My True Story," his own first-person narrative, following a preface that announces that he "is preparing to forsake the art of fiction for a while and embark upon an autobiographical narrative."[11] In imitating the autobiographical voice in this last, most powerful rendering of Tarnopol's struggle, Roth seems to support the principle that the least displaced material—the facts given narrative shape but not imaginatively altered detail—offers the most knowledge and, perhaps, the greatest therapeutic satisfaction. In the closing line of the novel, "This me who is me being me and none other,"[12] Tarnopol seems to assert the truth value of the unmasked persona. But this assertion is undermined by our awareness that Peter Tarnopol is simply a persona, a useful fiction, an invention of Roth's imagination and not a determinate projection of his life. There is no autobiography here, only the illusion of one. The "my" in the title *My Life as a Man* has no referent, at least not in the real world.

Although *My Life as a Man* may not have invited autobiographical interpretations from its first readers—since few may have known the details of Roth's life as they were later rehearsed in *The Facts*—it nevertheless presaged the enticements to such interpretations upon which Roth was to dilate in later works. The title, for example, is a bold stroke. Any reader who looks at the cover of a book with the pronoun "my" in the title is likely, fleetingly, to link that pronoun with the proper name—"Philip Roth"—printed below it, if only because no other antecedent yet exists in the reader's mind. Roth follows this impression with the disorienting "Note to the Reader" in the book's front matter, which asserts baldly that "Useful Fictions" and "My True Story" are "drawn from the writings of Peter Tarnopol." Pretending to create a context of facticity for what follows, the note instead reminds us of the novel's fictiveness, of the need for a writer to create an illusion of fact.[13] Roth's reflexive play here concerning the origin and authority of his narratives not only instigates the main concern of this novel but also informs the central epistemological and aesthetic question that gives shape to his subsequent work.

In order to understand the scope of Roth's explorations into this question, and to see how he might have moved from making use of autobiographical reference to foregrounding the problem of distinguishing fiction from autobiography, it is worth trying to outline the contexts out of which the question arises. The most obvious is perhaps Roth's repeated use of first-person narration, a device conventionally intended to heighten verisimilitude by lending the authority of an experience to the voice that narrates it as eyewitness and participant. Such a narrator, by the enunciation of "I," collapses the distance between the participant in the story-events and the norms of the implied author who, in Wayne Booth's terms, is "the sum of his [narrative] choices."[14] Tautologically the only possible voice of self-narration, the first-person narrator by definition promises to inscribe autobiography, to speak the authorial self in an unmediated fashion.[15] This is, of course, the central conceit of all fiction narrated in the first person. The autobiographical effect of Roth's fiction, then, is overdetermined not only by his extratextual self-references, but also by the forms he chooses, from the psychoanalytic monologue in *Portnoy's Complaint* to the first-person narration of the Zuckerman novels, from the pseudo-autobiography of *My Life as a Man* to the "real" autobiography of *The Facts* and *Patrimony* (1991)[16] and the "confession" of *Operation Shylock*.

Up to this point, I have been eliding an important distinction: between a narrative whose form represents an autobiographical act—the result of an author who chooses to narrate his or her life experiences—and a narrative interpreted by a reader as autobiographical. The former implies intentionality, and even if the life story is displaced into other characters and events—is fictionalized, that is to say—such a narrative represents an author's efforts to construct a coherent perspective on the self and the self's history in the world. Such a narrative may be considered either "autobiography," as typically conceived, or, following Eugene Stelzig, a work of "confessional fiction."[17] The type of narrative that must be distinguished from these is necessarily fictional and, in regard to the design of the work, it matters little to what degree an author's life story may be buried there. The act of deciphering the clues to an author's lived experience, however, becomes central to the way in which the reader constructs the meaning of this sort of text, in part because the relation between text and author is emphatically undecidable. Any reader can, of course, perform such an interpretive operation on any text, but certain texts are more prone to such a reading because they cue the reader to detect, accurately or otherwise, such traces of the author in the narrative. As I have suggested, Roth offers both sorts of narrative, and sometimes within a single text. This dual perspective on life writing is the source of my own title, since the fictions of self-exposure Roth writes are at once works of fiction that expose the self and lies that only pretend to do so. My intention is to follow the intertwined trails of both versions of the "autobiographical"—the writerly and the readerly, so to speak—in order to see how Roth avails himself of the implications of each.

When Roth has spoken about the relationship between fiction and an author's life, he has suggested that readers are largely at fault for seeing autobiography in his work—no Roth where none intended. To Alain Finkielkraut, for example, Roth asserted

> I have nothing to confess and no one I want to confess to. . . .
> To label books like mine "autobiographical" or "confessional" is not only to falsify their suppositional nature but . . . to slight whatever artfulness leads some readers to think that they must be autobiographical. You

don't create the aura of intimacy by dropping your pants in public; do
that and most people will instinctively look away.[18]

Roth's protestations, while sensibly describing the process of fiction
making, still seem somewhat disingenuous; even he reads other writers' fiction to an extent biographically, as when he sees in Kafka's
story "The Burrow" inklings of Kafka's relationship to Dora Dy-
mant.[19] Similarly, the very notion of an alter ego like Zuckerman
who narrates as a stand-in for the writer—a situation dramatized by
Peter Tarnopol in *My Life as a Man*—implies that there is some referent external to the text, an ego presented as "alter," an authorial
self that, logically, still exists in the displacements and erasures of
the imaginative process which leave traces in the completed artifact.[20] As Jay Halio notes, then, of Tarnopol's story, "Roth knows that
the artistic problem involves getting the proper distance, or detach-
ment, from his subject, particularly when his subject is himself."[21]

Roth's fictional practices indicate more ambivalence about the
place of autobiography in fiction than do his statements about his
aesthetics. On one hand, Roth renders a powerful critique in *My Life
as a Man* of the narcissistic writer whose writing is always and only
about him or herself. In urging judgment against Tarnopol, Roth
seems dutifully to satisfy the readerly mandate for authorial "objec-
tivity"—however inherently fallacious a notion—that Wayne Booth
described when he observed that "signs of the real author's untransformed loves and hates are almost always fatal."[22] On the other
hand, Roth serves up a significant rejection of just this aesthetic of
the "authorless" work,[23] descended from Henry James and pursued
by the modernists, precisely by refusing at times to gain the "proper
distance" from the subject. The trilogy collected in *Zuckerman Bound*
(1985) contains numerous examples.[24] Like the rabbis who condemned Roth for *Goodbye, Columbus*, for example, Zuckerman's
father in *The Ghost Writer* (1979) criticizes him sharply for his representations of Jews in his story "Higher Education." In *Zuckerman Unbound* (1981), Roth allows Nathan to become the victim of his own
celebrity for writing the sexually explicit novel *Carnovsky*, an obvious
allusion to *Portnoy's Complaint*. And in Zuckerman's comic invective
against Milton Appel in *The Anatomy Lesson* (1983), Roth plays out
his thinly disguised vendetta against Irving Howe for Howe's notori-
ously stinging reappraisal of Roth in 1972.[25]

I would hazard several reasons for Roth's contradictory treatment
of self-reference. First, Roth feels considerable allegiance to the

Jamesian realistic tradition—a debt he alludes to in *The Ghost Writer* when Zuckerman reads "The Middle Years" just before he recounts his invention of Amy Bellette's alternative life as Anne Frank. Even when Roth is most engaged in the play of postmodern narrative form and epistemologies of identity—as in *The Counterlife* or *Operation Shylock*, for instance—he clearly strives for verisimilitude. Like Zuckerman who, faced with the manic inventiveness and tenacity of his döppleganger, Alvin Pepler, marvels "Priceless. The *vrai*. You can't beat it,"[26] Roth welcomes when the world shows forth in its manifold strangeness. He is committed to character and incident (and the Jamesian interdependence between them), and prefers to embed contrary norms within the views expressed by characters rather than in the voice of an omniscient narrator—hence the extended and unresolved dialogues (or arguments) that fill up the pages of his novels. As Roth insisted to Ian Hamilton, "I *want* belief, and I work to try to get it. If all these subtle readers can see in my work is my biography, then they are simply numb to fiction—numb to impersonation, to ventriloquism, to irony, . . . numb to all the delicate devices by which novels create the illusion of a reality more like the real than our own."[27] The second, and opposing, reason for Roth's contradictoriness is buried in the two metaphors above—impersonation and ventriloquism—both of which appear centrally in Roth's later work and which bespeak the provocations to the imagination inherent in inventing and projecting a self. If every autobiography is a song of myself, every work of fiction that posits displacement and difference from the authorial self is nevertheless a song of myself as well. Realism exploits the fact that inventing selves and worlds requires a strong leavening from the observable self and world, a truism that has interesting consequences because of the paradox that "self" is a contested concept.

My Life as a Man again supplies a useful example. Essentially a novel about a writer struggling to tell his story in order to define his own subjectivity, the novel in representing that struggle anticipates poststructural commonplaces about identity. *My Life as a Man* begins from the premise that "self" is a textual product, the result of its varied tellings. What Tarnopol anxiously intuits, as Patrick O'Donnell notes, "goes beyond the idea that the 'self' is a collection of its different versions to a questioning of what, *if anything*, defines these as variations of some single . . . subject" (emphasis added).[28] The implication for autobiography is thus: despite our convention that autobiography is a genre, that it is possible to write the self, the

genre is effectively self-canceling. There is no self to write, at least
not as a stable entity with presence in the world that can be mirrored
in language, and what the autobiographical act reveals to the writer
is the abyss of subjectivity, the final impossibility of performing such
an act. O'Donnell continues: "Even though . . . it is possible at times
to discuss 'Tarnopol' as a character who has a history, personality,
and motives, this version of the self, the novel convinces us, is simply
one more 'useful fiction' which allows us to discuss the subject . . .
[which] is more a process than a character—a process of self-inscrip-
tion that leads to an awareness of the subject as multiple."[29] Tarnopol's final line in the novel can then be reinterpreted: "This me who
is me being me and none other"[30] no longer asserts that a subject
can reach autobiographical truth by assuming the first-person voice
named "Peter Tarnopol," but rather represents an essentially disem-
bodied voice whistling in the dark, attempting to stave off the exis-
tential vertigo implied by the recognition that neither the proper
name nor its pronoun has a locatable referent. In the assertion of
the "me" in the text, Roth offers his consummate irony about the
nonexistence of the "me." The biographical reading of Tarnopol's
story dismantles itself.

If autobiography is, so to speak, a self-contradictory genre, at
least—as Roth presents it in *My Life as a Man*—the fiction more or
less negates biographical readings of his work in general. If there is
no "I" in the text, nor an "I" outside the text to which the pronoun
refers, then Roth cannot be discerned in his writing—except, perhaps, as "Roth," a discursively constructed and ephemeral entity.
For Peter Tarnopol, this logical conclusion is a source of considerable dread, but for Roth, this recognition seems to be tremendously
liberating, never mind the anxiety that we might interpret him as
projecting into Tarnopol. The freedom to invent selves is a writer's
special privilege. From the late 1970s, Roth has particularly enjoyed
this privilege in his numerous experiments with the representation
of subjectivity. He has been aided by poststructuralist epistemologies, such as those descending from Derrida's notion that linguistic
signs mark the referent's absence rather than its presence.[31] If one
accepts this premise, the subject that attempts to write itself in an
autobiographical act is, in fact, only transcribing its own lack, since
language displaces the subject. This seems to suit Roth just fine. As
Avrom Fleishman points out, there are two very different possible
responses to the poststructuralist insight into autobiography. In the
first, which we might see as Tarnopol's, "language becomes the

model of the self's inclinations toward self-alienation—toward the evasion of identity and the responsibilities of identification with/as oneself."[32] In the second, which we might see as Zuckerman's in *The Counterlife*, "the tendency of the self to become other in writing is seen neutrally as a process of self-alteration. Altering, becoming other, need not be taken as making strange but may be remaking. From this position, the death of self in autobiography may be seen as a sloughing off of the dead self, as exorcism of the living yet baleful one, or as the inveterate need or habit of tinkering with oneself in language."[33] What I have identified as Zuckerman's view is closer to the one Roth has expressed in interviews, quoted above. That stance frees him of responsibility to the "facts" of his life from which the fiction emerges, because it frees him from the expectation that "fact" exists as anything verifiable beyond the language in which experience is presented. If a fact is simply an event under description, one can proliferate selves merely by narrating them, by putting each version of self in possession of "facts," without loss of truth value.

Roth's evident pleasure in the potentialities of self-invention caused Mark Shechner to find in his work "fables of identity, variations upon the theme of the self designed to heighten and refine essential elements, highlight basic terms of being, and dramatize recurring conflicts."[34] That his novels constitute "fables" in no way diminishes their access to knowledge; rather, Roth simply points up the paradox that Michael Riffaterre finds in realism: "fiction emphasizes the fact of the fictionality of a story at the same time it states that the story is true. Furthermore, verisimilitude is an artifact, since it is a verbal representation of reality rather than reality itself: verisimilitude itself, therefore, entails fictionality."[35] Fables of identity are the useful fictions by which we attain a coherent vision of subjectivity. Such fables at once acknowledge their distance from a fixed subject—from the "ideal" autobiography, for example—and present understanding through the reader's recognition of their verisimilitude, which, in Riffaterre's terms, offers the "real" by way of the fictive. For Roth, the failure to discover what he calls in *The Counterlife* an "irreducible self"[36] serves to reinforce the primacy of fiction—and fiction making—as a way of knowing, and allows him to explore through brilliant invention the manifold contradictions implicit in representing the self.

With the exception perhaps of *Patrimony*, each of Roth's books from *The Counterlife* through *Sabbath's Theater* has offered at least one central trope by which Roth has revealed his preoccupation with these contradictions. In *The Counterlife*, for example, the trope is named in the novel's title. Roth develops the figure of the counterlife through a series of narratives answering the question "what if," each of which provides an alternative version of Nathan Zuckerman's life story, and which refuse to come together into a single coherent narrative of the self.[37] The very form of the novel, with its juxtaposed, oppositional chapters, suggests the potential for the stories of the self to proliferate endlessly. Like Tarnopol, Zuckerman represents a writer's activity of narrating his autobiography, with the difference that in Nathan's story, Roth prohibits the reader from distinguishing "real" event from its imaginative projections. The ultimate joke of the book is that a "counterlife" ought to presuppose a prior or "real" life to which alternatives are being posed, but Roth declines to supply—or at least to identify—the "life" that is countered in the novel.[38] The prior or real referent (by antithesis) for the "counterlife" is either missing or unknowable. At the end of the novel, Roth has Zuckerman elaborate a related theory around a cluster of theatrical metaphors—"impersonation," "act," "performance"—similarly denying the existence of some primary selfhood. When Nathan tells his (invented) lover Maria that "Being Zuckerman is one long performance and the very opposite of what is thought of as *being oneself*,"[39] he undercuts the meaningfulness of those last two terms. "There is no you, Maria, any more than there's a me," he writes.[40] Failing a self, Zuckerman is left with what could be termed subject-positions—which Paul Smith defines as "the conglomeration of *positions*, . . . provisional and not necessarily indefeasible, into which a person is called momentarily by the discourses and the world that he/she inhabits."[41] Nathan's subject-positions in *The Counterlife* are delineated variously by such roles as writer, brother, lover, husband, Jew, and even dead man. The self-writing that is autobiography turns out to be the projection of each subject-position into a narrative with its own facts.

At the end of *The Counterlife*, Roth has Maria introduce the trope that he will develop at greater length in the next work of fiction, *Deception*, where the verbal declaration of subject-positions is dramatized most vividly. Maria writes a farewell letter to Zuckerman in which she follows the example of "characters rebelling against their author" because she is no longer willing to be his "'character,' just one of a series of fictive propositions." In the letter, she announces, "You want to play reality-shift? Get yourself another girl."[42] Reality shift is the game that "Philip," the voice consistent across the dialogues that make up the narrative of *Deception*, plays with his lover who, in the conceit of the novel, is the "real-life" model for Maria in *The Counterlife*. In various conversations, the two lovers engage in extended bouts of invention, each taking the role of some imagined character or self-projection, and, beginning with certain "facts" or premises, working through the conversations these selves might have with each other. In a broad sense, the dialogue form of *Deception* can be seen as one version of reality shift, because it illuminates how "reality" is shaped for a perceiver. Dialogue exposes complementary activities: the way a subject constructs selves and the way an audience apprehends the other, both through language. In this novel, Roth strips away the illusion of mediation provided by a narrator, who must be seen to weigh and interpret "facts" as he or she presents them. The uncontextualized presentation of speech gives the appearance of reportage rather than of invention, deepening the credibility of the speakers who seem to be offering themselves to direct apprehension, without prejudgment. Because the reader is confronted by the need to create the context of events within which to place the conversations "reported," filling in the gaps of normal colloquy and supplying action and scene, the reader's role is much more obviously active than in most novels. The novel's form underscores the speculative and engaged nature of the reading process, with the consequence that the "selves" perceived therein are clearly as much the reader's product as the writer's. Any reader plays reality shift during the interpretive process.

Primarily, however, reality shift is a metaphor for the verbal constructions of subject-positions, and Roth links the game explicitly to the way the process of writing obscures the distinction between fact and fiction. He has "Philip" play Zuckerman while his lover plays Zuckerman's biographer, who, he surmises, is interested in "the terrible ambiguity of the 'I,' the way a writer makes a myth of himself and, particularly, *why*."[43] As a game in which the players know the rules, reality shift seems harmless enough, and clearly fruitful for a writer, whose life's work depends on the capacity to meddle with the facts. At one point, however, "Philip's" friend Ivan makes the case for a reality distinct from its linguistic representations: "The undevelopedness, the unplottedness, what is merely latent, that is actuality. . . . Life before the narrative takes over is life."[44] Subsequently, Roth shows what is at stake in this distinction—how reality shift is more than just a game and how there may be consequences to interpreting a narrative as autobiographical "fact" or as unmitigated invention. When the woman he lives with reads "Philip's" notebooks, where the conversations with the lover are recorded, she accuses him of actually recording such conversations rather than making them up. He assures her that " 'I have been imagining myself, outside of my novel, having a love affair with a character inside my novel," that the notebook contains "the story of an *imagination* in love"[45] as distinct from the story of himself in love with a real person. When she refuses to accept his explanations—refuses to be guided by the author toward an intentional interpretation—she substitutes for precisely the readers who read Roth biographically, and her sense of betrayal is palpable. The erotic betrayal stands for the epistemological betrayal experienced by readers whom a writer frustrates when he plants autobiographical clues in fictional narrative, and both betrayals are brought together in the titular figure of "deception."[46] In the perception of both readerly and sexual betrayal, one person has promised intimacy to another, and both texts and lovers are deliberately ambiguous about whether such intimacy has been achieved—whether actual insight into the normally guarded self has been offered to another or, to the contrary, whether the self remains stubbornly elusive to the other. The larger betrayal is to suggest that intimacy is impossible because there is no "self" to be offered.

Since the form of the novel invites a reader to be conscious of his or her interpretive process, and since the reader can feel betrayed by the veiled references to Roth's own life, his decision to name his central speaker "Philip" provides a particular irritant. For the first time in his fiction, Roth's readers are openly encouraged to read the text as autobiography. Yet he thwarts such interpretations by posing these apparent self-revelations against the novel's repeated discussions of the fiction-making process, which are most poignant in but not limited to "Philip's" defense of his imaginary affair to the woman he lives with. This flagrant gesture of self-naming allows Roth to tweak his critics: "I write fiction and I'm told it's autobiography, I write autobiography and I'm told it's fiction, so since I'm so dim and they're so smart, let *them* decide what it is or it isn't."[47] Herein lies the active "deception"; Roth deliberately avails himself of the obscurity that exists between the categories of fact and fiction to place the ball in the reader's court. We have no choice but to become active ourselves.

The second clause in "Philip's" bitter comment—"I write autobiography and I'm told it's fiction"—refers to *The Facts*, the first time

"Philip" appears in one of Roth's narratives, not named but as an explicit referent for the "I" in the text. By some measures, "Philip" appears in *The Facts* in a less problematic way than in *Deception*, since the book announces itself in the subtitle as *A Novelist's Autobiography*. But the "novelist" here is a clue that all is not as simple as it might appear, a hint that is elaborated when we open to the first page of the text to find Roth's letter to his character, Zuckerman. While this epistolary preface asserts that the book "embodies my counterlife, the antidote and answer to all those fictions that culminated in the fiction of you,"[48] it nevertheless exposes the irony of Roth's title when he points out that "the facts are never just coming at you but are incorporated by an imagination that is formed by your previous experience. Memories of the past are not memories of facts but memories of your imaginings of the facts."[49] In this manner, "fact" itself becomes the central trope by which Roth inquires in this book into the problem of representing subjectivity. Even as he provides a detailed rendition of the "facts" of his first thirty-five years, he reminds the reader that this is but one possible telling, and a muted one at that, since, as Zuckerman argues, in "the mask of Philip" he is incapable of "telling the truth about his personal experience."[50] If it weren't for Roth's admission that a breakdown in 1987 caused him to seek the thinner air of autobiography, it would be perfectly reasonable to ask why he would, after *The Counterlife*, prefer to recount the untransformed events of his early years. But the answer is that, through the deft move of the framing device, Roth manages to pursue the point that self-exposure is always a work of fiction.[51] Zuckerman makes much the same point: "With autobiography, there's always another text, a countertext, if you will, to the one presented. It's probably the most manipulative of all literary forms."[52] Indeed, as Elaine Kauvar has argued, in this autobiography, Roth "overturns the entire enterprise of factual discourse" with the result that the book "materializes an affirmation of the imagination's power and a refutation of facticity."[53]

So why write autobiographically in the first place? It seems that *The Facts* provided Roth a necessary stage in the process of assessing life writing, an excuse to hold the artifact of his past in his hand like Yorick's skull and examine it in the contours of its own untransformed events much as he did the various counterselves he developed in David Kepesh, Peter Tarnopol, and Nathan Zuckerman. The same might be said for *Patrimony*, though the form of this memoir is not nearly as self-conscious as that of *The Facts*. Although the book is ostensibly about Roth's father, even the title implies its relational character—the father is perceived through the lens of his legacy to his son. Herman and his legacy are intricately bound up with Philip's identity as a writer. It is Herman who is the "bard of Newark," whose stories have grounded his son in the place that has largely been the material of his fiction. It is Herman, too, who gave Philip his language: "he taught me the vernacular. He was the vernacular, unpoetic and expressive and point-blank." It is, finally, Herman, with his endless storytelling, whose unspoken motto is "You mustn't forget anything," for whom "To be alive . . . is to be made of memory."[54] Herman is the proto-novelist and the book obliquely recalls the Dedalus myth to which Roth alludes directly in *The Ghost Writer*—it is a portrait of the artist as the son of Herman. What this proves is not so much the inescapability of narcissism as that any account of the real is inevitably from a point of view, the first-person perspective of the narrating consciousness. The logical extension of this effect is that any narrative is in some sense both a work of fiction and a song of myself.

So it is that Roth expresses anxiety over the representation of the actual. At the very end of the memoir, Roth reports a nightmare that occurred after Herman's death: "he came in a hooded white shroud to reproach me. He said, 'I should have been dressed in a suit. You did the wrong thing.' . . . All that peered out from the shroud was the displeasure in his dead face. And his only words were a rebuke: I had dressed him for eternity in the wrong clothes."[55] As he recognizes, the dream alludes to the book itself. His unconscious is expressing anxiety over how he "dresses" his father for posterity and public view—how, that is, he presents the "facts" of Herman's life while simultaneously remaining faithful to the truth of Herman's experience of his own life and giving narrative shape to that experience. This anxiety takes a very different form in the next work of fiction, *Operation Shylock*, which leaves behind the focus on the representation of the other to return it to the representation of the self. Once again, "Philip" appears in the narrative, presumably without quotation marks—and in fact appears with a vengeance, in both the narrator and his double, also named Philip Roth. Here, the double is the obvious trope for the inquiry into self-exposure. This "confession" moves seamlessly from Roth's account of his drug-induced breakdown—documented as "factual" in *The Facts*—into the far less plausible encounter with the double and the significations of identity the double portends. The form of the book as "confession" clearly raises the point that to represent "untransformed" reality has ethical as well as epistemological implications—even though, by a contorted logic, it is a fiction that the facts are untransformed here. Roth addresses the question directly in the epilogue, which announces his supposed suppression of an account of "Philip's" undercover operation for the Israeli intelligence agency. While the novel refuses definitive judgment concerning the writer's obligation to adjust his fictions to the needs of the external world, the concluding statement suggests that the voice of conscience will have the last word. The expression that lingers in the reader's mind—Smilesburger's advice to "Let your Jewish conscience be your guide"—demands that "reality" remain unrepresented.[56]

It is not only because *Operation Shylock* invokes the ethical implications of novel writing that the quasi-autobiographical "I" telling the story—the Philip Roth in the text—seems to have a curious effect for the reader, quite unlike that of most fictional narrators. Normally, a reader is said to identify with characters in a text, and that identification is especially intense when the reader is drawn into being the subject of the first-person "I" speaking the narration. Georges Poulet argues that, in the process of reading, the reader thinks the thoughts of someone else, such that the "I" the reader mentally thinks is not the reader him or herself: "I am the subject of thoughts other than my own. My consciousness behaves as though it were the consciousness of another."[57] As a result, author and reader converge in a common consciousness, such that "This *I* who thinks in me when I read a book, is the *I* of the one who writes the book."[58] Wolfgang Iser finds that the conflation of subjectivities in the reading process implies "the cessation of the temporary self-alienation that occurs to the reader when his consciousness brings to life the ideas formulated by the author";[59] the reader's "own individuality temporarily recedes into the background, since it is supplanted by these alien thoughts."[60] This process depends, according to Iser, on "two conditions: the life-story of the author must be shut out of the work and the individual disposition of the reader must be shut out of the act of reading."[61]

When Roth makes clear that the referent for the "I" in *Operation Shylock* is "Philip Roth," which happens in the very first sentence of chapter 1—"I learned about the other Philip Roth in January 1988"—he demonstrates that the first of these conditions will not be met in the text.[62] Instead, the reader is displaced from identification with the narrating voice when the author seems to hold the position of the subject. The novel resists the imaginative act that every reader engages in when confronted by a work of fiction. Roth's strategy has several effects. Most obviously, it returns the reader to facticity. By being excluded from the narrating voice, the reader is unable to participate except at a distance in the events related, and this distance paradoxically seems to verify the status of events as factual, as "out there" in the world. Furthermore, the thoughts of the narrator remain other—they are Philip Roth's thoughts, not our own, even if we are able to engage them fully and empathetically, because we know that there exists in the world an *actual* Philip Roth to have these thoughts.[63] The reader is therefore more likely to interpret the narrative as "fact," not just as "true" (in the sense of "true to life"), because it seems to relate a reality into which we cannot fully project our own subjectivity. We do not live through these events because someone else already has. The tactic renders the narrative "historical," lacking the sense of continuous presence otherwise resulting even from fictional narratives related in the past tense. This allows the reader's individuality to recede. Roth's tactic reminds us that the sense of the fictive relies on our ability to identify with otherness, to become imaginatively absorbed into a world that is not-us—or at the very least that the experience of fiction resides in our oscillation between that phenomenon of absorption and the intermittent awareness that what we are reading is not factual.

The apparent return to facticity Roth creates in the invention of the autobiographical "I" elicits a complex response. Since, as I have suggested, the autobiographical act is founded on the textualizing of the self, a reader of Roth's novel gets a heightened awareness of the "I" as a textual product. We become implicated, too. Not only is this allegedly self-revealing author inventing the self he reveals, but our own selves must be invented as well. Paradoxically, the appeal to fact undermines factuality as a recoverable entity. As in *The Facts*, then, the conclusion one draws from *Operation Shylock* is about the primacy of fiction. Smilesburger's final appeal to conscience rather than the freedom to represent the real is made ironic in that it is followed by white space. Roth's answer is indeterminate, because he does not include the words of assent that would adopt Smilesburger's position. The reader is left poised between a silence that suggests agreement—since, after all, the offending chapter does not appear in the published text—and a silence that suggests a rejection of "Jewish conscience" in favor of representing the world just as it exists.

If one reads Roth's books chronologically, it would seem that his unspoken choice is the latter—to represent the real no matter what conscience dictates—since the next novel that appeared was *Sabbath's Theater*, with its unfettered focus on sex, death, and emotional abuse. But in this novel and the more recent *American Pastoral* (1997),[64] the "real" is no longer autobiographical reality, at least insofar as Roth may be said to be projecting events in any recognizable way from his personal life into the likes of Nathan Zuckerman in *Zuckerman Bound* or "Philip Roth" in *Operation Shylock*. Instead, he seems for a time to have exhausted the activity of self-exposure for its own sake, and no wonder, given the tour de force performance of selves in *Operation Shylock*.[65]

Nevertheless, the concerns expressed by the various tropes in the preceding works that represent the indeterminacy of the subject— the counterlife, reality shift, "fact," and so forth—appear in these two late novels in relation to what might be termed the "Roth" persona. This persona encompasses the variety of roles with which Roth's fiction and, inescapably, the public's interpretation of his life, have been associated: the Jew, the writer, the anxious male, the breaker of sexual taboos. I do not suggest that Roth is writing covert autobiography in this recent work, but rather that the impersonations tempting his imagination draw to some degree on the images that his readership associates with his life as well as his art. In both novels, "autobiography" and "biography," in their broad reference to the writing of a life story, provide metaphors rather than determinate puzzles for readers to solve concerning the relationship between the fiction and the "facts" of Roth's life. I suggest further that in these novels, Roth pushes his consideration of the problem of positioning and representing the self beyond where he went before. *Operation Shylock* seems to demand, through such features of the novel as Smilesburger's injunctions and the tragedy of "Philip's" double, that Roth consider the effect of the narrativized subject on the other. Once Roth brings his "self" into the full glare of narrative exposure, he begins to think in even more comprehensively relational terms than he has done in earlier works, where the interest of relationships remained largely focused on the narrators like Kepesh in *The Breast* (1972) and *The Professor of Desire* (1977), Tarnopol, and Zuckerman.[66]

The most obvious example in *Sabbath's Theater* appears in the character of Mickey Sabbath. Sabbath is what Alex Portnoy might have become if he had left therapy, joined the merchant marine, and

taken up puppetry as a vocation. Because Sabbath revels in the art
of transgression and identifies himself with the principle of chaos,
he inverts the image of Portnoy's neurosis, defining his health by his
ability to disrupt social codes and force his will on those around him.
If, to adopt Roth's own distinction, Portnoy was traumatized by the
desires that prohibited him from enacting the role of the "nice Jewish boy," Sabbath is delighted to perform as the "Jewboy," as Roth
puts it elsewhere, with "all that word signifies to Jew and Gentile
alike about aggression, appetite, and marginality."[67] Sabbath represents the transgressive features of the "Roth" persona, and thereby
allows him to test the effects of such transgressiveness on those upon
whom Sabbath exerts his will, such as his two wives, Nikki and Roseanna. The metaphor Roth wraps his inquiry around is ventriloquism—the activity by which Sabbath as puppetmaster projects his
voice into others. This self-projection is a logical extension of the
way Roth's characters have always engaged in self-invention, in developing the narratives of their lives, with the difference that the excesses in which Sabbath engages highlight the way that self-
invention requires others to serve as objects for the self's ends. A
ventriloquist needs a dummy, a puppetmaster a puppet. Nikki's disappearance and Roseanna's alcoholism both suggest the damage
that Sabbath's objectification of them causes: they lose their grasp of
their own subjectivity. Only when Roth permits a view of Sabbath's
tremendous anxiety about death do we come to see that self-projection is a desperate gesture against the annihilation of self. The theater of self-performance Sabbath erects around himself can be seen
as an extreme expression of the urge toward autobiography as an
act of self-preservation, toward making somehow permanent the
vanishing self.

The vanishing subject likewise becomes the central concern of
American Pastoral. Like *Sabbath's Theater,* it cannot be mistaken for an
autobiography, except insofar as Nathan Zuckerman reappears as
narrator and, through his familiarity to Roth's readers as a writerly
alter ego, may be taken as a mouthpiece for the author. Where writing as a primary vehicle for the invention of subjectivity is virtually
absent as a theme from *Sabbath's Theater,* it comes to the fore again
in *American Pastoral* as Nathan, driven by profound nostalgia, struggles to write a biography, to imagine the selfhood that would support the "facts" he has learned about Swede Levov's life. Here, the
parts of the "Roth persona" Roth engages include the writer (in Nathan) and the Jew (in Swede and in Nathan's recovery of his New

Jersey past), where both subjects are more acted upon than acting. Like *My Life as a Man*, the novel has a Chinese box structure, not of narrators exactly, but of consciousnesses trying to apprehend unknowable others. Zuckerman wants to know Swede, who remains elusive and larger than life to him, and who, he imagines, wants to know his daughter, Merry Levov; Merry, in turn, is literally elusive (since she has gone into hiding) and so large as to have absorbed Swede's life into her tragedy. Zuckerman's endeavor is perpetually frustrated: "When it comes to illuminating someone with the Swede's opacity, to understanding those regular guys everybody likes and who go about more or less incognito, it's up for grabs."[68]

Like the gloves stitched together with such care at Swede's factory, the story Zuckerman pieces together must withstand the stretch of the manipulating hand—the will of the other to remain other—only to pull apart at the missed stitch. Nathan bemoans the limitations of the biographer:

> You get [people] wrong before you meet them . . . ; you get them wrong while you're with them; and then you go home to tell somebody else about the meeting and you get them all wrong again. Since the same generally goes for them with you, the whole thing is really a dazzling illusion empty of all perception, an astonishing farce of misperception. And yet what are we to do about this terribly significant business of *other people* . . . ? . . . The fact remains that getting people right is not what living is all about anyway. It's getting them wrong that is living, getting them wrong and wrong and wrong and then, on careful reconsideration, getting them wrong again.[69]

The "astonishing farce of misperception" that is the game of interrelationships replicates the complex game of self-knowing and self-exposure, and the unknowability that Roth explores here echoes the problem the double, Pipik, poses to "Philip Roth" in *Operation Shylock*. The difference is that *American Pastoral* extends the farce to show how it is contextualized by history—by Swede's place as a second-generation Jewish American and by the contradictions and confrontations of American culture during the 1960s. Swede might be seen as Roth's effort to imagine a counterlife for Sabbath. He is the "nice Jewish boy," a man who offers the antithesis of Sabbath's will to transgress, who desires simply to do and to be good, to conform his subjectivity to the ruling norms of his world, only to be battered and baffled and emptied of selfhood when the rules seem to change. What he is left with is a void within the structures of life he has most

cherished—his family, his business, his country. He loses his grip on
his life as an American, about which he once could think "Everything he loved was here,"[70] a thought which reverses Sabbath's final
assertion about the force that drives him to live despite himself:
"Everything he hated was here."[71] Because Merry has inexplicably
vanished from his life, Swede must confront the instability of all his
knowledge about himself and his world. He pursues a quest to understand her, to find the causes that might explain the monstrosity
which finally seems to define what she becomes, and it is necessarily
a quest without closure. Nathan pursues a parallel and equally unsat-
isfiable quest to explain Swede's opaque life, developing a series of
narrative hypotheses that enclose Swede's hypotheses about his
daughter. Ultimately, neither biographer can ever grasp his *subject*,
in both senses of the term. The topic, the object of concern for each,
remains beyond reach, with the result that—since most quests for
knowledge, whatever their guise may be, are inevitably about knowing ourselves—the self that each biographer would define through
his project of knowing the other evaporates into thin air. The attempt to expose the other to one's view is analogous to the attempt
at self-exposure that Roth questions in so much of the previous fiction, and I think this is why he arrives at the initially bewildering
strategy of introducing Zuckerman as narrator only to have him disappear as an identifiable presence a quarter of the way through the
narrative. Zuckerman's vanishing act is a structural metaphor for
Roth's theme: the unreadable "reality" of the visible world renders
the perceiving subject as fleeting as his object of perception.[72]

Much of Roth's work since *My Life as a Man* complicates and undermines conventional notions of personality as moderately stable
and detectable. While the postmodern epistemologies of identity
Roth has explored are far from new, his particular narrative approach, through the exploitation of his own persona, provides fresh
angles on the issue of how subjectivity is represented and poses fascinating interpretive puzzles for readers. When he uses himself as the
object of representation, he offers a special case of the problem of
writing the self, more intimate because seemingly more verifiably
"real" than an obviously invented self, and therefore more disturb-
ing when he explores the less socially acceptable corners of the self's
desires. When Roth experiments with the form of his narratives,
drawing on genres as various as autobiography, biography, memoir,
confession, dialogue, psychoanalytic monologue, and fiction-about-
fiction, he draws upon readers' expectations about the "truth" value

of each genre in such a way that he can simultaneously offer and refuse self-exposure. As a result, readers experience the absolute indeterminacy of the narrated subject. Confessional fiction—the work that transforms the identifiable events and concerns of an author's life into fiction—masks the self in order to unmask it, to produce knowledge about the self through the defamiliarizations of metaphor and plot. Roth's fictions of self-exposure, however, appear to unmask the self only in order to mask it, to invent a not-self or counterlife that is an alternative to what is allegedly known; as Roth told Hermione Lee, when a writer "dons the mask of the first-person singular," it "may be the best mask of all for a second self."[73] Autobiography is the magician's best trick: now you see him, now you don't.

Like Zuckerman in *American Pastoral* and the earlier double, Alvin Pepler in *Zuckerman Unbound,* Pipik in *Operation Shylock* performs a vanishing act. Aptly enough, Pipik—the exemplar of self-exposure as deception—is central to my closing story about how a reader attempting to interpret the "Roth" in the text meets frustration, even when the "Roth" under scrutiny is not a public face offered in a published work. Early in *Operation Shylock,* the "Philip Roth" who narrates the novel visits the trial in Israel of John Demjanjuk, the alleged Ivan the Terrible of Treblinka. He observes: "When I entered the courtroom . . . I forgot completely why I had come; when, after sorting out the dozen or so figures on the raised platform at the front of the courtroom, I realized which one was the accused, not only did my double cease to exist, but, for the time being, so did I."[74] "Philip" energetically attempts to understand the mysterious otherness of Demjanjuk. His meditation begins "There he was" and notes the defendant's vigor, indifference, and appearance as a "cheerful palooka of sixty-eight,"[75] none of which squares with the horror of the accusations against him. When "Philip" subsequently thinks "There he was. Or wasn't,"[76] Roth captures the elusiveness of personality and the "farce of misperception" that, in denying that identity is ineffable, misguidedly asserts that it can be narrated. "Philip's" response to the muteness of identity signified by Demjanjuk's physical presence is salutary—he feels that he ceases to exist. The unapproachability of a given subject erodes the presence of any subjectivity. The "Philip" who narrates is finally no more there than the "Philip" he purports to narrate.

Demjanjuk's appearance is a metonymy for the question of identity posed even more forcibly in this novel by "Philip's" double, the

"other Philip Roth."[77] Included in the materials Roth has deposited
at the Library of Congress are notes and drafts for *Operation Shylock*
and among these, in Draft 1, is the first version of this passage narrating "Philip's" appearance at the Demjanjuk trial. Although the
alterations Roth made in this passage between the draft and the published version are for my purposes insignificant, what is arresting is
a handwritten note that appears below the typed text: "Moishe Pipik
(When I was clowning as a child, my nickname)."[78] A reader of these
papers would be tempted to see several things going on here, each
of which resists verification. First, this page seems to be an artifact
bearing witness to the creative act. Juxtaposed to the typed draft, the
handwritten note that relates in no immediate way to the content of
this page of the draft seems to capture a moment of the composition
process: for whatever reason, in rereading this passage, Roth had the
insight, apparently deriving from a memory, that caused him to discover the name that "Philip" brilliantly bestows on his double. A
reader of this manuscript then interprets—and thereby invents—
Roth's own biography, both the time of his childhood and the time
of his writing this book. Second, the parenthetical phrases are more
complicated than they look at first. Given that the narrative to which
this note is appended is written in the first person, to whom does
that "I" refer? Is this the "Philip Roth" in the text, or the Philip
Roth with historical existence outside the text? Is the writer making
use of a memory (in which case, why would he have to remind himself on paper that this was "my nickname"?), or is the writer inventing a past for his character and noting it in his character's voice? In
whose childhood was who called Moishe Pipik?

The answers to these questions may be trivial, but their implications are not. When Roth flaunts self-references and invites autobiographical interpretations, he performs a kind of seduction of his
readers, promising an "objective" truth and then failing to deliver.
The dizzying effects of self-exposure, like the betrayals outlined in
Deception, not only frustrate a reader's impatient desire to sort out
the truth of what he or she is reading, but also strike at fundamental
assumptions about how one can trust and interpret any evidence.
Because a reader takes the cognitive process of encountering a narrative as equivalent to the cognitive process of encountering real
perceptual experience in the world, Roth's decision to break the
contract with the reader, to refuse to earn or justify a reader's faith
by satisfactorily distinguishing fact from fiction, becomes deeply unsettling. Roth places the reader in Swede Levov's position, baffled

by the uninterpretable world and no more able than Roth's various narrators to capture a life story. To write autobiography is to lose assurance that one records subjectivity rather than evanescent subject-positions. Roth's gambit is to bring his readers to this point by thinking that they are coming to know him.

NOTES

1. Philip Roth, *Deception: A Novel* (New York: Simon and Schuster, 1990), and *Operation Shylock: A Confession* (New York: Simon and Schuster, 1993). A revised and expanded version of this essay appears in chapter 5 of my book, *Philip Roth: Countertexts, Counterlives* (Columbia: University of South Carolina Press, 2004).

2. Philip Roth, *The Counterlife* (1986; repr., New York: Penguin, 1989), and *Sabbath's Theater* (Boston: Houghton Mifflin, 1995).

3. For a full discussion of a range of autobiographical references in Roth's work, see Alan Cooper, *Philip Roth and the Jews* (Albany: State University of New York Press, 1996), esp. 51–71. For a cogent description of the "coquettish game with his readers" (46) that Roth has played, see Hillel Halkin, "How to Read Philip Roth," *Commentary* (February 1994): 43–48.

4. Philip Roth, *Goodbye, Columbus* (Boston: Houghton Mifflin, 1959), and "Writing About Jews," *Reading Myself and Others* (1975; rev. ed., New York: Penguin, 1985). Rabbis criticized Roth from pulpit and periodical for failing to translate his observations of assimilated American Jews in *Goodbye, Columbus* into a portrayal sensitive to the impressions he might make on his non-Jewish readership. Unwilling to believe that Roth was inventing rather than recording life around him, these readers felt betrayed. See "Writing About Jews."

5. Philip Roth, *Portnoy's Complaint* (New York: Random House, 1969).

6. Philip Roth, "Imagining Jews," *Reading Myself and Others*, 274.

7. Philip Roth, *My Life as a Man* (1974; repr., New York: Vintage, 1993).

8. Ibid., 174.

9. Philip Roth, *The Facts: A Novelist's Autobiography* (New York: Farrar, 1988).

10. In *The Facts*, Roth notes the degree to which *My Life as a Man* retells the story of his marriage to Margaret Martinson Roth. He especially makes use in the novel of the trick by which she caused him to marry her: "Probably nothing else in my work more precisely duplicates the autobiographical facts. Those scenes represent one of the few occasions when I haven't spontaneously set out to improve on actuality in the interest of being more interesting" (*The Facts*, 107).

11. *My Life as a Man*, 100.

12. Ibid., 334.

13. Roth's move here is much like what he does with closure in *Operation Shylock*, where the "Note to the Reader" following the last page of the novel, with its final ironic line that "This confession is false," simultaneously asserts and denies the historical truth of the narrative that has just concluded.

14. Wayne Booth, *The Rhetoric of Fiction* (Chicago: University of Chicago Press, 1961), 75.

15. Needless to say, the notion that autobiography is itself an unmediated form

is highly contested. For discussion of the inherent duplicity of autobiography as a narrative of "fact," see Paul John Eakin, *Fictions in Autobiography: Studies in the Art of Self-Invention* (Princeton: Princeton University Press, 1985), and Paul Jay, *Being in the Text: Self-Representation from Wordsworth to Roland Barthes* (Ithaca: Cornell University Press, 1984). For a discussion of the broader issues involved in consideration of narratives of fact, see Hayden White, "The Value of Narrativity in the Representation of Reality," in *On Narrative*, ed. W. J. T. Mitchell (Chicago: University of Chicago Press, 1981), 1–23.

16. Philip Roth, *Patrimony: A True Story* (New York: Simon and Schuster, 1991).

17. Eugene L. Stelzig, *Hermann Hesse's Fictions of the Self: Autobiography and the Confessional Imagination* (Princeton: Princeton University Press, 1988), 3.

18. Philip Roth, "Interview with *Le Nouvel Observateur*," 1981, with Alain Finkielkraut, *Reading Myself and Others*, 117. See also Roth, "Interview with *The Paris Review*," 1984, with Hermione Lee, *Reading Myself and Others*, 147.

19. Philip Roth, "'I Always Wanted You to Admire My Fasting'; or, Looking at Kafka," 1973, *Reading Myself and Others*, 313.

20. Despite its conventional usage, the "alter ego" seems to me a misnomer, since the term suggests something approaching a one-to-one correspondence between the facts of a life and their fictional counterparts. To assume such a correspondence is to adopt an unreliable interpretive device.

21. Jay Halio, *Philip Roth Revisited* (New York: Twayne, 1992), 140.

22. Booth, *Rhetoric of Fiction*, 86.

23. Ibid., 326.

24. Philip Roth, *Zuckerman Bound* (New York: Farrar, Straus and Giroux, 1985). This volume contains the trilogy of Zuckerman novels: *The Ghost Writer* (1979), *Zuckerman Unbound* (1981), and *The Anatomy Lesson* (1983), as well as an epilogue, *The Prague Orgy*.

25. Irving Howe, "Philip Roth Reconsidered" *Commentary* (December 1972), rpt. in *Critical Essays on Philip Roth*, ed. Sanford Pinsker (Boston: G. K. Hall, 1982), 229–44. For a useful defense of the Howe/Appel episode in the context of Roth's transgressive explorations of the nature of desire, see James D. Wallace, "'This Nation of Narrators': Transgression, Revenge and Desire in *Zuckerman Bound*," *Modern Language Studies* 21, no. 3 (1991): 17–34.

26. Roth, *Zuckerman Unbound*, in *Zuckerman Bound*, 319.

27. Philip Roth, "Interview with *The London Sunday Times*," 1984, with Ian Hamilton, *Reading Myself and Others*, 130.

28. Patrick O'Donnell, "'None Other': The Subject of Roth's *My Life as a Man*," in *Reading Philip Roth*, ed. Asher Z. Milbauer and Donald G. Watson (New York: St. Martin's Press, 1988), 154.

29. Ibid., 157. See also Sanford Pinsker, *The Comedy That "Hoits": An Essay on the Fiction of Philip Roth* (Columbia: University of Missouri Press, 1975), 103–5. For the countering view that *My Life as a Man*'s "skepticism is less epistemological than moral" (263), see Howard Eiland, "Philip Roth: The Ambiguities of Desire," in *Critical Essays on Philip Roth*, ed. Sanford Pinsker (Boston: G. K. Hall, 1982), 255–65.

30. Roth, *My Life as a Man*, 334.

31. See Jacques Derrida, *Of Grammatology*, trans. Gayatri Spivak (Baltimore: Johns Hopkins University Press, 1976), 145.

32. Avrom Fleishman, *Figures of Autobiography: The Language of Self-Writing in Victo-*

rian and Modern England (Berkeley and Los Angeles: University of California Press, 1983), 32.

33. Ibid.

34. Mark Schechner, *After the Revolution: Studies in the Contemporary Jewish American Imagination* (Bloomington: Indiana University Press, 1987), 225.

35. Michael Riffaterre, *Fictional Truth* (Baltimore: Johns Hopkins University Press, 1990), xv.

36. Roth, *Counterlife*, 320.

37. See Ellen Levy, "Is Zuckerman Dead? Countertexts in Philip Roth's *The Counterlife*," *Caliban* 29 (1992): 126–27; Michael Greenstein, "Ozick, Roth, and Postmodernism," *Studies in American Jewish Literature* 10 (1991): 60–62; and Debra Shostak "'This obsessive reinvention of the real': Speculative Narrative in Philip Roth's *The Counterlife*," *Modern Fiction Studies* 37 (1991): 198–200.

38. "Counterlife" even more precisely implies a relationship of binary opposition, such that there would be only a single narrative to oppose the "real." Roth with this term uncovers an analogous terminological flaw to that implied by the notion of the "alter ego," which I mentioned above (see note 20). Part of Roth's joke, embedded in the form of this novel, is to undermine his own terminology; Zuckerman (and the reader) should be so lucky as to have just two possible narratives to choose from.

39. *Counterlife*, 319.

40. Ibid., 320.

41. Paul Smith, *Discerning the Subject* (Minneapolis: University of Minnesota Press, 1988), xxxv.

42. *Counterlife*, 312, 319, and 318.

43. *Deception*, 98.

44. Ibid., 94.

45. Ibid., 183, 189.

46. Rodger Kamenetz, in "'The Hocker, Misnomer . . . Love/Dad': Philip Roth's *Patrimony*," *The Southern Review* 27 (1991): 942, captures the cognitive predicament of the reader confronted by the conflicting stories of "Roth" and his housemate: "the reader, in searching for the autobiographical 'truth' of the situation, forgets that, as in Poe's story of the purloined letter, the secret is hidden in being exposed."

47. *Deception*, 190.

48. *Facts*, 6.

49. Ibid., 8.

50. Ibid., 191.

51. And, for some readers, satisfyingly so. In a thorough reading of *The Facts* as a crucial stage in Roth's "growing recognition of the indeterminacy of all forms of textuality," Brian Finney concludes that "It is not simply impossible to disentangle fact from imaginative invention, it is impoverishing." Brian Finney, "Roth's Counterlife: Destabilizing *The Facts*," *Biography* 16 (1993): 372, 378.

52. *Facts*, 172.

53. Elaine Kauvar, "This Doubly Reflected Communication: Philip Roth's 'Autobiographies,'" *Contemporary Literature* 36 (1995): 415, 420.

54. *Patrimony*, 125, 181, and 124.

55. Ibid., 237.

56. *OS*, 398.

57. Georges Poulet, "Phenomenology of Reading," *New Literary History* 1 (1969): 56.

58. Ibid., 58.

59. Wolfgang Iser, "The Reading Process: A Phenomenological Approach," in *Reader-Response Criticism: From Formalism to Post-Structuralism*, ed. JaneTompkins (Baltimore: Johns Hopkins University Press, 1980), 66.

60. Ibid., 67.

61. Ibid., 66.

62. *OS*, 17.

63. This is true even if we don't quite believe that these thoughts happened in this particular order and in this particular context—if, that is, we still cling to the premise that we are reading a work of fiction—since there is still a *real* Philip Roth writing the book. He thinks these thoughts at the time of writing, if nothing else. They can't be our thoughts.

64. Philip Roth, *American Pastoral* (Boston: Houghton Mifflin, 1997).

65. Roth's pendulum, however, does seem to have swung back in the other direction with the publication of *I Married a Communist* (Boston: Houghton Mifflin, 1998). Nathan Zuckerman is not only the interlocutor who allows the ninety-year-old Murray Ringold to tell his and his brother, Ira's, story—and, along with it, a version of midcentury American history—but he also has a phantom life existing on the borders of the narrative, a story of idealistic youth turned to withdrawal from the world, a story that never gets told. In describing Ira's rural shack, where Nathan now lives, he hints darkly at this untold story: this is the "place where you are stripped back to essentials, to which you return . . . to decontaminate and absolve yourself of the striving. . . . where you shed your batteredness and your resentment, your appeasement of the world and your defiance of the world, your manipulation of the world and its manhandling of you. . . . [The aging man] has entered vigorously into competition with life; now, becalmed, he enters into competition with death, drawn down into austerity, the final business" (72).

The eschatological tone of these musings, coupled with Zuckerman's refusal to narrate his present life, might lead a reader to discern in Nathan's predicament the aging and embattled Roth, holed up in Connecticut. This impression is exacerbated by Roth's placement of an actress, Eve Frame, and her harpist daughter, Sylphid, at the center of Ira's story—for many readers an inescapable reference to Roth's ex-wife, Claire Bloom, and her daughter, the singer Anna, a reference that, given the narrative judgments Roth performs against Eve and Sylphid, can make the novel seem like retaliation for Bloom's exposé of Roth in her memoir, *Leaving a Doll's House* (Boston: Little, Brown, 1996). See, for example, Robert Kelly, "Are You Now or Have You Ever Been . . . ," review of *I Married a Communist*, by Philip Roth, *New York Times Book Review*, October 11, 1998, 6–7, as well as the more withering treatment of Roth's self-references in John Leonard, "Bedtime for Bolsheviks," review of *I Married a Communist*, by Philip Roth, *The Nation*, November 16, 1998, esp. 28–29.

66. Philip Roth, *The Breast* (1972; repr., New York: Vintage, 1994), and *The Professor of Desire* (1977; repr., New York: Penguin, 1985).

67. Philip Roth, "In Response to Those Who Have Asked Me: 'How Did You Come to Write That Book, Anyway?'" *Reading Myself and Others*, 35.

68. *AP*, 77.

69. Ibid., 35.

70. Ibid., 213.

71. *ST*, 450.

72. Though Zuckerman remains the audible narrator in *I Married a Communist*, the vanishing act in *American Pastoral* has prepared us for his teasing presence/absence as a figure in the later work.

73. "Interview with *The Paris Review*," 145.

74. *OS*, 59–60.

75. Ibid., 60, 61.

76. Ibid., 62.

77. Ibid., 17.

78. "Two-Faced (Early Draft of *Operation Shylock*)," Mar. 25, 1990, marked as "Draft 1,"86a, unprocessed Philip Roth papers, Manuscript Division, Library of Congress. Interestingly enough, this draft as a whole is titled "Duality" and, attached to the top is a title page that reads "Two-Faced: An Autobiography in Four Acts," followed by a listing: "1. *The Facts*, a Novelist's Autobiography 2. *Deception*, a Novel 3. *Patrimony*, a True Story 4. *Duality*, a Novelist's Fantasy." Clearly, Roth thought of the novel that was to become *Operation Shylock* as the conclusion of a tetralogy about autobiography.

Textualizing the Self: Adultery, Blatant Fictions, and Jewishness in Philip Roth's *Deception*

G. Neelakantan

PHILIP ROTH'S *DECEPTION* (1990) RETURNS TO SOME OF THE NOVELIST'S familiar concerns,[1] even while its techniques of narration are radically experimental.[2] The story at the core of the narrative is "the story of an *imagination* in love."[3] In *Deception*, Roth for once dispenses with Nathan Zuckerman, his alter ego, in narrating the events that comprise the novel. Enmeshing fiction with autobiography[4] and thereby creating intriguing possibilities of reading a situation or a character, Roth succeeds in addressing certain concerns characteristic of metafiction[5] in this novel. The novel nearly abandons exposition in favor of dialogues for narrative purposes, and this technique often creates a vivid dramatic impact.

The protagonist of *Deception* is thinly disguised Philip Roth himself, an American-Jewish novelist who, for the most part of the novel's present, lives in London. Owing to "cultural displacement" (50) as he puts it, Philip spends most of his day in his one-room studio working on his novel *The Counterlife* (1986).[6] He falls in love with "Maria," a married Englishwoman, who seeks solace in his company for the troubles of her unhappy married life. Though she is unnamed in the novel, she is later identified as modeled on Maria in *The Counterlife*. As in *The Counterlife*, Roth conflates her with other women whom he knew intimately in order to implicate himself deeper into his "story of an *imagination* in love." Accordingly, the sections where Philip and Maria converse are juxtaposed by sections where Roth talks to ex-patriot Czechs, former lovers, and even a Polish woman interested in politics. As Jay Halio aptly points out, "Counter-pointing, heightening, and sometimes mirroring the dialogues with Maria, they [these sections] are on sex, infidelity, family and work, psychotherapy, sleeplessness, divorce lawyers, English anti-Semitism, and other subjects."[7]

Philip, the protagonist, clearly has an adulterous relationship with Maria. "Roth's new novel," [*Deception*], Brian Johnson argues, "is about adultery, in a manner of speaking."[8] If adultery is the theme, it also serves to structure the narrative in ways that make it possible to see the Rothian artist as an incorrigible adulterer.[9] To commit adultery and to write fiction both, in effect, mean a sanction for deception. There is nothing pristine or sacred, according to Roth, about the artistic process: it is a game where the artist constantly betrays others, stealing their words and deceiving them. Halio observes, Roth "plays games of deception and betrayal, 'impersonates' himself, 'ventriloquizes' himself, and has a thoroughly good time experimenting with what for him is also a new form of fiction."[10] In an interview shortly after *Deception* was published, Roth had expressed his passion for play. "What a writer has on tap," he said, "is the capacity . . . to play. I'm in here trying to find out what the game is . . . What I'm doing is looking to find out how to play."[11]

The artist and adulterer in Philip is drawn to only those women who have a way with words. Appropriately, when confronted with his wife's charge that he had portrayed his affair with Rosalie Nichols in his notebook,[12] Philip loses his temper and rants: "She's not, she's *words*—and try as I will, I cannot fuck words!" (192). He exhibits an irresistible fascination for the seductive movement of the narrative. To Maria's complaint that he is often indifferent when she talks to him, Philip responds: "I'm listening. I listen. I'm an écouteur—an audiophiliac. I'm a talk fetishist" (44). Maria is quick to understand that his libidinal urges translate into the act of listening.[13] She says, "It *is* erotic, you just sitting there listening" (44). Philip often, however, does more than listen. What he does listen to intently is subjected to his habit of "fictionalizing," a second nature with him, so that in his fictional work the narrative would bristle with dramatic possibilities. By practicing such "blatant fictionalizing" (95), he throws himself open to attack. But Philip being what he is—a manic given to excesses of imagination—carnivalizes these complications. As he himself confesses, "I portray myself as implicated because it is not enough just to be present. . . . What heats things up is compromising me. It kind of makes the indictment juicier, besmirching myself" (183–84). The projected confrontation of Ivan and Philip in the novel over Olina's betrayal of Ivan is a classic instance of this.

Olina, wife of Ivan, Philip's refugee friend, leaves Ivan to live with

a "big black" man. It is true that Philip had found Olina attractive
and that he was privy to some of her personal problems. However,
in his notebook Philip contrives a situation that shows Ivan accusing
him of betraying him with his wife and also of "rotten fictionalizing"
(94). Philip thus makes Ivan at some level conflate him with the
black, i.e., as a betrayer. In Ivan's view, "He [the black] did not fuck
her the way you [Philip] fucked her, for her stories. He fucked her
for fucking. You are more interested in listening than in fucking,
and Olina is not that interesting to listen to" (92). Further, Ivan is
exasperated when Philip tries to refute his charge of betraying him
with Olina: "You are a treacherous bastard who cannot resist a narrative even from the wife of his refugee friend. The stronger the narrative impulse in her, the more captivated you are. And all of this, I
must tell you, limits you not only as a friend but as a novelist" (93).
Philip is even told in which respect he fails as a novelist: "Maybe you
should have been a wonderful actor instead of a terrible novelist
who will never understand the power of a narrative that *remains* latent. You don't know how to leave *anything* alone. Just to give voice
to the woman is never enough for you. You will not just drown in
her cuntliness. You must always submerge and distort her in your
hero's stupid, artificial *plot*" (95). Though Philip tries to defend
himself, he also realizes that Ivan's charges are not wholly baseless.

Philip's accomplice in his games of deception and betrayal, Maria,
often herself doubts if he is entirely altruistic in empathizing with
her condition. On one occasion, she tells him without mincing
words that he has "no scruples" (105). Charging him with being her
"guilty secret" (154) and also of having "distracted [her] from the
central concerns of [her] life" (150), Maria even parts ways with
him. Her expectations of him, Philip realizes, are unrealistic and
confused. He tells her, "it didn't work out that way, you know. Because I became a temptation: a source of fantasy in the beginning, a
source of possibility after that, and then, eventually, a disappointment" (150).

Toward the end of *Deception*, Maria is seen making a transatlantic
call and telling Philip, among other things, that she has a second
child. In his characteristic way, Philip responds: "Well, ironies
abound. You had the son all right but not by my character and not
in my book. I imagined it but he did it. That's the difference between us; that's why you live with him and not me" (197). However,
Philip's declaration that his wife thinks Rosalie Nichols is the woman
who is depicted in the book incites Maria into saying: "Not only do

you steal my words, you've given them to someone else" (200). Nichols, as Philip reports to Maria, herself reacts in a similar fashion: "All the time I thought you loved me for my body when in fact it was only for my sentences" (200). Enraged at Philip's "blatant fictionalizing" (95), Maria herself accuses Philip of "taking down what I say" (202) and quoting her verbatim in the book. She is confused by Philip's loud way of depicting their affair in the book, while earlier he seemed paranoid about keeping the whole thing a secret. His only justification then was that he wanted to protect his wife "from something she couldn't be expected to be happy about" (199).

Maria shows mixed feelings toward Philip's book. To her query why he should fictionalize her character, Philip replies: "You also exist and also I made you up. 'Also' is a good word to remember. You also don't exist as only you" (206). Philip, one guesses, is fully convinced of his right to be endlessly inventive in fleshing out his fiction. As a writer, he is self-avowedly a "thief" who is "not to be trusted" (207). Speaking for herself, Maria makes a comment on Philip, with which other women in his life, including his wife, would concur: "What it comes down to is that a woman comes to a man to chat a little, and all the man is really thinking about is his typewriter. You love your typewriter more than you could ever love any woman" (207).

Like Maria, Mrs. Roth also expresses her sense of revulsion with Philip's book. She is fully assured that the woman in the book is real and it is on account of this affair that Philip is "distracted and totally uninterested in [her] for months" (181). She learns from him that the exchange with Rosalie Nichols is partly real and partly invented. Since Mrs. Roth takes it into her head that the female character in the novel is Rosalie, Philip does not bother himself to prove that it is modeled on Maria. This insincerity, he knows, would ensure a less stormy domestic environment. Philip also lets her know that the entire section on Ivan accusing him of betraying him with his wife Olina is made up and that in reality no such exchange took place. When Mrs. Roth insists that she is sure that the woman in the book is real, Philip confesses to "imagining myself, outside of my novel, having a love affair with a character inside my novel" (183). To assuage her suspicions, he tells her that the English woman depicted in his novel is Rosalie Nichols, who used to live upstairs with her husband on Eighty-First Street after she had moved from England. He accepts that, like most men and women who fancy other partners during actual sexual congress, he also imagines but with the difference that he compulsively commits it to writing: "The difference is that what I impurely imagine, I am impelled to develop and write down. A mitigating circumstance: my work, my livelihood. In my imagination I am unfaithful to everybody, by the way, not just to you. Look, think of it as an act of mourning, because it is that too—a lament of sorts for a life I did lead before you" (185).

Even though she is not fully convinced by Philip's explanations, Mrs. Roth finally agrees to a truce if only he would drop his name when he gets his notebook published. Philip rejects this, saying that the character in the novel is Zuckerman, and that the notebook is himself. He makes light of her apprehension that, if published, the notebook might create misunderstandings and complications: "I write fiction and I'm told it's autobiography, I write autobiography and I'm told it's fiction, so since I'm so dim and they're so smart, let *them* decide what it is or it isn't" (190). Philip tells her categorically that as a novelist "discretion" and "shame" (190) are not for him and that he would publish the notebook as it is when it pleases him.

The portrait of Philip as an artist would not be complete without problematizing his Jewishness as well as his compulsive fictionalizing. In section 3, we learn that it is "cultural displacement" which has driven Philip into an adulterous relationship with Maria. Maria then rightly concludes that theirs is not "a love story, really—it's a cultural story" (50). Dissatisfied with "England" and "Englishness," Philip often sympathizes with other displaced persons from other cultures who live in England. Lee views *Deception* as "also about obstacles to freedom, which is why the novel has other voices cutting across the lovers' voices of Roth's obstructed Eastern European characters."[14] It dawns upon him that in England his Jewish identity is rudely thrust upon him. The blatant anti-Semitic remarks that assail his Jewish self in England make him long for Newark, the veritable Zion.

Playing confidante, Philip becomes privy to the agonies of many women. The Czechoslovakian girl who seeks his help to get published engages his attention because she has suffered the trauma of cultural displacement. Emigrating to the USA in 1968 after the Russian tanks had arrived, she manages to survive by holding on to a variety of positions such as babysitter, model, apartment decorator, and even a call girl. Being hopelessly in love with the idea of love, she seeks fulfillment in love but sadly enough all her quests for love end in disappointment. Philip empathizes with her when she remarks,

I want to be myself. I want somebody who's going to love me, whom I'm going to love. I'm not necessarily going to be married to someone, I just want. . . . But people here, or people anywhere, have rules. I hate Czechoslovakia because it has very set rules. You can't breathe. I don't particularly like England because it has another set of rules. Of little houses and little vegetable gardens, and all their life is to get something like that. I can't be like that." (63)

Hasn't Philip himself suffered in Czechoslovakia? Is he not suffering in England, too?

Talking to one of his former students with whom he probably had an affair, Philip recalls how articulate and insightful she used to be. Now devastated by drugs and failed relationships, she, he reminisces, was once "the smartest girl in the seminar" (122) who struck him as "intellectually stubborn and very shrewd-looking and boldly aloof for a kid" (124). In Philip's class, she literally "[laid] down the law on Kafka" (125). Rejecting the popular view that Kafka's *Metamorphosis* and *The Trial* derive from his relationship with his father, she argued: "By the time a novelist worth his salt is thirty-six, he's no longer translating experience into a fable—he's imposing his fable onto experience" (125). Philip is again found talking to a Polish woman interested in politics. She recounts to Philip how she saw recently one of her former lovers, an American Jew, pass her by at the Charing Cross station. Being culturally displaced, Philip understands her torments of being misplaced; in counseling her he counsels himself, too. He tells her, "It isn't hard to make you explode. Or go off. You happen to be suffering the human predicament times ten. Anybody who spends, as they say, two weeks in another town, is always a little susceptible but you're even more so" (175).

Though not orthodox, Philip wakes up to the realization that inasmuch as he is a Jew his personal destiny is tied up with the larger Jewry and that he is a misfit in England. He wonders why Israel and America, "two greatest scourges" (84) with whom he is allied, should inspire so much ill will in England. Confessing to Maria, Philip says, "Because being a Jew and being an American in this country of yours is making me into a very contentious fellow. I'd forgotten about both, really. Then I moved to England and started attending smart dinner parties" (88). Philip performs to Maria the English response to his dismay over an anti-Semite in London: "Oh, why do you Jews make such a fuss about being Jewish?" (110). Finally, Philip would candidly tell her that England was too suffocat-

ingly Christian for him when she would phone him in New York. He
would let her know that he is happy being among Jews in New York.
In sharp contrast to the anemic ways of the English, Philip's Jews
burst with vitality and force. Describing the Jews of New York, Philip
says: "Jews with force . . . , Jews with appetite. Jews without shame.
Complaining Jews who get under your skin. Brash Jews who eat with
their elbows on the table. Unaccommodating Jews, full of anger, in-
sult, argument, and impudence. New York's the real obstreperous
Zion" (204).

The theme of deception foregrounded in the title of the novel
derives from the adulterous relationship of the lovers as well as from
the versions of reality that ensue when fictions constantly invade reality resulting in its adulteration. The deception we practice on one
another by marauding reality springs from the pathological deter-
minism of the self. Being a writer, Philip compulsively superimposes
fictions on undramatic reality and creates his own versions of reality.
To do this, he would run afoul of any inhibitions, taboos, or even
intimate confidences. In *Deception*, one of the games that Maria and
Philip play to beguile time is called the "reality shift" (67). This involves "exchanging places and speaking from the other's or from an
imagined perspective."[15] In one episode, Maria plays the biographer
of the dead Nathan Zuckerman and interviews Philip for information on Zuckerman.

However, she warns Philip of the dangers of placing both Zuckerman and Philip in the same narrative. Maria, as biographer, invents
for us details of an interview she had conducted with Zuckerman in
connection with the biography of E. I. Lonoff, the recluse writer. In
the novel's present, the biographer works on Zuckerman's biography because he can make a fast buck: "He was forty-four years old,
only four books, and the literary criticism isn't that difficult. It's the
dream biography—the author died young, he led a juicy life with
lots of women, he outraged popular opinion, he had an instant audience, and he made a lot of money. Also, he's a serious writer whose
books are readable and I can go to town on the autobiographical
issue" (100). In talking about Lonoff, Maria as biographer makes
pronouncements about what a writer's true nature is and these appear to be in tune with Philip's own nature as a writer: " *Caprice* is at
the heart of a writer's nature. Exploration, fixation, isolation,
venom, fetishism, austerity, levity, perplexity, childishness, *et cetera.*
The nose in the seam of the undergarment—*that's* the writer's nature. *Im*purity, but these Lonoffs—such a suffocating investment in

temperance, in *dignity*, of all damn things. As though the man wasn't an American novelist but was ambassador to the Holy See!" (103). Maria's sympathies unmistakably seem to lie with the Lonoffs, though she had played the role of the biographer with verve and gusto. Thrilled and amused that he is, Philip urges her to continue. As biographer, Maria recalls Zuckerman telling her about Lonoff's comment on his (Zuckerman's) appearance: "You're not so nice as you look" (104).

In another episode, Roth derides the feminist critics who misread into his work a strident form of misogyny. Maria in this "reality shift" assumes the role of the female prosecutor and Philip that of the accused writer:

> The women in your work are all vicious stereotypes. Was *that* your aim as a writer? . . .
>
> Why did you portray Mrs. Portnoy as a hysteric? Why did you portray Lucy Nelson as a psychopath? Why did you portray Maureen Tarnopol as a liar and a cheat? Does this not defame and denigrate women? Why do you depict women as shrews, if not to malign them?
>
> Why did Shakespeare? You refer to women as though every woman is a person to be extolled.
>
> You dare to compare yourself to Shakespeare?
>
> I am only—
>
> Next you will be comparing yourself to Margaret Atwood and Alice Walker! (114–15).

Maria plays the role of the prosecutor with élan and Philip, dazzled by her performance, moves toward her with great desire.

By his endless inventions, whom has Philip Roth deceived? The answer is at once everybody and nobody. At one level, his fictions, if they assault reality, are also nothing more than lies and concealment; at another level, these fictions have made others, including Maria and Mrs. Roth, become organized and defend their versions of the real. Philip's testament of faith as a novelist writing in the late twentieth century remains, "The treacherous imagination is everybody's maker—we are all the invention of each other, everybody a conjuration conjuring up everyone else. We are all each other's authors."[16] Angered by Philip's blatant exposure of their affair, Maria also admits to having experienced moments of tenderness when reading the novel. Philip's fiction is thus, paradoxically, like reality itself—a mélange; if it deals with adultery and the adulteration of reality, it also strangely enough exposes the tenderness and contingency characterizing all affairs of the heart.

NOTES

1. To quote Johnson, the familiar concerns include "the dilemmas of being male, being Jewish and being a writer." See Brian D. Johnson, "Intimate Affairs," *Maclean's* (April 30, 1990): 66–67. Review of *Deception*, reprinted in *Conversations with Philip Roth*, ed. George Searles (Jackson: University of Mississippi Press, 1992), 254.

2. In *Deception*, Roth almost does away with exposition and structures the novel around dialogues like the novels of Ivy Compton-Burnett. See Jay L. Halio, *Philip Roth Revisited* (New York: Twayne Press, 1992), 216. Wendy Steiner notes that *Deception* is an exercise in metafiction which offers "no insights into Jewishness or the act of writing." See Steiner's review of *Deception* in *Times Literary Supplement* (August 31–September 6, 1990), 917. Alan Cooper recognized *Deception* as "an experiment in an art form" which deserves "credit(s) for taking risks." See Alan Cooper, *Philip Roth and the Jews* (Albany: State University of New York Press, 1996), 241. However, Cooper faults the novel for lacking in "compelling conflict" in the character of the protagonist. He further observes that the novel "forfeits mimesis for technique, experience for teasing curiosity about the source of the experience" (232).

3. Philip Roth, *Deception* (New York: Simon and Schuster, 1990), 189. Hereafter cited parenthetically.

4. Roth's fiction had always shown autobiographical affinities. Alan Cooper views Roth's post-*Counterlife* works—*The Facts, Deception*, and *Patrimony*—as autobiographical fiction or autobiography using devices of fiction (228).

5. Some critics find Roth's use of metafictional technique unconvincing. Martyn Harris suggests such disapproval in commenting, "as the imagined lover reappears in an appended chapter, discussing her portrayal in the book, we reel giddily again in the intertextual dazzle." See Martyn Harris, "Damsels in Distress," *New Statesman and Society* 3, no. 7 (September 7, 1990): 42.

6. Philip Roth, *The Counterlife* (New York: Farrar, Straus & Giroux, 1986).

7. Halio, *Roth Revisited*, 197.

8. Johnson, "Intimate Affairs," 254.

9. I would go with Lee's position that Roth in *Deception* is more interested in "adultery as the occasion for authorial deception" than in "adultery as sexual or social plot." See Hermione Lee, "Kiss and Tell," review of *Deception*, by Philip Roth, *New Republic* (April 30, 1990): 39–42. In this sense, *Deception* is different from Updike's *Couples* or even Flaubert's *Madame Bovary*. It is also intriguing to note that in the novel Philip and Maria discuss *Madame Bovary*, the classic text on adultery. My guess is that Roth is fascinated by "adultery" as a metaphor for the act of writing itself.

10. Halio, *Roth Revisited*, 197.

11. David Klinghoffer, "Roth for Roth's Sake," *National Review* 42 (August 20, 1990), 48–50.

12. It is possible to view *Deception* as a notebook for *The Counterlife*, though one

could also see it as "the notebook for the novel that it itself is." See Steiner review, 917.

13. Talking about *Deception*, Roth says: "This book is a momentary escape from all kinds of narrative building blocks that I have been playing with for a long time. It is primarily about two people in hiding. They have a sexual life, but the rest of their life is only talk—talking and listening are almost erotic activities." Roth, quoted in Johnson, "Intimate Affairs," 255.

14. Hermione Lee, "Life *Is* and': Philip Roth in 1990," *The Independent* (September 2, 1990). Reprinted in Searles, Roth, 265.

15. Cooper, *Roth and the Jews*, 236.

16. *Counterlife*, 145.

Texts, Lives, and Bellybuttons: Philip Roth's *Operation Shylock* and the Renegotiation of Subjectivity

Derek Parker Royal

IT IS NOT AN EXAGGERATION TO STATE THAT PHILIP ROTH IS OBSESSED with the play between the world that is inscribed on the page and the world that is not. Ever since *My Life as a Man* (1974) he has engaged in a relentless negotiation between life and art, a metafictional realm of instability where narrative is an uncertain combination of creator and creation. Critics have accused him of filling his fictional worlds with nothing more than a thinly veiled chronicle of his own life and the real lives around him. Indeed, his Zuckerman novels and the "autobiographical" works that followed have been dismissed as mere personal—and, some would argue, narcissistic—disclosure. But Roth is engaged in a more philosophical investigation, an exploration that highlights interrelationship between autobiography and fiction. He calls this textual preoccupation, in one of his earlier essays, "the relationship between the written and the unwritten world":

> the worlds that I feel myself shuttling between every day couldn't be more succinctly described. Back and forth, back and forth, bearing fresh information, detailed instructions, garbled messages, desperate inquiries, naïve expectations, baffling challenges . . . in all, cast somewhat in the role of the courier Barnabas, whom the Land Surveyor K. enlists to traverse the steep winding road between the village and the castle in Kafka's novel about the difficulties of getting through.[1]

Roth has spent the better part of his career traveling between these two worlds, so many times in fact that one would be hard pressed to tell which is the village and which is the castle. Is the castle a metaphor for the written world, the modernist high ground of art, as the young Nathan Zuckerman would believe; or is it instead the domain of "the facts," the lived world from which art ultimately emanates and takes its sustenance? For literary critics, of course, this distinction is moot. The "garbled messages" and "baffling challenges" themselves are the points of departure, arrival, and the message, all rolled into one.

This relationship between the written and the unwritten worlds has gained attention in recent years, at least within Roth studies, especially when viewed in light of how autobiographies are constructed. The publication of an autobiography, especially one from the bright spotlights of the entertainment industry (and, given both the "scandal" of *Portnoy's Complaint* (1969) and his more recent breakup with actress Claire Bloom, Roth has found himself a reluctant celebrity), always brings with it both a sense of titillating expectation and high risk. Will the book be nothing more than an exaggerated kiss-and-tell-all, leaving a trail of publicity-damaged figures in its wake; or will it be an earnest attempt at recreating a life that reveals just as much about the act of writing autobiography as it does of its subject matter? When Roth published *The Facts: A Novelist's Autobiography* in 1988, he was doing outright what many had already accused him of doing most of his career: writing about himself. In the highly revealing last section of *The Facts*, where Nathan Zuckerman questions his creator's autobiographical intentions, Zuckerman tells him "you've written metamorphoses of yourself so many times, you no longer have any idea what *you* are or ever were. By now what you are is a walking text. . . . With autobiography, there's always another text, a countertext, if you will, to the one presented. It's probably the most manipulative of all literary forms."[2] What is more, Claire Bloom's 1996 memoir, *Leaving a Doll's House: A Memoir*, underscores the project of Roth's more recent fiction. Not only is it a countertext to Roth's own—much as Maria provides to Zuckerman's in *The Counterlife* (1986)—but it is also a demonstration by example of the "walking text" that is Philip Roth.

One of the recurring themes in Bloom's memoir, especially in the last chapters, is her inability to read Roth. "Which was the real Philip Roth?" she asks at one point, echoing the question Roth himself asks in *Operation Shylock: A Confession* (1993).[3] And readers (of both Bloom's book and Roth's novels) are encouraged to speculate on the same: are we to take Roth's autobiographical writings as autobiography? But instead of playing the celebrity game and reading Bloom's memoir as a fair or unfair portrait of Roth, perhaps it would

be more fruitful to approach her text as one of the latest contribu-
tions to the "walking text." It is necessary to keep in mind that the
persona of Roth is far from being the sole product of the author
himself. From the very beginning of his career he has been the subject of multiple countertexts, both popular and critical: the self-
effacing Jew, the scandalous cultural phenomenon behind *Portnoy's
Complaint,* the stand-up comedian (as opposed to the "serious" novelist), the narcissistic author, the pornographer, the good and dutiful
son, and the misogynist. These representations of Roth, regardless of
their validity, have gone on to further inspire Roth and fuel his fiction. Without the fame of and reaction to *Portnoy's Complaint,* there
may never have been a Zuckerman nor a literary character named
"Philip Roth" obsessed with the production of the self. These texts
and countertexts live in a symbiotic manner, and it is in this complementary relationship that the subject of fiction and autobiography
comes into play. What Roth's works (especially the more recent "autobiographical" pieces) directly address, and what Bloom's memoir
indirectly asks us to consider, is the construction of autobiography
and its resemblance in many ways to the craft underlying fiction.
Roth's post-Zuckerman books and Bloom's memoir reveal how both
authors create a text of the self and a countertext of the other (and
in the former's case, countertexts to the text of the self). While
Roth's postmodern awareness of the self is both honest and potentially liberating, there is nonetheless a danger in the realization that
identity may be nothing more than a construction. An unanchored
self, inscribed to obsessive lengths, can lead to what the character of
Roth experienced in *Operation Shylock*: "Me-itis" or "drowning in the
tiny tub of yourself."[4] The publication of Bloom's autobiography,
and of Roth's works themselves, asks us to consider this relationship
between fiction and autobiography, the dynamics involved, and the
implications of this mixture. Put another way, it raises questions of
the authenticity of autobiographical writing and of the self. If
Bloom's *Leaving a Doll's House* provides us with the opportunity to
raise these issues, it is Roth's most ambitious work to date, *Operation
Shylock*, to which we can turn for a sustained analysis.

    While most critics—scholarly and otherwise—have wisely aban-
doned their search for the actual man behind Zuckerman, Peter
Tarnopol, Alexander Portnoy, David Kepesh, and even "Roth,"
there is nonetheless a persistent confusion over the forms through
which Philip Roth the author chooses to reveal himself (or his
selves). A relatively recent manifestation of this phenomenon oc-

curred with the publication of *Operation Shylock*. Whatever its short-comings, reviewers welcomed Roth's latest text as a return to his strong "novelistic" abilities. Michiko Kakutani, one of the first to review the book, stated that "the reader is encouraged to read this *novel* as a *kind of* autobiographical confession" (emphasis added).[5] John Updike called "this novel, which purports to be a confession," an international, medical, and psychological thriller in the vein of Dostoyevsky and Mann.[6] D. M. Thomas read "Philip Roth's new novel" as a work in the literary tradition of creative doubles.[7] Robert Alter, likewise seeing in *Operation Shylock* the well-worn theme of the dopplegänger, found "a fictional character named Philip Roth, who shares with the author of this novel a biography . . . a wife and a list of publications from *Goodbye, Columbus* to *Patrimony*." However, Alter continued, if reading the book as a novel proved problematic, then one could better read it as "a looser and less realistic fiction of the sort that Gide had in mind when he designated several of his longer narratives as *soties*—roughly, farces."[8] Harold Bloom, perhaps one of the book's more perceptive early critics, not only noticed the double play at work, but also identified the fictive game in which Roth was engaging.[9] Alan Cooper, writing a few years after the novel's publication, similarly noted the book's labyrinthine exploration into identity by referring to the hero of his post-Zuckerman works as "Zuckerroth."[10] For his part Roth himself said that his book should be read as neither novel nor farce, but should instead be taken as he subtitled it. "The book is true," he states during one interview, "I'm not trying to confuse you. . . . This happened. I stepped into a strange hole, which I don't understand to this day. . . . I tell [the critics], 'Well, how can I make it up since you've always said I am incapable of making anything up?' I can't win!"[11] He claimed that in 1988 he actually confronted an exact double who called himself "Philip Roth" and who appropriated his own reputation for purposes that were as fantastic as they were ridiculous. "Inasmuch as his imposturing constituted a crisis I was living rather than writing, it embodied a form of self-denunciation that I could not sanction, a satirizing of me so bizarre and unrealistic as to exceed by far the boundaries of amusing mischief I may myself have playfully perpetuated on my own existence in fiction."[12] Significantly, one year later he would make a claim that curiously resembles the unlikely assertion he made with *Operation Shylock*. Roth held that the first sentence from each of his nineteen works of fiction, beginning with *Goodbye, Columbus* (1959) and ending with *Operation Shylock*'s opening ("For legal reasons, I have had to alter a number of facts in this book") derived from an abandoned piece of paper he found in the Chicago cafeteria he used to frequent in the mid-1950s. The writer tells us that this piece of paper is one that has "never before been disclosed to anyone and which I have kept securely hidden all these years in a safe-deposit box in my bank."[13] He asks that we sincerely believe this improbable event to have actually happened. Despite the farcical nature of this episode, it highlights the mischievous side of Roth, where he can simultaneously look his reader straight in the face, so to speak, in all seriousness, and at the same time wink knowingly. This is one way the author responds to his lamentations over two decades earlier, "the actuality is continually outdoing our talents."[14]

Only those who are not familiar with Roth's many fictions would imagine taking him at his word, and even then those reading *Operation Shylock* would be hard pressed to find any verisimilitude in the text. In fact, given his past frustrations over critics trying to discover "Philip Roth" within one of his characters, one would expect that a representational reading would be the *last* thing he would want his readers to bring to his latest book.[15] Updike's, Alter's, and Thomas's "novelistic" readings do allow for a fictional or constructed approach to the text, but they nonetheless fail to consider (especially in light of his earlier works) the larger issues in which Roth is engaged. It is obvious that Roth's own disclosures are as duplicitous as they are revealing. They, along with the actual text of *Operation Shylock*, are a significant commentary on his ongoing fascination with the relationship between author and subject as well as the playful, yet highly revealing, nature of fiction. As with the Zuckerman works, *Operation Shylock* (as well as the three texts that preceded it) is a variation on the theme of constructed identities, but this time he explores more fully that paradoxically revealing Yiddish proverb, "Truth is the safest lie." Or, put another way, Roth engages in a literary act similar to the unlikely encounters his cousin Apter creates, "fiction that, like so much of fiction, provides the storyteller with the lie through which to expose his unspeakable truth."[16] This notion, in many ways, is similar in kind to that found in Emily Dickinson's "Tell all the Truth but tell it slant—." As the poem suggests, direct truth is so powerful that it is capable of overwhelming the one who pursues it and, as a result, the best way to encounter it is askance. What is more, as a philosophy of narrative, this approach allows the author latitude, so that she or he may engage in fictive exercises of ambiguity, thereby challenging the reader and encouraging an active participation in the reading process. In *Operation Shylock* Roth confronts his subject matter in much the same manner. His "unspeakable truth"—whether it be of the Holocaust, the profound effects of Zionism, the benefits and costs of the Diaspora, the place of the Jew in both assimilated and non-assimilated communities, or the very fragmented and decentered nature of ethnic identity itself—is best revealed through a "lie," and in this case the lie is the text, the mischievous text Roth would probably admit, of *Operation Shylock*. The late twentieth-century Jewish American novelist would most wholeheartedly concur with the nineteenth-century Dickinson when she asserts, "Success in Circuit lies."

Many Roth critics have approached his texts almost solely in terms of his ethnicity and his (early) Jamesian realism. For critics who privilege a more poststructualist approach to texts and desire an alternative to the literature of exhaustion, this relegated him to a category of historically fixed and (for many) antiquated styles. However, since the 1980s there has nevertheless been a growing number of readings concerning the postmodern assumptions and structures underlying Roth's works, assumptions that include such issues as the decentered subject, the emphasis on metafiction, and the breakdown of traditional narrative. For instance, *My Life as a Man* explores the (male) self as a socially constructed subject. Peter Tarnopol's story is not about how he determines himself, but how others determine him. *The Ghost Writer* (1979) can be read as a deconstructive exercise in textual authority and responsibility, where the author underscores the constructed nature of text as well as of self so as to recreate freely an alternative narrative. For instance, Zuckerman, the "author" of the living Anne Frank, uses his creation to serve as a countertext to the stifling rhetoric of Judge Wapter's. *The Counterlife* challenges us to transcend the anxiety of the interpretive act, to embrace and be liberated by the duplicity of reality itself (i.e., the variety of subjective perceptions to phenomena) and not merely the duplicity of language. And the more recent autobiographical works establish a context for the psychological writer self.[17] Such postmodern readings of Roth's fiction serve as a cogent response to the anxieties underlying some contemporary theories of autobiography (pertinent theories in the case of Roth, who questions the assumptions of autobiography within his fiction). Scholars who see in autobiographical fiction—of Roth, Nabokov, Barth, and others—a privileging of textual representations of the subject worry that the authors are evading the responsibilities of history, or in other words, are not being true to the events of the unwritten world. Working with *My Life as a Man*, Philip Dodd concludes that "my charge against autobiography-as-fiction, whether practiced by writers or celebrated by critics, is that autobiography becomes a safe and reserved space in which the harried self is released from the demands of history to become the product either of art (conservative version) or textuality (radical version)."[18] What Dodd apparently does not see in Roth's novels is the desire to articulate the historical context surrounding a specific subject position, one grounded in the unwritten world and more pertinent than any preoccupation with the self: "my life as a *Jewish* man." Throughout most of his fiction, Roth has explored issues of Jewish ethnicity within various postmodern assumptions. His protagonists have always been constructed (and reconstructed) within the context of competing ethnic, social, economic, and gender-based historical forces. Roth has never been one to withdraw into a Barthian world of intertextual play without first packing with him the sights, smells, and sounds of Newark and Jerusalem. He is not merely interested in the intertextual interplay among author, text, and interpretation (in many ways a solipsistic and exhausted exercise in itself). Reading him purely as an intricately self-conscious writer would be as limiting and unjust as reading him purely in terms of his ethnicity. The path between his written and unwritten worlds is a two-way street where neither "reality" nor "fiction" collides and subordinates the other. What is more, both of these realms interact in a complementary manner, creating a narrative space that allows Roth to explore Jewish American identity on his own terms. As Mark Shechner so clearly puts it, "the writer may play fast and loose with the *I*, doing anything with Zuckerman that suits his fancy or his vision of life, but he dare not tamper with the *we*. Jewish history is not something to be arbitrarily reinvented."[19] Roth, in other words, is a writer most genuinely concerned with both his history and his aesthetics. He brings the postmodern "play" of textual creation into the realm of the Jewish experience and in doing so explores the ways in which Jews in general, and Jewish Americans in particular, have "created" or defined themselves against the backdrops of both their ethnic heritage and the non-Jewish culture at large.

Since *The Counterlife*, Roth has further explored the fictional(ized) boundaries between the written and the unwritten worlds. Yet whereas his previous novels focus by and large on the interplay among characters that resemble their creator (e.g., Jewish American writers and/or professors), the immediate post-Zuckerman works concern the author himself. In *The Facts, Deception* (1990), *Patrimony* (1991), and *Operation Shylock* the subject under consideration is no longer Zuckerman or Tarnopol, but "Philip Roth."[20] Just as in Roth's life, Philip's is populated by a father named Herman, a wife (or lover) named Claire, and a brother named Sandy who all live in and travel between Newark, New York, Connecticut, Chicago, London, and Jerusalem. If Nathan's words to Henry—"We are all each other's authors"[21]—epitomize Roth's Zuckerman fiction, then Philip's tirade in *Deception* stands as *the* representative passage of his "autobiographical" project: "I write fiction and I'm told it's autobiography, I write autobiography and I'm told it's fiction, so since I'm so dim and they're so smart, let *them* decide what it is or it isn't."[22] Roth has been well acquainted with this guessing game of autobiographical presence almost from the very beginning of his career, and most certainly since the publication of *Portnoy's Complaint*. But as the above words of Philip demonstrate, Roth, in no uncertain terms, is here throwing down the gauntlet to his readers and critics, challenging them to distinguish between the author and the artifice, to discover within the twists and turns of his narratives a figure that *is* Philip Roth the writer.

The determination between fact and fiction, however, is inconsequential, and Roth of course is aware of this. In contrast to all of his previous novels, and to his most recent works, each text within the "autobiographical" tetralogy possesses a subtitle that on the surface serves as a directive for interpretation: *The Facts* should be read as "A Novelist's Autobiography," *Deception* is presented as "A Novel," *Patrimony* is "A True Story," and *Operation Shylock* professes to being "A Confession."[23] Taken at face value, only one of texts should be read as fiction while the others stand out as bare-bones autobiography. However, this distinction between the purely fictional and the purely autobiographical is undermined from the outset, in the very book where Roth is supposed to shed his masks. *The Facts* is framed by two letters, one from Philip to Zuckerman and the other from Zuckerman to Philip, and together these "fictions" make up a quarter of the "facts." The ideas of autobiography and the coherent self are deconstructed from the very first page. In his letter, Philip confides to Zuckerman that he has suffered a Halcion-induced depression and felt himself "coming undone."[24] To put himself back together, he "had to go back to the moment of origin," the facts prior to fiction, despite the naiveté of such a movement.[25] But Roth is not convinced, and in perhaps the book's most moving chapter, "Girl of My Dreams," the author indirectly reveals his suspicions of representing reality as it is truly lived. In what is supposed to be the "factual" part of the book, the author gives an account of his painful experience with his first wife Josie (whose fictional embodiment is Maureen in *My Life As a Man*), and laments the fact that he had ever fallen for her deceptive acts, behavior which he describes in artistic and novelistic terms. He calls her "the greatest creative-writing teacher of them all," and then admits that he is at a loss to determine which of her stories are lies and which are true: "who can distinguish what is so from what isn't so when confronted with a master of fabrication?"[26] Even if the reader neglects to notice the ample associations between Josie's creative duplicity and Roth's artistic flair, these very words ought to reverberate as the height of irony. One can easily imagine Roth mischievously reveling in these narrative bouts with his marital nemesis.

As does Roth, Zuckerman easily sees through Philip's textual facade and the futility of trying to recover any factual origins for the purposes of understanding himself (or at least in helping his readership understand him). What Philip (Roth) has been engaged in all along, from the creation of Neil Klugman to that of Nathan himself, is the reinvention of the self: "you've written metamorphoses of yourself so many times, you no longer have any idea what *you* are or ever were. By now what you are is a walking text."[27] Besides, Maria Zuckerman reminds him, by sticking to the facts, Philip is engaging in *occupatio*, a Latin rhetorical strategy whereby one broaches something by saying that he is not going to mention it. This act is as deceptive, as "fictional," as fiction. Even Zuckerman, the supposedly fictional embodiment of his creator, believes that autobiography is highly manipulative and is at a loss to determine what self in *The Facts* is being countered. As he tells Maria, "having this letter at the end is a self-defensive trick to have it both ways. I'm not even sure any longer which of us he's set up as the straw man. I thought first it was him in his letter to me—now it feels like me in my letter to him."[28] For his part, even Philip acknowledges the labyrinth he has entered—*Begging the Question*, he says, may have been a better title than *The Facts*—but he nonetheless needs to undergo this autobiographical exercise in order "to transform myself into *myself*."[29]

This is exactly what Philip Roth has done: transform Roth into Philip. After deconstructing the binary of fiction-autobiography and ushering Zuckerman out of his texts, Roth turns solely to his counterself.[30] This transformation is certainly apparent in *The Facts, Deception*, and *Patrimony*, but only in *Operation Shylock: A Confession* does it reach its fullest expression. As with the two books before it, this "confession" takes as its protagonist the counterself Philip, and like *The Facts*, it defiantly challenges the reader to differentiate between "reality" and "fiction." But what distinguishes *Operation Shylock* from the previous books, and what makes it such a distinctively experimental work, is not only its ambitious scope, but also how it reveals the symbiotic relationship between the written and unwritten worlds. Roth structures the text so that author and subject become indistinguishable, and it appears that the subject writes the author as much as the author writes the subject.

The plot of this "true" story is as fantastical as many in Roth's novels, filled with ongoing crises and unexpected turns, and because it can get twisted at times it may help to recount it here in brief. Everything begins around the time of the John Demjanjuk trials, when Philip receives a call from his cousin in Israel telling him that there is a man attending the trials who not only looks like him, but calls himself Philip Roth. Looking into the matter, he discovers that there is actually an impostor in Jerusalem using his name and publicly advocating Diasporism as the only solution to the "Jewish Problems" in the Middle East. After flying to Jerusalem, against the wishes of Claire Bloom, Philip encounters the double, a fanatical admirer of his novels and whose appearance he finds frighteningly similar to his own—facial features, clothes, and all. The other Philip and his girlfriend are working to convince Israelis that if European Jews aren't soon relocated back into Europe, the Arab-Israeli tensions will lead to catastrophic war, resulting either in another Jewish holocaust or in Israel using nuclear weapons on its neighbors, which in itself would result in a moral holocaust. Against his better judgment Philip gets involved in the plot, along the way encountering suspicious characters whose relations to the PLO, the Mossad, or to the other Philip are suggested but never fully disclosed. The storyline ends with an agent asking the real Philip (who is by this time extremely paranoid) to undertake intelligence operations for the Mossad.

As in many of Roth's novels, *Operation Shylock* is filled with texts that attempt to transcribe a life, or as Nathan Zuckerman once put it, "*the kind of stories people turn life into, the kind of lives that people turn stories into.*"[31] There are the oral texts of Aharon Appelfeld, interviewed by Philip for the *New York Times* (the transcripts of which actu-

ally did appear in the book review section and were later reprinted
in Appelfeld's *Beyond Despair*); the "fictional" stories of Philip's
cousin Apter; the recording of the spurious Anti-Semite Anonymous
workout tape from Pipik,[32] Philip's double; and the dialog taken
from the minutes of the John Demjanjuk trial. More significant, especially when viewed in light of Roth's own position as a writer, are
the many written texts that suffuse book. Among these are the travel
diaries of Leon Klinghoffer, the Jew who was killed by the PLO during the *Achille Lauro* highjacking. Philip comes to the diaries
through David Supposnik, a Mossad agent posing as a rare book
dealer, and is asked by him to write an introduction for their publication so that they may reach a wide audience. What Eleanor Roosevelt did for *The Diary of Anne Frank*, Supposnik urges, Philip Roth can
do for *The Travel Diaries of Leon Klinghoffer*. The problem, as Philip
later discovers, is not only that Supposnik is an agent, but that the
diaries are fabrications created to lure him into espionage. There
is also the Treblinka memoir of Eliahu Rosenberg, a Jewish "death
commando" whose job it was to empty and clean the gas chambers
that he claimed Demjanjuk operated. His memoir, written in 1945
and describing the "death" of Ivan the Terrible at the hands of his
captors, contradicts the positive identity he made of Demjanjuk in
earlier testimony. When the defense establishes that he had escaped
Treblinka before the revolt, Rosenberg argues that the memoir was
nonetheless a collective one, based on hearsay from supposed eye-
witnesses. In addition to these texts, there are the Hebrew sentence
on Smilesburger's blackboard that Philip cannot read and two
pieces of writing that Philip "imagines" into his tale: a letter from
Philip to Pipik's girlfriend, Wanda Jane "Jinx" Possesski;[33] and *His
Way*, the secret exposé of Philip that Pipik writes, and whose content, significantly enough, turns out to be nothing but blank pages.
In each case, the authors generate a text whose authenticity is either
refuted or placed in doubt. As in *The Ghost Writer*, Roth here is questioning the notions of originality, the possibility of representation,
and the overall authority of the text.

Roth's most extensive critique of textual reliability is the book itself. Just as with all the other "texts" that Philip encounters, the one
he actually creates, *Operation Shylock*, is filled with gaps and inconsist-
encies. Nowhere is this more apparent than in the book's structure,
beginning with its narrative frames. Bracketing the story proper are
two narrative qualifiers, each of which stands in stark contrast to the
other. In the preface, Roth outlines the true life conditions under

which the book was written: "I've drawn *Operation Shylock* from note-book journals. The book is as accurate an account as I am able to give of actual occurrences that I lived through during my middle fifties and that culminated, early in 1988, in my agreeing to under-take an intelligence-gathering operation for Israel's foreign intelli-gence service, the Mossad."[34]

Like *The Facts* before it, Roth professes to be taking his story straight from his notebooks (he's an avid note taker) and without the varnish of fiction. The only "facts" altered are for legal reasons, and "these are minor changes that mainly involve details of identi-fication and locale and are of little significance to the overall story and its verisimilitude.[35] His "Note to the Reader" at the end of the book, on the other hand, is something else entirely. In addition to the standard Simon and Schuster disclaimer—"This book is a work of fiction. Otherwise, the names, characters, places, and incidents are either products of the author's imagination or are used ficti-tiously. Any resemblance to actual events or locales or persons, living or dead, is entirely coincidental"—the Note mentions the two non-fiction exceptions: the interview with Appelfeld and the minutes from the Demjanjuk trial. The Note then ends with the words, "This confession is false."[36] Outside of the obvious discrepancy, these two qualifiers reveal several suspect traces that are difficult to ignore. First, the wording in the above quoted section of the Preface should raise suspicion in the astute reader. "The book is *as accurate an ac-count as I am able to give* of actual occurrences . . ." (emphasis added). Coming from a writer with a history of creating fictive labyrinths, these words would seem to suggest more of a narrative temperament or predisposition than a limitation or inability of style. Between the lines, they read as a backhanded acknowledgment of his addiction to fictional "mischief," and coupled with the "minor changes" that are of "little significance," they leave the reader on his guard.

Furthermore, there is the ambiguous meaning behind the final admission, "This confession is false." Is it the "confession" of fiction uttered in the Note that is false, or is the entire text itself, that pro-fesses verisimilitude and whose subtitle bears the word "confes-sion," that is false? Roth gives the reader no indication of and is noticeably—in mischief?—absent concerning any textual clues. The positioning of the Note raises similar questions. For Simon and Schuster and its imprints, it is standard practice in every work of fic-tion to insert the disclaimer in small type on the copyright page im-mediately underneath the publisher's address. There is no such

disclaimer on the copyright page of *Operation Shylock*, perhaps because the legal department thought that the subtitle "A Confession"
was sufficient. Yet Roth nonetheless places his amended version of
the disclaimer at the very end of the book, a space normally reserved
for notes on the author or type. His "Note to the Reader" not only
appears in exactly the same type as the rest of the book (suggesting
continuity of the text), but, more significantly, is also listed prominently in the table of contents. It works more as a narrative slap in
the face than as an unobtrusive legal formality.

Even more suspect is the "missing" chapter 11 at the end of the
book. In chapter 10 Philip discovers that Smilesburger, an elderly
agent of the Mossad posing as a retired jeweler, wants him to do
some intelligence gathering for the agency in Athens. It's never explicitly reveled what he is to do in Athens, but there is a hint that it
may involve PLO leader Yasir Arafat. Yet when the reader finishes
that chapter and turns to the next, he finds no climax to the story
that has been building all along, but instead an epilogue entitled
"Words Generally Only Spoil Things." Philip says that he chose to
delete the last twelve thousand words to his book because "the contents of chapter 11, 'Operation Shylock,' were deemed by [Smiles-
burger] to contain information too seriously detrimental to his
agency's interests and to the Israeli government."[37] For his part,
Smilesburger suggests that Philip perform that "sacrosanct prank of
artistic transubstantiation,"[38] and turn the confession into fiction.
"If I were to do as you ask," Philip replies, "the whole book would
be specious. Calling fiction fact would undermine everything," and
given Roth's privileging of the former, would be a highly suspect
posture.[39] These last lines resonate with a narrative impishness so
common in much of Roth's writings. In actuality, the prank of transubstantiation—a mischievous word choice on Roth's part—has already taken place. By substituting an epilogue for the story's
conclusion, Roth conflates our notions of "fact" and "fiction" and
places the product of textual duplicity directly into the hands of the
reader. The text that the reader literally holds, *Operation Shylock*, is
every bit as unreliable as Rosenburg's memoir, Klinghoffer's diaries,
and Pipik's workout tape. It is no small fact that the title of the book
is the same as the title of the deleted chapter (as well as the code
name of the intelligence operation). "Operation Shylock" both is
and isn't there. In a deconstructive act of erasure, Roth has undermined the course of his entire creation, problematizing its origin as

well as its teleology. With its narrative frames and missing chapter, the text begins in question and ends in fragmentation.

Along with the unreliable texts, the book is populated with fragmented subjects who attempt to (re)create themselves. Most of the characters in the story are either artists, such as Apter and Appelfeld, or artist-like figures who are in the process of "authoring" their lives. Standing behind the entire plot almost as a specter is John Demjanjuk, the historical figure who found himself the center of controversy in being mistaken for "Ivan the Terrible" of Treblinka (in August 1993, approximately four months after the publication of *Operation Shylock*, the Supreme Court of Israel later unanimously acquitted him of any crimes).[40] For Philip, he is in many ways the most riveting part of the story. He goes to the trial as soon as he arrives in Jerusalem, before investigating Pipik, and once he sees the accused on the stand, "not only did my double cease to exist, but, for the time being, so did I."[41] And so does the accused, for when Philip muses on Demjanjuk or "reimagines" his life as Ivan, all he can repeat to himself is "So there he was. Or wasn't."[42] The identity of Demjanjuk is at this point uncertain and constantly called into question. The cohesion of Philip is also problematic. Just as in *The Facts*, Philip alerts the reader to his condition in 1987 due to "Halcion madness":

> My mind began to disintegrate. The word DISINTEGRATION seemed itself to be the matter out of which my brain was constituted, and it began spontaneously coming apart. The fourteen letters, big, chunky, irregularly sized components of my brain, elaborately intertwined, tore jaggedly loose from one another, sometimes a fragment of a letter at a time, but usually in painfully unpronounceable nonsyllabic segments of two or three, their edges roughly serrated. This mental coming apart was as distinctly physical a reality as a tooth being pulled, and the agony of it was excruciating.[43]

Philip calls this condition "Me-itis. Microcosmosis. Drowning in the tiny tub of yourself."[44] As he suggests, there is a symbiotic relationship between mental existence and physical reality, and the agent that binds the two together is the word, the text where Roth has placed so much of his artistic investment. (This "confessional" account of Philip's breakdown, along with the author's mischievous play with reality and fiction, is given an added twist when read in light of Claire Bloom's *Leaving a Doll's House*. She states in her memoir that the account of her husband's mental disintegration in *Operation Shylock* was "neither inaccurate nor overblown."[45] If Bloom is correct, then this accurate confession, placed within the context of unlikely and spurious accounts, further complicates the autobiographical premise of the book.) Furthermore, when Philip first talks to Pipik over the telephone, he uses as a disguise the name of Pierre Roget, author of the famous thesaurus (and whose initials are the same as his). As is suggested by his choice of masks, Philip finds himself trapped in a game of synonymous intrigue where one identity, much like the words in a thesaurus, is substituted for another. In yet another act of "artistic transubstantiation," Roth takes the figure of Philip and turns him into a text—or looked at another way, takes the "text" of his own identity and deconstructs it into "unpronounceable nonsyllabic segments."

While Philip's sense of self is breaking down, Pipik is in the process of constructing his, and the one he constructs is Philip's. He is the writer's true counterself, the one who not only appropriates the other's identity as his own, but constructs Philip's as well. "I know your books inside out," he tells Philip when they first meet. "I know your *life* inside out. I could be your biographer. I *am* your biographer."[46] He appears as Philip's doppelgänger, the chaotic reality behind the well-crafted sentences: "I AM THE YOU THAT IS NOT WORDS."[47] Here Pipik becomes for Philip the flesh and blood embodiment of the fictional double, stripped of any possible linguistic subterfuge and in control of his own destiny. Unlike the characters that populate Philip's novels, Pipik has the potential to create problems for the author that the author does not bring on himself. He is, for Roth the novelist, a creation that helps delineate as well as recreate—much like a biographer—the life of Philip, the novelist's fictional surrogate. Pipik's relationship with Philip, in conjunction with the mock-confessional premise of the novel, places into question any traditional notions of autobiography in that Philip/Roth is as much determined by his creation as he determines it.

Almost from the beginning, Philip is both attracted to and repulsed by his double. At times he assumes a passive acceptance of Pipik, thinking him a ridiculous but nonetheless harmless neurotic, and at others he is consumed by a manic desire to annihilate him. Whatever the case, as long as Pipik remains alive he poses a threat to Philip's tenuous mental state, thereby causing him to "dwell in the house of Ambiguity forever."[48] The only way Philip can gain control over the entire situation is for him to become the "counterlife" of Pipik (who is himself a counterself to Philip), to reimagine or re-create the existence of his nemesis. He does this by doing what he does best: turning Pipik into a parody. The writer muses, "In pseu-donymity is his anonymity, and it's that anonymity that's killing me. Name him!"[49] It is the naming that is so significant here. Philip chooses the name "Moishe Pipik," which translates from Yiddish into "Moses Bellybutton." It's a name that Roth's family used to des-ignate a ridiculous, funny, but nonetheless innocuous character—significantly enough, one that isn't real—and it gets its effect from being two dissimilar and antithetical words yoked together: Moses, the Jewish lawgiver, juxtaposed to bellybutton, a purposeless ana-tomical mark. After he signifies his double into something com-pletely absurd, Philip feels that "never had anybody seemed less of a menace to me or a more pathetic rival for my birthright. He struck me instead as *a great idea* . . . yes, a great idea breathing with life!"[50] Here, Philip engages in yet another act of transubstantiation where the flesh is made word—the opposite of what Pipik had attempted when he called himself the Philip "that is not words"—this time so that he may begin to free himself.

The name Moishe Pipik takes on an even deeper meaning when viewed in the context of ethnicity. Very early in his career, and con-trary to what many of his critics believed, Roth was uncertain about the direction of the contemporary American Jew. In *Goodbye, Co-lumbus* Neil Klugman was caught between the assimilated world of the Patimkins and the more ethnically rooted life in Newark, yet for all the material promise of Short Hills, the sights and smells of his Newark neighborhood seemed more real and in many ways more attractive to him. In "Eli, the Fanatic," another fable of the double, Roth's privileging of his ethnic roots is even more apparent. When Eli puts on the greenhorn's black Eastern European garb, he feels himself transformed and connected to some part of his ethnic past. He is overcome by the "blackness" and it becomes a fixed part of his identity, so much so in fact that when the orderlies attempt to anesthetize Eli, "the drug calmed his soul, but it did not touch it down where the blackness had reached."[51]

In Roth's early fiction, there is a possibility, however tenuous, that some sort of ethnic bedrock can be reached, and that by turning back to one's ancestral origins one could construct at least part of a fixed identity. This idea changed, however, as his career evolved. Whereas once there had been the deep "blackness" of the soul that nothing could ever reach, as we find in "Eli, the Fanatic," in *Opera-*

tion Shylock there is a remnant of origin that leads to nowhere and is nothing more than a meaningless trace. The "pipik," as Roth describes it, is "the silliest, blankest, stupidest watermark that could have been devised for a species with a brain like ours. It might as well have been the omphalos at Delphi given the enigma the pipik presented. Exactly what was your pipik trying to tell you? Nobody could every really figure it out. You were left with only the word, the delightful playword itself, the sonic prankishness of the two syllabic pops and the closing click encasing those peepingly meekish, unobtrusively shlemielish twin vowels."[52]

Roth may not make the same kind of overt ethnic link as he did with the circumcised penis in *The Counterlife,* but it is not too difficult to see the symbolic significance of the bellybutton. Here, Roth has taken the postmodern problem of identity and origin, and placed it within the context of ethnicity. The flesh, this time associated with his Jewishness (especially in being paired with the central figure of the Torah), is once more turned into word, a playful oral event made up of "syllabic pops" and "clicks." Like the circumcised penis, the bellybutton is a signifying mark, but unlike circumcision it suggests more of an absence than a presence. For Zuckerman, circumcision is a unifying act, one acknowledging a male individual's place within the ethnic community. The bellybutton, on the other hand, is nothing more than an anatomical relic of a once-present connection to the womb. Similar to a physical link to the nurturing body being severed at birth, any cohesive and unified understanding of ethnic identity, especially as it springs from a myriad of voices within the Jewish community, is called into question. Whereas in earlier metafictional works such as *My Life as a Man* or *The Ghost Writer* Roth had either marginalized his Jewishness or used it as a vehicle to disarm his critics, here he directly confronts his ethnicity by using a style that had once allowed him to confront his aesthetics. His ethnic aesthetics have shifted from a modernist focus on origin and depth to a postmodern privileging of surface and dissemination. He has moved from souls to bellybuttons.

Philip's sense of identity is never static. He defines himself, and is defined by others both within and outside of his ethnic community, through a series of unlikely binaries such as Zionist and Diasporist, prophet and pariah, comedian and straight man, many times all at once. In other words, Philip becomes a "post-subject" whose sense of self is constantly deferred and resists closure. The text reflects an intermediacy or a betweenness, but it is important to note that the various dialogues in the book are contextualized within the disinte-grated subject, Philip, and that they are never fully resolved. Such a dialogical emphasis on subjectivity gives the text a rather postmod-ern quality. "Where is Philip Roth," Philip asks at one point, "Where did he go?"[53] What is more, this "crisis" is inextricably linked to his ethnicity. It is the Pipik-inspired subject of Israel—the question of how Jews should best define themselves—that casts Philip into an identity vortex. This becomes apparent when he speaks with his old friend, George Ziad—significantly enough, a Pal-estinian nationalist—and finds himself easily slipping into the role of Pipik: "On I went, usurping the identity of the usurper who had usurped mine, heedless of truth, liberated from all doubt, assured of the indisputable rightness of my cause—seer, savior, very likely the Jews' Messiah."[54] In this context, it is no accident that once again the bellybutton, or the pipik, becomes one of the most striking im-ages in *Operation Shylock*. The bellybutton can be seen as one of our most primitive links to identity. It is the remnant of a connection that once provided us with life and bound us to our (parental and ethnic) history. But as with Philip's unlikely double, it represents something that is both there and not there. The bellybutton, the "scar" of identity, no more determines the self than do authorized or fixed notions of Jewishness. As Philip learns, not only can he eas-ily slip into alternate identities when the need arises, but when con-fronted with a destabilizing force such as Pipik, he undergoes a crisis where he is forced to question his own identity as an author writing for the general public and as a Jew. Meeting Pipik for the first time, Philip is profoundly struck by the identical appearance of the two of them, right down to the threadbare elbows of gray herringbone jacket that both men sport, and realizes that "everything inexplica-ble became even more inexplicable, *as though what we were missing were our navels*" (emphasis added).[55] Philip's identity is usurped—or in a deconstructive sense, deferred—by one who believes himself to be a modern-day Moses, the grand patriarch who embodies Judaism.

Roth again addresses the question of ethnicity in the classroom scene where Philip tries unsuccessfully to translate from Hebrew the telling passage from Genesis inscribed on the blackboard, "So Jacob was left alone, and a man wrestled with him until daybreak" (which also serves as one of the book's epigraphs). He reminisces about He-brew school and realizes that, despite its many drawbacks, it is none-theless central to his identity: "What could possibly come of those three or four hundred hours of the worst possible teaching in the

worst possible atmosphere for learning? Why, everything—what
came of it was *everything!* . . . Yes, all and everything had originated
there, including Moishe Pipik."[56] These last words are telling, for as
Roth makes clear throughout the text, Pipik (the man as well as the
bellybutton) represents something in the process of erasure. The
nostalgic reverie is undermined from the outset. At the very moment that Philip is reaching back to what he believes is an ethnically
defining beginning, he is nonetheless unable to translate the letters
on the blackboard, the very letters he once learned in the Hebrew
school. If, as Roth states, Philip's understanding of the ethnic community and his place in it spring from his time in that religious classroom (and one may assume, by association, other ethnic
experiences that the young Philip may have undergone), then his
inability to decipher the Hebrew script suggests a problem in acquir-
ing any sense of a unified identity. What Philip may not realize, and
what Roth the author understands all too well, is the dubiousness of
fixed meanings and points of origins, especially as it relates to notions of self.

One of the last speeches in the book—and the text is filled with
speeches—underscores the unanchored and heteroglossic nature of
identity, in particular ethnic identity. Smilesburger, the deceptive
and enigmatic instigator of Operation Shylock, tries to persuade
Philip not to publish the book, *Operation Shylock*, by preaching on
the underlying causes of Jewish conflict:

> The divisiveness is not just between Jew and Jew—it is within the individ-
> ual Jew. Is there a more manifold personality in all the world? I don't say
> divided. Divided is nothing. Even the goyim are divided. But inside every
> Jew there is a *mob* of Jews. The good Jew, the bad Jew. The new Jew, the
> old Jew. The lover of Jews, the hater of Jews. The friend of the goy, the
> enemy of the goy. The arrogant Jew, the wounded Jew. The pious Jew,
> the rascal Jew. The coarse Jew, the gentle Jew. The defiant Jew, the ap-
> peasing Jew. The Jewish Jew, the de-Jewed Jew. Do I have to expound
> upon the Jew as a three-thousand-year amassment of mirrored fragments
> to one who has made his fortune as a leading Jewologist of international
> literature? Is it any wonder that the Jew is always disputing? He *is* a dis-
> pute, incarnate![57]

As with almost every other speech in the book, here is Roth, or one
of the voices of Roth, disclosing with force what his characters are
often slow to realize. Other speeches—those by Moishe Pipik,
George Ziad, Aharon Appelfeld, Jinx Possesski, David Supposnik,

even Philip himself—express varying if not outright contrary views on the subject of the Jew. These also are the voices of Roth. Like Philip's successor, Mickey Sabbath, Roth slips on the puppets in this "confessional theater" and gives voice to the mob of Jews inside of him. In a text that explores the writing of the self, especially the ethnic writing of the self, it is of no small significance that author and subject are conflated. Both the author and the text itself serve as case studies in the fluidity of subjectivity. What makes Smilesburger's speech stand out is its centrality to Roth's project, its critique on ethnic identity. Even Philip—probably the most intimate of Roth's voices in the text—realizes the importance of the Mossad agent when he admits to himself, "Smilesburger is my kind of Jew, he is what 'Jew' *is* to me, the best of it to me."[58] Perhaps this is why Philip follows his advice on publication, "Let your Jewish conscience be your guide," and fails to include the "Operation Shylock" chapter of *Operation Shylock*.[59] As with the text of the self, the written text in front of the reader both is and isn't there.

Overall, the entire book reads as an exercise in public relations, an elaborate PR game of texts and lives whose objectives are nothing less than a grand duplicity. It is a deceptive act, a bit of "Jewish mischief," that engages the reader in a seductive plot (in both the sense of story and secret plan) that is never fully realized, and makes of him an accomplice to the fact. In engaging the text, the reader by association becomes a participant in the deceptive act of fiction making. As a result, *Operation Shylock* stands as the most successful of Roth's post-Zuckerman works, and one of his most ambitious efforts to date. Not only does he parallel the issues of textual authority and identity construction, at the same time he places them alongside the problems of nationality and Jewish identity.[60] With all of these issues there are never any complete resolutions, but by confronting them together Roth shows that the realm of the written world is not entirely disengaged from that of the unwritten world. This, in many ways, is an answer to Philip Dodd's anxiety over the hermetic quality of contemporary autobiography-as-fiction. As O'Donnell and Shostak have suggested, Roth does indeed seem to reject the nihilistic impulse in much postmodern writing by redefining "reality" as a process of ongoing construction. The language may be duplicitous, but it is no more duplicitous than lived reality itself. In fact, Roth concludes, reality is even less centered than language and texts. During one of his interviews, Appelfeld, the survivor of an unimaginable destruction of life, confides to Philip that "Reality, as you know, is always stronger than the human imagination. Not only that, reality can permit itself to be unbelievable, inexplicable, out of all proportion. The created work, to my regret, cannot permit itself all that."[61] These, one could argue, are—almost—Roth's words exactly. One way out of this query of reality, *Operation Shylock* so daringly suggests, is to constantly renegotiate the bellybuttons of subjectivity, to engage the genres of autobiography and the novel in a mischievous dialogue of mutual definition.

Such a strategy, then, problematizes the "tell-all" qualities of biographies and autobiographies, such as Roth's *The Facts* and Claire Bloom's *Leaving a Doll's House*. What is more, it foregrounds the act of writing the ethnic self. Regardless of whether or not Bloom's memoir is accurate, whether or not it invites us into the personal lives of her and Philip Roth, and thereby sanctions or condemns their actions, readers should take from both *Operation Shylock* and Bloom's book a cue to reinvestigate the construction of texts. Autobiography, as well as fiction, isn't so much a window into the true lives of individuals as it is a glimpse into the ways in which the author constructs his or her reality. Bloom herself, working within the genre that most readers assume to be "true to reality," engages in fiction much in the way that Roth does. In the final pages of her memoir, she relates the details of her last encounters with Roth, after the marriage had ended. Following a nervous meeting at a coffeehouse, Roth tells her, "I want our old life back," and the two of them return to the house in Connecticut to begin anew. She ends this reverie with the words "I knew I had finally come home," suggesting a point of closure to her life with Roth, a "they lived happily ever after" quality reminiscent of fairy tales.[62] But, as Bloom tells us immediately after this episode, this happy ending is nothing but a fiction, a constructed finale that is not true, but which nonetheless gives us a possible clue as to what could be read as her own desires for the outcome of this relationship. What is more real: the actual event or the wish? In light of the nature of autobiography, it doesn't matter. If we engage in the game of ferreting out "the real" from the imagined, we could wind up running in circles. The relationship between autobiography and fiction is most illustrative when it provides us with a means to observe how authors construct their reality, thereby their lives. Roth's *Operation Shylock* provides us with a rich text in which to do so. It is indeed a "confession," but one that tells us more about the self, and the very nature of narrative, than it does its subject.

NOTES

1. Philip Roth, "Author's Note," *Reading Myself and Others* (New York: Farrar, Straus and Giroux, 1975), xi–xii.

2. Philip Roth, *The Facts: A Novelist's Autobiography* (New York: Farrar, Straus and Giroux, 1988), 162, 172. Hereafter referred to as *Facts*.

3. Claire Bloom, *Leaving a Doll's House: A Memoir* (Boston: Little Brown, 1996), 223.

4. Philip Roth, *Operation Shylock: A Confession* (New York: Simon and Schuster, 1993), 55. Hereafter referred to as *OS*.

5. Michiko Kakutani, "Roth within a Roth within a Roth: Where's Roth?" review of *Operation Shylock: A Confession*, by Philip Roth, *New York Times*, March 4, 1993, 4C; emphasis mine.

6. John Updike, "Recruiting Raw Nerves," review of *Operation Shylock: A Confession*, by Philip Roth, *New Yorker* (March 15, 1993): 110.

7. D. M. Thomas, "Face to Face with His Double," review of *Operation Shylock: A Confession*, by Philip Roth, *New York Times Book Review*, March 7, 1993, 1.

8. Robert Alter, "The Spritzer," review of *Operation Shylock: A Confession*, by Philip Roth, *New Republic* (April 5, 1993): 32–33.

9. Harold Bloom, "Operation Roth," review of *Operation Shylock: A Confession*, by Philip Roth, *New York Review of Books*, April 22, 1993, 45.

10. Alan Cooper, *Philip Roth and the Jews* (Albany: State University of New York Press, 1996), 219.

11. Quoted in Esther B. Fein, " 'Believe Me,' Says Roth with a Straight Face" *New York Times*, March 9, 1993, B1-B2.

12. Philip Roth, "A Bit of Jewish Mischief," *New York Times Book Review*, March 7, 1993, 1.

13. Philip Roth, "Juice or Gravy?: How I Met My Fate in a Cafeteria," *New York Times Book Review*, September 18, 1994, 22.

14. Philip Roth, "Writing American Fiction," *Reading Myself and Others* (New York: Farrar, Straus and Giroux, 1961), 120.

15. Almost from the beginning of his career Roth has had to contend with the willed and unwilled fragmentation of his identity as both an author and a "character." Two illuminating sources can be found in "Document Dated July 27, 1969," *Reading Myself and Others* (New York: Farrar, Straus and Giroux, 1975), 23–31, and the various interviews collected in *Conversations with Philip Roth*, ed. George J. Searles (Jackson: University Press of Mississippi, 1992).

16. *OS*, 58.

17. For critical analyses on these issues, see, respectively, Patrick O'Donnell, " 'None other': The Subject of Roth's *My Life as a Man*," in *Reading Philip Roth*, ed. Asher Z. Milbauer and Donald G. Watson (New York: St. Martin's, 1988), 144–59; Sanford Pinsker, "Jewish-American Literature's Lost-and-Found Department: How Philip Roth and Cynthia Ozick Reimagine Their Significant Dead," *Modern Fiction Studies* 35 (1989): 223–35; Mark Shechner, "Zuckerman's Travels," *American Literary History* 1 (1989): 219–30; Debra Shostak, " 'This Obsessive Reinvention of the Real': Speculative Narrative in Philip Roth's *The Counterlife*," *Modern Fiction Studies* 37 (1991): 197–215; and Elaine M. Kauvar, "This Doubly Reflected Communication: Philip Roth's 'Authobiographies,' " *Contemporary Literature* 36 (1995): 412–46.

18. Philip Dodd, "History or Fiction: Balancing Contemporary Autobiography's Claims," *Mosaic* 20 (1987): 65.

19. Shechner, "Zuckerman's Travels," 225.

20. By placing Roth's name in quotation marks, I am referring to the "Roth" who is the subject of his last four works, not to Roth the author of that constructed subject. In order to differentiate between Philip Roth the creator and "Philip Roth" the creation, I will from here on refer to the actual author as Roth (as I have throughout this essay) and the subject or protagonist of his works as Philip (without quotation marks for ease of reading).

21. Philip Roth, *The Counterlife* (New York: Farrar, Straus and Giroux, 1986), 145. Hereafter referred to as *Counterlife*.

22. Philip Roth, *Deception: A Novel* (New York: Simon and Schuster, 1990), 190.

23. My grouping is similar to that of Harold Bloom's, who also reads these texts as a tetralogy, and at odds with Elaine M. Kauvar's, who excludes *Deception* from this list in favor of a trilogy. In an otherwise insightful essay on Roth's psychology of the self, Kauvar is conspicuously silent on *Deception*'s place within the autobiographical writings. What is more, she misinterprets Bloom's textual grouping, claiming it to include *The Counterlife, The Facts, Patrimony,* and *Operation Shylock* (when in fact Bloom sees the earlier work as a precursor to the autobiographical tetralogy).

24. Roth actually underwent a serious bout of depression in 1987. Although the conditions of this breakdown are identical to those revealed in Philip's letter, the difference between the two is again the difference between Roth's written and un-written worlds. The very act of writing the incident on a page transforms it into narrative, text, the "written" world.

25. *Facts*, 5.

26. Ibid., 111, 112.

27. Ibid., 162.

28. Ibid., 192.

29. Ibid., 5.

30. By "counterself" I do not mean to imply the textual self that runs counter or differs from the authorial self. Such a designation would suggest the very binary that Roth attempts to discard. The counterself is a self that appears in the text (or written world), but it does not necessarily contradict, erase, or mimic its author. It suggests fluidity between author and subject, a relationship that is more symbiotic than in traditional narratives. Just as the "real" self is socially and personally con-structed, the counterself is inscribed upon the page.

31. *Counterlife*, 111.

32. In another effort to avoid confusion, I will refer to the impostor or "fake" Philip Roth as Pipik, the name given to him by Philip early in the story.

33. In light of Roth's play between fact and fiction, it is significant to note that the purportedly real Wanda Jane Possesski makes a brief appearance in his next book, *Sabbath's Theater*. In this work, a text with no claims to be anything other than fiction, Mickey Sabbath describes her as his dying lover's nurse, "a good-natured buxom blond named Jinx." In *Sabbath's Theater* (Boston: Houghton Mifflin, 1995), 415.

34. *OS*, 13.

35. Ibid.

36. Ibid., 399.

37. Ibid., 357.

38. Ibid., 361.

39. Ibid., 387.

40. In her memoir, Claire Bloom states that *Operation Shylock* was completed in winter of 1992, meaning that the Demjanjuk trial was still underway as Roth was writing his book. The implication here is that the unresolved and ongoing Demjanjuk trial served as an appropriate backdrop for the ambiguous underpinnings of Roth's text.

41. *OS*, 60.

42. Ibid., 62.

43. Ibid., 20.

44. Ibid., 55.

45. Bloom, *Doll's House*, 178.

46. *OS*, 73.

47. Ibid., 87.

48. Ibid., 307. This allusion to the end of Psalm 23 is just one of the many intertexts that appear throughout the book. Among the others are references to Henry James's "House of Fiction," *The Ghost Writer*, *The Diary of Anne Frank*, "Eli, the Fanatic," and (obviously) Dostoyevsky's *The Double*.

49. *OS*, 115.

50. Ibid., 83.

51. Philip Roth, "Eli, the Fanatic," in *Goodbye, Columbus and Five Short Stories* (Boston: Houghton Mifflin, 1959), 298.

52. *OS*, 116.

53. Ibid., 22.

54. Ibid., 156.

55. Ibid., 76; emphasis mine.

56. Ibid., 312.

57. Ibid., 334.

58. Ibid., 394.

59. Ibid., 398.

60. Cynthia Ozick, for these reasons as well as others, was quite effusive in her praise of the book, calling it "the Great American Jewish Novel" and Roth "the boldest American writer alive." Interview with Elaine M. Kauvar, *Contemporary Literature* 34 (1993): 394, 370.

61. *OS*, 86.

62. Bloom, *Doll's House*, 243.

The Travels of the American *Talush*

Alexis Kate Wilson

IN PHILIP ROTH'S *OPERATION SHYLOCK* (1993) AND *THE COUNTERLIFE* (1986), an American Jew traveling in Israel becomes part of an experiment in the postmodern motifs of projected, multiple, constructed, and possible worlds. At the same time, however, Roth invokes the language of the modernist trope of the artist who stands outside culture in a way that allows him to represent the experience of modernity. Some modernist artists even thought it necessary to see themselves as "Jews" in some way. "All poets are Jews"—Anna Akhmatova says. Indeed, Alfred Kazin has argued that the Jew, being the "symbol of exile," is the prototypical modern writer given that, while he exists on the margins of society, he can most accurately exemplify the dilemma of the modernist subject and artist. He can also be the best commentator on culture and society from this outsider position.[1]

In this paper, I explore the ways Roth not only echoes but also alters this modernist trope for a postmodern world. What is the significance of this trope in a postmodern context? How has the "role" of the Jewish writer changed? S. Lillian Kremer argues that the shift in Jewish-American literature has been one from a focus on marginality and alienation, to the "post-alienated" writers who focus on Jewish thought and values, the Holocaust, and the state of Israel—although less so.[2] I am interested in the way that the modernist themes of marginality and alterity unavoidably surface for Roth in Israel.

Roth's American characters in Israel find themselves in this place of ambiguity where they are both insiders and outsiders at the same time. They are in between worlds, experiencing the complexities of their Jewish *American* identity in the Jewish homeland, an experience noted by other Jewish literary figures as well. Leslie Fiedler has said of his experiences in Israel: "Never in my life have I felt less like a Jew. I have gone back five or six times over the years, only to leave each time further confused and dismayed."[3] However, Roth uses this

92

place of marginality and estrangement to voice the postmodern concerns about the constructed nature of reality—not only through the experience of his characters, but also through the technique of his narrative. *How* do Roth's characters differ from their alienated literary ancestors? Why do the modernist subject and the postmodern world meet in Israel?

Roth explores the Jewish American relationship with Israel in his experimental novel *The Counterlife.* In five chapters, Roth presents overlapping and contradicting stories about Nathan Zuckerman and his brother, Henry. In the spirit of postmodernism, Roth has created an antinovel. With multiple variations on each character, Roth eradicates the conventional structures of fiction and does away with the master narrative. In one section, Henry is suffering from impotence and dies from the surgery to correct it; yet in another he survives the surgery and decides to make *aliyah.* In the last two sections, Zuckerman is impotent and not Henry. Roth presents two variations of this scenario as well: in one Zuckerman dies from the surgery; and in another he survives and moves to England with his new wife. The reader is never sure which story is "real," so to speak, or if one story is fiction within another story. *The Counterlife* offers all these possibilities existing at the same time with no one world dominating. Multiple worlds and counterlives coexist between the covers of the book, in that they represent the endless number of choices available, emphasizing the performative nature of identity that this approach entails. Zuckerman explains: "The burden isn't either/or, consciously choosing from possibilities equally difficult and regrettable—it's and/and/and/and/and as well. Life *is* and: the accidental and the immutable, the elusive and the graspable, the bizarre and the predictable, the actual and the potential, all the multiplying realities, entangled, overlapping, colliding, conjoined."[4]

Roth uses this postmodern formulation as a springboard for an insightful discussion about Jewish identity, and all that condition encompasses. He does so from a variety of perspectives: American, English, and Israeli; Jewish and non-Jewish. As Nathan Zuckerman travels from America to England to Israel, readers are presented with a range of figures and voices from the Hasidic world to a Zionist religious settlement in the West Bank to anti-Semitism in England. Some of the amusing perspectives include the view of an Israeli friend of Zuckerman's that Israel "has become the American-Jewish Australia,"[5] and the enthusiastic young traveler Jimmy Ben-Joseph's own concern for Israel: "How can there be Jews without baseball?"[6]

Jimmy argues that "Not until there is baseball in Israel will Messiah come!"[7] and Jimmy wants to play center field for the Jerusalem Giants!

But I am especially interested in the role that Zuckerman plays here as traveler and writer. At a visit to the Wailing Wall, he positions himself beside the bookshelves, "*so as to look on unobstrusively from the sidelines.*"[8] Zuckerman wants to stand completely outside the scene and observe, but he is repeatedly drawn into various discussions. Later, he is traveling in England, but thinks back on his experience at the Wall: "It never fails. I am never more of a Jew than I am in a church when the organ begins. I may be estranged at the Wailing Wall but without being a stranger—I stand outside but not shut out, and even the most ludicrous or hopeless encounter serves to gauge, rather than sever, my affiliation with people I couldn't be less like."[9] In England, the distinction between "worlds" is clear-cut, but in Israel, he is in this interesting, conflicted position of being both an insider and an outsider at the same time.

As a tourist in Israel, Zuckerman moves from discourse to discourse—able to create a dialogue, but then he is also able to step back outside it and thoughtfully reflect on it. For example, after refusing to join a *minyan*, Zuckerman thinks about the "pious worshippers" at the Wall: "Leaning forward, their elbows on their knees, they reminded me of poor souls who'd been waiting all day in a welfare office or on an unemployment line. Low lozenge-like floodlights did not serve to make the place any cozier or more congenial. Religion couldn't come less adorned than this. These Jews needed nothing but that wall."[10] And after a lengthy evening of "word-whipping" with Mordecai Lippman—the fanatic Zionist of whom Zuckerman's brother has become a follower—Zuckerman reflects on his brother's decision to create his own counterlife by moving to Israel and changing his name to Hanoch:

Losing his way may actually have been the vital need that Henry had been fumbling toward during his recuperation . . . once he'd discovered it, [it] would deliver him from his baffling depression. If so, then it wasn't *roots* that he had unearthed sitting on the sunlit windowsill of that cheder in Mea She'arim; it wasn't his unbreakable bond to a traditional European Jewish life that he'd heard in the chanting of those Orthodox children clamorously memorizing their lessons—it was his opportunity to be *uprooted*, to depart from the path that had been posted with his name the day he was born, and in the disguise of a Jew to cunningly defect. Israel instead of Jersey, Zionism instead of Wendy, assuring that he'd never again be bound to the actual in the old, suffocating, self-strangulating way.[11]

Henry, by choosing this exclusive "world," one which is about shutting down all other possibilities, is unable to do what Zuckerman can: to step back outside it and to write about it. Zuckerman's previous writings, such as his scandalous book *Carnovsky*, have served to alienate him; however, his alienation also *generates* his ability to write. Interestingly enough, as Zuckerman stands in this Kazin-like position as a commentator on the various constructions of Jewish identity he encounters, Zuckerman/Roth continuously draws attention to the fact that the story is just a construction—just as the entire book constructs multiple fictional worlds. In the midst of a discussion on "Who is a Jew?" and "What does it mean to be Jewish in America, and in Israel, and in England?," Roth emphasizes the postmodern skepticism of an essential or single self.

Roth probes the question of the American Jewish relationship with Israel further in his ambitious novel *Operation Shylock: A Confession*.[12] Here these questions of Jewish identity are profoundly coupled with postmodern questions of "what is real?" Brian McHale describes postmodernist fiction as a foregrounding of ontological questions, rather than the epistemological questions that modernism deploys.[13] These questions of postmodernism might be: "Which world is this? What is to be done in it? Which of my selves is to do it? What happens when different kinds of world are placed in confrontation, or when boundaries between worlds are violated?"[14]

His *Operation Shylock* is part of a tetralogy in which Philip Roth deceptively uses his own name in the novel, thus leaving the reader unsure at times if he is reading fiction or autobiography. As in *The Counterlife*, the ontological boundaries between fiction and reality and between different worlds are violated. In *Operation Shylock*, people, historical events, and historical memory all have at least one "counterlife," thereby raising McHale's question of "what is real?"

Philip Roth (the character) travels to Israel to interview Aharon Appelfeld, but instead is preoccupied the entire time with a man who also claims to be Roth—a "counter-Philip Roth." The impersonator Philip Roth, whom Roth renames "Moishe Pipik," is an "ardent Diasporist." He urges Israeli Jews to return to the European countries from which they came to avert a second Holocaust. Protagonist Roth describes his dilemma: "Coming here I had it all figured out: desubjectified in Jerusalem, subsumed in Appelfeld, swimming in the sea of the other self—the other self being yours. Instead there is this me to plague and preoccupy me, a me who is not even me to obsess me day and night—the me who's not me encamped boldly in Jewish Jerusalem while I go underground with the Arabs."[15] Through his being in Israel, Roth is forced to think about questions of identity. He is constantly being brought back to his own subjectivity because of this "other me," as well as being bombarded with paradoxes.

At one point, protagonist Roth attends the trial of John Demjanjuk, accused of being "Ivan the Terrible" of the Treblinka concentration camp. Demjanjuk claims, however, that he is a churchgoing family man from Ohio. Roth wonders, "So there he was—or wasn't. I stared and I stared, wondering if, despite all I'd read of the evidence against him, his claim that he was innocent was true."[16] *Everything* in *Operation Shylock* has multiple versions, including the history of Israel, the role of the Jewish writer, and the rights of Palestinians. Even anti-Semitism isn't merely pure hatred; Moishe Pipik argues that it is a disease that needs to be treated with his twelve-step program "Anti-Semites Anonymous."

Some critics have argued that American Jewish fiction has been slow to respond to the disconcerting subject of Israel. However, Andrew Furman praises Roth as being the "most courageous voice to probe this gap" and to "engage Israel with far greater intellectual rigor than any other contemporary writer."[17] Alvin Rosenfeld as well has said that "it is to Philip Roth that one must look for a writer who has shown the strongest inclination to open his fiction to the challenges of Zionism and Israel."[18] Roth's Israel novels become a polyphonic discourse, one representing the ambiguities and paradoxes a visitor might experience talking to a variety of people in Israel.

Israel, for Roth, seems to present the perfect situation to explore the ontological questions of postmodernity. What is real? How can incongruous identities—worlds—exist simultaneously? In what ways are all identities constructions? How is historical memory a construction? What happens when a fantasy of a homeland becomes a reality? Brian McHale even prefaces his chapter on constructed worlds by quoting Ronald Sukenick: "Here in Israel the extraordinary is run-of-the-mill. We are capable of living in a state in which certain things that have happened have not. At the same time that they have. This is The State of Israel."[19] However, more like modernist fiction, as Kremer describes it, Roth articulates these questions through the voice of the alienated writer who is uprooted from his home—the home, in his case, being America. Zuckerman describes his relationship to America:

> To be the Jew that I was . . . I didn't need to live in a Jewish nation. . . . My landscape wasn't the Negev wilderness, or the Galilean hills, or the coastal plain of ancient Philistia; it was industrial, immigrant America— Newark where I'd been raised, Chicago where I'd been educated, and New York where I was living. . . . My sacred text wasn't the Bible but novels translated from Russian, German, and French into the language in which I was beginning to write and publish my own fiction—not the semantic range of classical Hebrew but the jumpy beat of American English was what excited me.[20]

Zuckerman's identity is *grounded* not in Israel but in America. It is where his Jewishness has been shaped.

The *talush* of my paper's title is the version of the character of the alienated writer that appears in modern Hebrew literature. It literally means "uprooted." This character, often assumed to be based on the author himself, is usually portrayed as sickly, depressive, emasculated; confused about women or where to go, and trying to make sense of his psyche. He wanders from place to place, leaving one world but not quite entering into another. When I began this paper, I chose to call Roth's characters *talush* because of the way in which this "uprootedness" (confused identity, alienation, and mistaken authorial identity) resonated strongly in these two novels. Debra Shostak points out that "Israel poses an identity crisis for the Diaspora Jew largely because of its symbolic power as the Jewish 'home.'"[21] Indeed, although Roth's characters are at home in America, their identities become more complicated and confused when *uprooted* to what is promised to be their real homeland. For Zuckerman, Israel proves "a Jewish homeland that couldn't have seemed . . . more remote."[22] However, in the postmodern world, Roth's *talushim* are able to do what the Hebrew modernists could not. In Yosef Haim Brenner's *Breakdown and Bereavement,* as well as S. Y. Agnon's *Only Yesterday,* the *talush* character moves to Palestine, but he isn't quite able to make it there. He and others like him can't settle the land, and they are so stuck in their splintered selves that the story itself becomes impenetrable. Roth's postmodern, American *talush's* return to Zion does not quite work either. Still, his "uprooting" becomes an *opportunity* for imagining, projecting, and constructing possible worlds, and for examining Jewish identity, rather than a burden of alienation. In the postmodern world and in a postmodern narrative, Roth's *talushim* are able to exit the self and create/construct destinies *"out of words,"* as in *The Counterlife.* In so doing, they are able to do justice to such complex issues as identity and history which, for Roth, are placed at the forefront of the American Jew's total experience in Israel.

Notes

1. Alfred Kazin, "The Jew as Modern Writer," *Commentary* (April 1966): 37–41.

2. S. Lillian Kremer, "Post-alienation: Recent Directions in Jewish-American Literature." *Contemporary Literature* 34, no. 3: 571–91.

3. See Alvin Rosenfeld, "Promised Land(s): Zion, America, and American Jewish Writers," *Jewish Social Studies* 3, no. 3 (1997): 117–18.

4. Philip Roth, *The Counterlife* (New York: Farrar, Straus and Giroux, 1986), 306. Hereafter referred to as *Counterlife.*

5. Ibid., 77.

6. Ibid., 94.

7. Ibid.

8. Ibid., 88, emphasis mine.

9. Ibid., 256.

10. Ibid., 88.

11. Ibid., 131–32.

12. Philip Roth, *Operation Shylock: A Confession* (New York: Simon and Schuster, 1993). Hereafter referred to as *OS.*

13. Brian McHale, *Postmodernist Fiction* (New York: Routledge, 1987), 10.

14. Ibid.

15. *OS,* 55.

16. Ibid., 65.

17. Andrew Furman, *Israel Through the Jewish-American Imagination* (New York: State University of New York Press, 1997), 128.

18. Rosenfeld, "Promised Land(s)," 120–21.

19. McHale, *Postmodernist Fiction,* 99.

20. *Counterlife,* 53.

21. Debra Shostak, "The Diaspora Jew and the 'Instinct for Impersonation': Philip Roth's *Operation Shylock,*" *Contemporary Literature* 38, no. 4 (1997): 742.

22. *Counterlife,* 53.

Autobiography: False Confession?

Margaret Smith

> By the time the imagination is finished with a fact, believe me, it
> bears no resemblance to a fact.
>
> —Philip Roth

AMONG SCHOLARS AND READERS ALIKE AN ELEMENT OF CONTROVERSY
has been that Philip Roth's fiction is often thinly disguised autobiography. This speculation was intensified after the publication of *The
Facts: A Novelist's Autobiography* in 1988. Alan Cooper, in his *Philip
Roth and the Jews* (1996), refers to *The Facts* categorically as autobiography, the nature of which would "finally disclose or confirm [that]
whole episodes and some key plots of the sixties' and seventies' novels were indeed drawn from Roth's young adult life, [and] that
major characters were fictionalizations of friends, relatives, lovers,
and his first wife."[1]

Cooper argues that prior to the publication of *The Facts*, all Roth's
narratives could be construed as fiction. But "in disclosing the limited facts of *The Facts*,"[2] Roth left his work wide open to "legitimate
speculations" that some scenarios enacted in his fiction were indeed
re-enactments of his past life. However, Cooper does caution that
such facts are not necessarily to be trusted. "For in merely being ap-
prehended" he states, "they have already been assaulted by the
imagination."[3] Hence any attempt to link life and fiction is mere
conjecture. It is not my intention here to point to positive sightings
in Roth's texts of wives and friends fictionalized. Neither is it my intention to relate the key plots drawn from so-called real life. However, I will discuss the introduction of certain "facts" and the way
they are transformed imaginatively into fiction.

I argue that Roth does not write autobiography as such and that
his fiction is not a mere rendition of facts colored by his imagination. On the contrary, Roth contrives to blur the boundaries of both

fiction and autobiography as a narrative strategy; indeed, this can be understood as his own personal stance regarding his work. Consequently, when a protagonist called Philip Roth, who happens to be a Jewish-American writer, appears in his text, it is all part of a considered narrative device. Similarly, Nathan Zuckerman, one of a series of Roth protagonists that includes Gabe Wallach, Alexander Portnoy, David Kepesh, and Peter Tarnopol, has been labeled both by critics and readers alike as Roth's hidden, or second, self. Counter to this supposition, Zuckerman appears in several novels as a fictional Jewish-American novelist advocating, as Roth's narrator, that his task is merely to show the power of fiction to "illuminate life."[4] However, according to Roth himself, Zuckerman is an act: "it's all the art of impersonation," which by this definition prohibits narrator-figures such as Zuckerman and his fellow protagonists from relaying any aspect of "truth" due to their singular fictional capacity within the text.[5]

From *The Ghost Writer* (1979) to *The Counterlife* (1986), and even to some extent in *American Pastoral* (1997), Zuckerman repeatedly insists that his fictional Jews are not those his mother, father, and brother refer to as *The Jews*. This is evident in *The Ghost Writer* in the constant battle Nathan encounters concerning his short story "Higher Education"; this story of Newark Jews causes his family to envisage "all of Jewry gratuitously disgraced and jeopardized by my [Nathan's] inexplicable betrayal."[6] This sentiment is also endorsed in the telephone conversation Nathan has with his mother, during which they argue about the ten questions prepared for Nathan by Judge Wapter. The questions are devised to underline the idea that the story harbored potential harm for the Jews—and that in answering Wapter's ten questions, Nathan Zuckerman would uncover his own potential for anti-Semitism:

> "He only meant that what happened to the Jews—"
> "In Europe—not in Newark! We are not the wretched victims of Belsen! We are not the victims of that crime!"
> "But we *could* be—in their place we *would* be. Nathan, violence is nothing new to Jews, you *know* that!"
> "Ma, you want to see physical violence done to the Jews of Newark, go to the office of the plastic surgeon where the girls get their noses fixed. That's where the Jewish blood flows in Essex County, that's where the blow is delivered—with a mallet! To their bones—and to their pride!"[7]

Through his textual "illusion of independent existence," Zuckerman maintains the power of fiction to be "so much more truthful" than nonfiction because it provides a medium that is free of the worry of "causing direct pain."[8] Indeed, his perceptions of the possible publication of "Higher Education" and its potential for family conflict are testament to this opinion. The "direct pain" this story has caused in Zuckerman's eyes stems from the interpretation the reader makes, rather than the imaginative transformation of the material itself. Cooper has said that misreaders of Zuckerman's narrative were guilty of "self-impoverishment, of reducing fiction to some petty biographic detective game. Only fiction . . . has the power to convey the many-sidedness of fact."[9] Here Cooper clearly prescribes Zuckerman's "art of illuminating life" as crucial to fiction's role in conveying versions of fact. However, on closer examination of the text, the father's interpretation of his son's story actually disputes this particular analysis. Zuckerman senior accepts that "Higher Education" is a fictional account and not the re-enactment of a real-life scenario and rejects it as such by his comment, "This story isn't us."[10] Yet he claims it is intended by its author to be read as truth, and not merely a variation of the fact. "You are not somebody who writes this kind of story and then pretends it's the truth,"[11] he says. The son's "belligerent" retort, "I *am* the kind of person who writes this kind of story,"[12] only admits responsibility to the writing of fiction and not to the reader response to it. Zuckerman does not believe his personal stance as a storyteller requires any further qualification. His father is creating any potential humiliation of the Jews entirely by his own imagination.

Roth himself has many times referred to the narrative strategies he employs, citing "sheer playfulness and deadly seriousness"[13] as aspects of his writing he now considers his closest friends. Nowhere is this strategic combination any more evident than in *Operation Shylock: A Confession* (1993). This is a fiction layered with Philip Roths. There is Philip Roth author, Philip Roth as double, and Philip Roth as Jewish-American writer who also narrates the events of the novel. Philip Roth narrator assures the reader that this is an accurate account of the facts. He details as fact actual occurrences that he claims to have lived through in his middle-fifties. He further qualifies this declaration of so-called truth with statistics and dates surrounding the Demjanjuk trial concurrently taking place in the Israeli Supreme Court. In an end note to the reader, when Roth states that "This book is a work of fiction," he refers to parts of the text as being products of the author's imagination, or facts used fictitiously, declaring finally, "This confession is false."[14] The "Note to the Reader" is presented outside the main body of the text, thus creating an ambiguity as to which Philip Roth is speaking. So successful is Roth's elusive writing technique in *Operation Shylock* that reviewers and librarians alike have had difficulty in its cataloguing. One reviewer from the *Spectator* claimed it to be a very buoyant book, part truth, part fiction.[15]

Another example of Roth's dexterous playful and serious combination is *Deception* (1990). Here the reader is deliberately coerced to associate the identity of the narrator, a writer of fiction named Philip, with that of the perceived Philip Roth who exists outside the fiction. Narrator Philip further compounds the narrative's duplicity when he tries to explain away his suspicious wife's accusations of infidelity. She had found an intimate notebook which Philip insists was written in conjunction with an unnamed novel on which he is currently working:

> You are having an affair with someone in your studio! . . .
> The only woman in my studio is the woman in my novel.
> Not your novel—your notebook![16]

This so-called description of "postcoital intimacy,"[17] it is implied, appears as an exterior text in which Philip, narrator, and by implication Philip Roth, writer, imagines himself to be having a love affair with the English female protagonist of his novel: "One is a figure sketched in conversation in a notebook, the other is a major character entangled in the plot of an intricate book. I have been imagining myself, outside of my novel, having a love affair with a character inside my novel."[18]

This explanatory sequence, rather like *Operation Shylock's* end note, implies an existence outside the text that displays a so-called bona-fide experience of authorial intent, in which "the desire for her *to* exist exists."[19] Thus, by definition, the novel *Deception* itself arguably casts an ambiguous shadow over the notebook's said purpose as blueprint for the unnamed novel. At this point it is also possible to separate the contents of the notebook from the text of *Deception*, as the narrative strategies of one fiction comments on the fictional processes of another. The Philip who discusses the implications of his notebook with his doubting wife freely admits that he has, as yet, to define its purpose and the ambiguities raised therein: "A portrait of what? Up till now I have been fiddling with it on the side."[20] Again he is distinguishing its contents from the major work in progress he is concentrating on—that is, he is mostly "worrying about the novel."[21] His wife, however, can make no such distinction in her interpretation of the notebook's contents. Her only requirement is that her husband withdraw his name from that context, as an advisable measure against the public construction of a personal account of "adulterous love."[22] Consequently, entries such as, "Philip, do you have an ashtray?"[23] were it ever to be published, would be changed to "Nathan,"[24] thereby denying the notebook's intention of exploring the process of authorial imagining, or that which narrator Philip had dubbed "the story of an *imagination* in love."[25] What Nathan Zuckerman's father had previously interpreted as an act of inexplicable betrayal of all Jews is again echoed throughout the text of *Deception*. Only now this strategy can be interpreted as narrator Philip's confessed betrayal of his marriage vows.

The last chapter of *Deception* does little to unravel the complex nuances of Philip Roth's narrative strategy. A telephone call to his narrator from a woman, who introduces herself simply as "It's me,"[26] becomes the reader's stimulus for establishing her "true" identity, and for deciding whether or not she is the woman of the narrator's imaginative desire. Is it she who appears in Philip's unnamed novel, the "blueprint,"[27] and who is sketched out through the various conversations recorded in his yet unpublished notebook? We are given that the woman's surname is Freshfield, a name Philip admits came by way of an English poem, "Tomorrow to fresh woods and pasture new."[28] Her retort, "I don't think Freshfield was at all a good name for me. . . . It was too easy,"[29] suggests to the reader that her name is fictional, and that she may, or may not, exist. She is English and has two children: one, a girl of whom Philip narrator has previous knowledge; the second, a boy, who comes as a surprise to him. But the fact that he feels inclined to question the parentage of the child and her reply, "It's, it's my husband's, . . . it is,"[30] establishes that she is indeed the female protagonist engaged in the conversations recorded in his notebook. Maria Freshfield is also the name of the woman Nathan Zuckerman makes his fourth wife in *The Counterlife*. In his letter to his creator in *The Facts*, he identifies her as "Maria Freshfield Zuckerman," who is English and Oxford educated: "She has a daughter from her previous marriage, . . . a sweet and placid four-year-old, and is nearing the end of the eighth month of pregnancy with our first child."[31] In this light *The Counterlife, The Facts: A Novelist's Autobiography*, and *Deception* can be read as self-reflexive texts whose subject matter revolves around each other's complex narrative strategies: in other words, these are narratives devoted to their own fictionality and as such may be referred to as works of meta-fiction.

When asked by Alan Finkielkraut, "[Should we] read your books as confession, [and] as autobiography barely disguised?" Philip Roth replied: "You should read my books as fiction, demanding the pleasures that fiction can yield. I have nothing to confess and no one I want to confess to. . . . To label books like mine 'autobiographical' or 'confessional' is not only to falsify their suppositional nature but, if I may say so, to slight whatever artfulness leads some readers to think they must be autobiographical."[32] That was Philip Roth speaking in 1981 and, interestingly enough using the term "artfulness," which is not necessarily a reference to his creative powers alone. Arguably, it could be a reference to the literary strategy of conceit and metafiction which his narratives continue to employ. Zuckerman underlines this point in the letter to Roth that appears as an end note to *The Facts: A Novelist's Autobiography*: "by projecting essentially fictional characters with manic personae out into the world, you openly invite misunderstanding about yourself. . . . people get it wrong and don't have any idea of who or what you really are. . . . Consider having tricked them into those beliefs a *success*; that's what fiction is *supposed* to do."[33]

Zuckerman's intervention here, in what is allegedly his creator's autobiography, again can be construed as another of Roth's disclaimers that "this confession is false." When asked "Where does autobiography stop and fiction start," in an interview with *La Repubblica*, Roth gave the most definitive description yet of how he undertakes his work:

> The problem doesn't exist. The fiction starts with the first line of a novel, autobiography with the first word of an autobiography. Using fragments of your life is exactly like putting pieces of beefsteak through the mincer to make hamburger. The mincer is your imagination. What comes out is something completely different, completely transformed: The result is still meat, but transformed, organised. Moreover, when I want to write autobiography as in *Deception* or *Patrimony*, I do it without mask.[34]

Although Roth seems to indicate that he sees a clear demarcation between the presentation of life history in autobiography and the narrative form of fiction, this is questionable. First, that *Deception* is referred to by him in this interview as autobiography is somewhat of a revelation in itself, as it was previously considered by critics and publishers alike as a novel. Second, Roth seems to be suggesting that both mediums or genres are reliant on each other, in that both autobiography and fiction involve the mediation of life experience. How they are presented, he implies, is governed by the application or removal of mask.

The focus here will be on the word "mask," what it represents in this context and what it means for Philip Roth's work. He has in the past related the term mask to the "lies people can sustain behind the mask of their real faces"; he refers to the "act" or "great performance" of people pretending to be themselves is in essence "to go around in disguise. To act a character."[35] For example, Zuckerman is accused of experimenting with himself by Maria's sister in *The Counterlife*. She declares: "He experiments with himself . . . to see how it feels and what it's like." He agrees, as his answer emphasizes that he is displaying himself as a character: "I can only exhibit myself in disguise. All my audacity derives from masks."[36] This is a remark Roth later clarified as being Zuckerman's understanding "that the best of his [Zuckerman's] vividness, daring, originality and flair surfaces only through artistic imposturing," which in turn could be read as a literary deception or device.[37] If Roth is making the point here that by association fiction is a masquerade, a concealment, or a fanciful conceit of the real (as the imposturing protagonist pretending to be himself represents), this is a statement in direct conflict with his many previous declarations, including those he makes through his protagonist Nathan Zuckerman—that to read his fiction as autobiography is to misread, thereby undermining the creative art of the fiction writer himself. Or, more interestingly, is he admitting to writing autobiography, which up to this point he has vehemently claimed he does not do? An examination of *how* Roth devises the concept of mask will have a bearing on whether he, or any other writer for that matter, has the ability to apply or remove it, especially if what is at issue is the notion of veiled autobiography.

Roth has been recorded as saying on more than one occasion that the difference between writers and those who do not write is imagination: "The writer has something beyond the self which is imagination," and what separates him from the other people is simply the ability to "make things up."[38] That is to say, if you had only the experience of self to draw upon, you wouldn't be a writer. This view would seem to support Roth's metaphor in *La Repubblica* that only fragments of life experience transformed by the "mincer" of imagination into the "hamburger" of fiction (or autobiography) has the power to "illuminate life." Roth's distinction between writer and non-writer is more interesting than it first appears. He does not differentiate here between fiction and autobiography, but cites the imagination as the writer's most important tool, which he further places *beyond* the "self."

If, before Freud, the self was said to be defined by the sum total of life experience, it can be said that, after Freud, the concept of self is defined by that which cannot be remembered; if true, how does this difference relate to Roth's creation of mask? If it is fashioned, or produced from the transformation of autobiographical experience or fragments of memory, the application or removal of mask as a narrative strategy and as a means of distinguishing between fact and fiction may well be redundant. Or, alternatively, can masks be self-consciously created as an imaginary means of preventing the imaginative transformation of so called "real life," or life as lived, as in autobiography? The "mincer" quotation suggests the latter; and in removing mask, or to write without mask in the production of autobiography, implies the introduction of yet another form of narrative strategy, one which may be construed as the implication of "real truth." Within the concept of Freudian thought, however, beyond the self, or the hidden true self, resides in the id, which serves as the repository of repressed memory. The id is said to house those taboos of a human society that have a prohibitive effect on human customs and social behavior, thereby governing what individuals should and should not do.

With *this* in mind, Roth's notion of mask may be a reference to a social structure of personality—that is, the socially accepted face of self that remains. Thus, when Roth refers to the application of mask, he is possibly emphasizing a literary strategy that looks to undermine this socially imposed, self-consciously performed "best self," or ego. In Roth's writing philosophy then, the *mincer* of the imagination can now be understood as stripping away that face of acceptability—the "beefsteak" becoming in his writing an imaginary exploration of that which acts as counter to "best self." Through the application of mask, Roth can present his protagonists in more depth. Narrator Philip's account of "postcoital intimacy," as portrayed in his notebook and carefully divorced from the voice of Nathan Zuckerman in *The Counterlife*, could be considered an imaginary exploration of the counterself. The notebook, set within the concept of the novel *Deception*, however, serves a deeper and more far-reaching purpose. Rather like the id itself, the so-called imaginary notebook of Roth's narrator Philip is based on the meta-fictional evidence gleaned from *The Counterlife*, *The Facts*, and *Deception*, the published version of the notebook. The texts supply examples of self-reflexive narratives, which are devoted to their own fictionality, and as such make no pretence of having a connection with the "facts" of any particular history. The id of the personality can also be considered in a similar light as a collective consciousness of material, classed as taboos, and portrayed as allegorical notions that in some way determine human behavior. The id cannot be constructed on a base of facts. What the id represents for Roth's fiction is an artificial corpus of potential human behavior, or a fabrication of rules that may or may not bear reference to any recognized historical fact. This suggests that metafiction as a narrative strategy requires the total compliance of its readership. It works to internalize the relationship between author and reader, suggest Jones and Nance, "to free our feelings from societal restrictions so that we may respond to an imaginative experience without the compulsion to judge in the same way we would in everyday experience, where we might be expected to act on our judgments. . . . or [as] Roth suggests, 'we drop into another layer of consciousness.'"[39] Consequently, Roth is able to reveal the true condition of his protagonist, or the internal conflict of the Jew who is depicted as acting counter to what his peers regard as the Jewish "best self." It would seem to an ideal Roth reader that the ego or "best self" has to be mediated through the "worst self" of the id. This can explain the distinction Roth has drawn between the apologists of society and its artists. Roth would maintain that the artist can imagine steps beyond the accepted moral codes that limit the behavior of society as a whole. Yet through the literary strategy of metafiction, the reader, in what can be termed the unconscious assimilation of authorial intent, is coerced into confusing the fiction of the text with that which is perceived as real. After all, Philip Roth the writer has always argued that he does not intend his writing to affirm or deny the principles held by society, Jewish or otherwise. He wishes in his fiction merely to produce the "hamburger" or art of the disinterested social observer.

On the surface, when Roth describes autobiography as writing without mask, without the transforming properties of imagination, as he purports he has done in *Deception* and *Patrimony*, there can be some substance to what he is saying—that is, if we believe as Paul John Eakin has noted, there is a legitimate sense in which autobiography is actually the rendition of personal testimony that testifies to the individual experience of the "I." This is opposed to the "artfulness" Roth exposes when he textually seeks to certify with facts, dates, and statistics his protagonist, narrator, and author as real people; he does so to validate the "autobiographer's conventional posture of truth-telling, leaving open the possibility they may not be telling the truth."[40] For example, we are asked to believe that *Patrimony: A True Story* and *Deception* can be read as examples of Roth writing autobiography; we are to assume that the so-called autobiographical material used is a truthful version of the facts. We are thereby led to believe the novelist's imagination has to be restrained to recount what is alleged to be the "true story." If so, in *Patrimony* there is still some evidence that one particular dramatic scenario may be dubious. Paul John Eakin discusses what he calls the "remarkable" sequence in *Patrimony's* narrative, where Roth describes the "humiliating experience that his father regards as the depth of shame and disgrace."[41] Despite his father's pleading that his son never reveal this traumatic event, "Roth pursues a policy of total disclosure."[42] Entrusted with his father's postoperative care, Roth gives an account of his father's "exploding bowels" after days of constipation, and the cleaning of the "befouled bathroom" that followed. This vivid "autobiographical" scene of father beshitting his son's bathroom shares particular resonance with an equally vivid but fictional sequence in *My Life as a Man* (1974), where Maureen, Peter Tarnopol's estranged wife, responds in a fashion similar to that of the father figure in *Patrimony*. Following a distressing encounter between wife and husband, the latter cries out: "YOU'RE TRACKING SHIT EVERYWHERE! WASH YOURSELF!"[43] We see Roth's protagonist Peter Tarnopol and Philip Roth his creator, years apart and in different texts, both throwing windows wide open to release the overwhelming smell while cleaning feces from the cracks in the floor with wads of paper toweling. Alan Cooper has referred to the similarity of these scenes, one fictional and the other allegedly autobiographical, as enjoying a certain element of "fictive convenience."[44]

Philip Roth's graphic last impressions of his father so also bear some similarities to the tortured Portnoy senior, described by his son Alex as "Oh, this father! this kindly, anxious, uncomprehending, constipated father!"[45] The young Alex, rather like the older Philip, seems sensitive to his father's needs as he sits with him in the family kitchen. He is aware of "the suppository melting invisibly in [his father's] rectum," and awaits the "miracle. . . . But the miracle never came."[46] The release young Alex Portnoy wishes for his distant, anally retentive father is part of his own "history of disenchantment,"[47] one illustrated by his growing awareness of his father's lack of sporting prowess or even a healthy enquiring mind. "If only he could read *this*. Yes! Read and understand . . . this schmuck, this moron, this Philistine father of mine!"[48] Young Portnoy's growing despair is reminiscent of the emotions Herman Roth's act of paternal release in *Patrimony* inspires in his son: "So *that* was the patrimony. And not because cleaning it up was symbolic of something else but because it wasn't, because it was nothing less or more than the lived reality that it was. There was my patrimony: not the money, not the tefillin, not the shaving mug, but the shit."[49] Although not the most enlightened father, "he was always teaching me something, not the conventional American dad stuff, . . . but something coarser."[50] His patrimony, his son concludes, was the "vernacular" with its "glaring limitations and all its durable force."

So how should we read *Patrimony: A True Story*? Is it a son's account of his father's last years, which is to be perceived as an autobiographical account of the son? Or is it simply a biographical account of the father's death? Roth himself has referred to it—as he has to *Deception*—as autobiography. But, as is clearly the case, *Deception*, whether or not we read it as truth, is fundamentally a novel of metafiction. Fiction is its subject, which, through its form, artfully explores the artifice of that fiction. Similarly, *Patrimony* also offers clues to this particular strategy: "I must remember accurately, I told myself," says Roth, "remember everything accurately so that when he is gone I can re-create the father who created me."[51] To refer to the re-creation of the father suggests an imaginative process has taken place; furthermore, only after subjecting memory to this imaginative process will the "I" or the "self" become apparent.

Roth's use of mask, in whatever guise, presents the reader with enough scope to explore the whole spectrum and issue of self. He has described the writer as a "performer" who "dons the mask of the first-person singular," suggesting that this indeed "may be the best mask of all for a second self."[52] Roth has also described his frequent textual movements as a spontaneous action. This use of the third person in describing the "I" or the "self" not only becomes a masking device in its own right, but it also acts to displace personality. As Roth explains, writing in the third person leaves him free "to say about Zuckerman what it would be inappropriate for him [Zuck-

erman] to say about himself";[53] in this way the author is able to mod-
ify his protagonist's discreet behavior with his own lack of discretion.
That is a point reinforced in *Deception* by narrator Philip, who insists
that "I cannot and do not live in the world of discretion, not as a
writer anyway. . . . Discretion is, unfortunately, not for novelists."[54]
The writing of fiction that Roth himself termed in *Reading Myself and
Others* as the "making of fake biography, false history" and "the sly
and cunning of masquerade"[55] belies the claims he makes for the
writing of autobiography, and shows that the "artfulness" of his narrative strategy lies in his ability to create mask.

Philip Roth is continually encouraged by critics and interviewers
to describe the textual process involved in his depiction of character.
He echoes Nathan Zuckerman's term for covering *his* use of impersonation and mask; in short Roth concludes that the effectiveness
and power of his writing arise from the "audacity with which the
impersonation is pulled off."[56] In this sense, Roth makes no precise
differentiation between autobiography and fiction; instead, he prefers a wider classification within which to discuss what for him is literature's highest priority: "the belief it inspires is what counts."[57]
"To pass oneself off as what one is not"[58] is clearly the audacious
point in Roth's work. Also, in considering the metafictional properties that are part of that audacity, what Roth would have us believe
is that "naked autobiography" is more than likely "autobiography
grandiosely enlarged."[59] Clearly, Roth undertakes this even before
being advised by his protagonist Nathan Zuckerman in *The Facts* to
consider that the conceits of his writing and their outcome are his
success. Zuckerman insists that "people get it wrong" and read fiction as autobiography; however, Roth holds that it is through the
"artfulness" of his narrative strategy that people get it absolutely
right.

In speaking about his work, Roth has invoked the image of the
ventriloquist whose art is to speak at a distance from himself—as
if the voice were that of someone else and out of his audience's
line of vision. However, if that were the case, there would be little
pleasure in his artfulness. As Roth has said of the novelist, "His art
consists of being present and absent; he's most himself by simultaneously being someone else, neither of whom he 'is' once the curtain
is down."[60] This, too, is a typical scenario in Roth's writing as this
short, edited extract from *Operation Shylock: A Confession*, will show. It
describes the meeting of the two men purporting to be the same
Philip Roth:

"I can't speak," he said. "It's you. You came!"

But the one who couldn't speak was I. . . . and I had imagined that confronted with the materialialization of *me*, he would recoil in fear and capitulate.

"Philip Roth! The real Philip Roth—after all these years!"

"And you," I said, shoving him a little as I stepped away, "you must be the fake Philip Roth."

"Fake, oh, compared to you, *absolutely* fake—compared to you, nothing, no one, a cipher. . . . imagine yourself in my place. For me—to meet you. . . . What brings you here?" . . .

I heard myself reply, "Passing through."

"I'm looking at myself," he said, ecstatically, "except it's *you*."

"What's your game my friend?"

"No game," he replied, surprised and wounded by my angry tone. "And I'm no fake. I was using 'real' ironically."

"Well, I'm not so pretty as you and I'm not so ironical as you and I was using 'fake' *unerringly*. . . . You go around pretending to be me."

This brought that smile back—"You go round pretending to be *me*," he loathsomely replied.[61]

The ventriloquist image is paramount to this edited sequence. The reader is at all times directed to consider who the ventriloquist of the piece actually is, which will ultimately help determine who the "real" Philip Roth is. Initially, the form Roth's construction of dialogue takes, as well as his use of the word "materialization," helps to establish the premise that the "me" who speaks is the "I" of the text: the "I" who speaks does so with the authority and audacity that arise from being the actual/real Philip Roth. The other voice now can be understood as the "other" or misleading Philip Roth voice—the one that comes from somewhere else and is therefore fake. However, the last retort of the so-called other Roth is an echo of Roth's accusation and, therefore, Roth himself, which brings this scenario into doubt. Who is "passing" for whom, creates a moment of acute tension within the text.

In a similar vein, the Philip Roth of the so-called autobiographical *Deception* explains, in defense of his imaginative blueprint, the duplicity of his own textual depiction: "It is *far* from myself—it's play, it's a game, it is an *impersonation* of myself! Me *ventriloquizing* myself. Or maybe it's more easily grasped the other way around—everything here is falsified *except* me. Maybe it's *both*."[62] Here, the ventriloquist device becomes a more complex issue. The textual "me" is subject to impersonation and even ventriloquy, as the discourse between

the two Roths of *Operation Shylock* previously suggests. Are there
really two Roths in the guise of artist and puppet? Or, is the impersonator merely the simplistic introduction of the narrator's present
state of mind? That will gradually become clearer as Roth develops
his impersonator's presence into a clearer figure in his imagination.
However, the narrator in *Deception* discussing his notebook questions
the very basis of the self. His notebook is a fictional rendition of the
narratives of memory, as Ivan's comments suggest: "[you] cannot
resist a narrative. . . . The stronger the narrative impulse in her, the
more captivated you are."[63] Ivan's further reference to "Schehera-
zade"[64] is also testament to this notion of narrative; his point is that
the narrative is based on a subjective account of personal life that
lacks any substance of historical memory, or, in his words, "you
[Philip] listen and rush to write it down and then you ruin it with
your rotten fictionalizing."[65] "Everything here is falsified";[66] therefore, autobiographical "truth" is brought into question. In this
sense, the ability to remove or write without mask seems to be rendered redundant. When narrator Philip told his wife, "the novel is
Zuckerman. The notebook is me," the "play" or "game"[67] to which
he refers becomes apparent. The game is to play with fragments of
memory that experiment with traditional and modern notions of
how autobiography is produced. The suggestion that Roth's fiction
contains autobiographical facts becomes, in this light, a sequence of
stories that narrator Philip uses to combine the so-called facts. The
meanings produced demonstrate that "memories of the past are not
memories of facts but memories of your imaginings of the facts."[68]
Using Roth's own analogy, the "beefsteak," or the metafictional account of the facts, is fed through the imaginative "mincer" of *Deception*, and the "hamburger" that appears is fiction easily confused
with autobiography.

In asking what "mask" represents in Philip Roth's work, perhaps
it may be more productive to ask, "What does he gain by wearing
this mask?"[69] This is a question he himself answered initially in *Deception* in reference to his notebook: "I portray myself as implicated because it is not enough just to be present."[70] Clearly, in the novelist's
own impersonation as a central character or characters within his
writings, he reinforces the illusion, or perhaps the deception, that
the novel is true and not to be "discounted as fiction."[71] Roth's
claim that the so-called novels *Deception* and *Patrimony* in particular
are autobiography can be given some credence—when these texts
are actually viewed as the autobiographical account of a literary

process. They are autobiographical because they are the accounts of an author's personal processing of imaginary material, or the self-conscious creations of mask through which each "confession" is rendered truly "false."

Notes

Epigraph. Philip Roth, "This Butcher, Imagination," *New York Times Book Review,* February 14, 1988, 2.

1. Alan Cooper, *Philip Roth and the Jews* (Albany: State University of New York Press, 1996), 52.

2. Ibid., 51.

3. Ibid., 53.

4. Philip Roth, *The Facts: A Novelist's Autobiography* (New York: Farrar, Straus and Giroux, 1988), 162. Hereafter referred to as *Facts.*

5. Hermione Lee, "The Art of Fiction LXXXIV: Philip Roth," in *Conversations with Philip Roth,* ed. George J. Searles (Jackson: University Press of Mississippi, 1992), 166.

6. Philip Roth, "The Ghost Writer," in *Zuckerman Bound: A Trilogy and Epilogue* (New York: Farrar, Straus and Giroux, 1980), 96. Hereafter referred to as *ZB.*

7. Ibid., 106.

8. *Facts,* 162.

9. Cooper, *Philip Roth and the Jews,* 1.

10. *ZB,* 94.

11. *ZB,* 95.

12. Ibid.

13. Philip Roth, *Reading Myself and Others* (1975; repr., New York: Vintage, 2001), 96.

14. Philip Roth, *Operation Shylock: A Confession* (New York: Simon and Schuster, 1993), 399.

15. Publisher's note taken from the back cover of *Operation Shylock: A Confession* (London: Vintage, 2000 edition).

16. Philip Roth, *Deception* (New York: Simon and Schuster, 1990), 180. Hereafter referred to as *Deception.*

17. Ibid., 187.

18. Ibid., 183.

19. Ibid., 188.

20. Ibid., 189.

21. Ibid.

22. Ibid.

23. Ibid.

24. Ibid.

25. Ibid.

26. Ibid., 193.

27. Ibid., 192.

28. Ibid., 202.

29. Ibid.

30. Ibid., 197.

31. *Facts*, 185.

32. Alan Finkielkraut, "The Ghost of Roth," in Searles, *Conversations with Philip Roth*, 121–22.

33. *Facts*, 167.

34. Irene Bignardi, "Che vergogna l'America di McCarthy," *La Repubblica*, June 25, 2000, 37.

35. Lee, "Art of Fiction," 167.

36. Philip Roth, *The Counterlife* (New York: Farrar, Straus and Giroux, 1987), 275.

37. Mervyn Rothstein, "Philip Roth and the World of 'What If,' " in Searles, *Conversations with Philip Roth*, 198.

38. Cathleen Medwick, "A Meeting of Hearts and Minds," in Searles, *Conversations with Philip Roth*, 134.

39. Judith Paterson Jones and Guinevera A. Nance, *Philip Roth* (New York: Ungar, 1981), 27–28.

40. Paul John Eakin, *How Our Lives Become Stories* (New York: Cornell University Press, 1987), 4.

41. Ibid., 183.

42. Ibid.

43. Philip Roth, *My Life as a Man* (New York: Holt, Rhinehart and Winston, 1974), 284.

44. Cooper, *Philip Roth and the Jews*, 244.

45. Philip Roth, *Portnoy's Complaint* (New York: Random House, 1969), 39. Hereafter referred to as *PC*.

46. Ibid., 5.

47. Ibid., 9.

48. Ibid.

49. *Patrimony*, 176.

50. Ibid., 181.

51. Ibid., 177.

52. Roth, *Reading Myself and Others*, 125.

53. *Deception*, 142.

54. Ibid., 190.

55. *Reading Myself and Others*, 125.

56. Lee, "Art of Fiction," 168.

57. Ibid.

58. Ibid., 167.

59. Ibid., 169.

60. Roth, *Reading Myself and Others*, 124.

61. *OS*, 71–72.

62. *Deception*, 190.

63. Ibid., 93.

64. Ibid., 94.

65. Ibid.

66. Ibid., 190.

67. Ibid., 189–90.

68. *Facts*, 8.

69. *Reading Myself and Others*, 125.

70. *Deception*, 183.

71. Ibid.

Death, Mourning, and Besse's Ghost: From Philip Roth's *The Facts* to *Sabbath's Theater*

James M. Mellard

> Memories of the past are not memories of facts but memories of your imaginings of the facts. There is something naïve about a novelist like myself talking about presenting himself "undisguised" and depicting "a life without the fiction."
>
> —Philip Roth

1

Oddly, perhaps, though it is a life in each case upon which they focus, it is death, not life, that lies behind Roth's two autobiographical works of nonfiction, *The Facts* (1988) and *Patrimony* (1991). *Patrimony* somewhat fills the gap of years between Roth, age about thirty-five, covered in *The Facts* and Roth, age about fifty-five when, in *Patrimony* he produced his affecting account of his father's life and death in 1989 of a brain tumor. *The Facts* ends in about September 1968, at a time just before the publication of *Portnoy's Complaint* made Roth rich and famous (well, rich and notorious). But it was neither wealth nor fame that drove Roth to write *The Facts*. According to Roth, that book was as much a response to death as was *Patrimony*. Whereas *Patrimony* emerged from Roth's foreknowledge that his father was dying of the tumor and thus was written from notes Roth made as the tumor progressed, the earlier *Facts* came as a response to the other parent's death, to the death of Besse Roth. In a "letter" to Nathan Zuckerman prefacing *The Facts*, Roth confesses some of the motives that underlay his writing the book. One motive, he suggests, is that he was tired of creating "self-legends" in his fiction; another is the "crack-up" that resulted from his having taken the drug Halcion while recovering from a knee surgery that went wrong; yet a third—and to Roth the most prominent—was his mother's death. "Though I can't be entirely sure," he tells Zuckerman, "I

wonder if this book was written not only out of exhaustion with making fictional self-legends and not only as a spontaneous therapeutic
response to my crack-up but also as a palliative for the loss of a
mother who still, in my mind, seems to have died inexplicably—at
seventy-seven in 1981."[1]

But this motive is augmented, says Roth, by another that, as we
will learn from *Patrimony*, has an oddly ironic, almost uncanny, por-
tentousness to it. The writing of *The Facts* may also have provided a
way, says Roth, "to hearten me as I come closer and closer and closer
to an eighty-six-year-old father viewing the end of life as a thing as
near to his face as the mirror he shaves in (except that this mirror is
there day and night, directly in front of him all the time)."[2] The
irony here occurs not in the father's knowledge, but in Roth's lack
of knowledge about his father's health. Thus *The Facts* provides
knowing readers an uncanny portent of *Patrimony* not only in its
most brutal "fact," but also in the metaphor of illness Roth uses to
speak of a father he still thinks is healthy. "Even though it might not
be apparent to others," says Roth of the earlier book, "I think that
subterraneanly my mother's death is very strong in . . . [it], as is ob-
serving my provident father preparing for no future, a healthy but
very old man dealing with the kind of feelings aroused by an incur-
able illness, because just like those who are incurably ill, the aged
know everything about their dying except exactly when."[3]

Soon enough, both Roth and his father will learn that the old
man's good health is an illusion and that the specter of his death
will become visible in the tumor's effect on his motor skills, facial
muscles, and ability to swallow. Thus the considerable irony of *The
Facts* is that it begins in one form of what Roth calls "parental longing" and ends without Roth's knowledge by foreshadowing another
form of it. But, however unaware of what soon was to befall his
father, Roth clearly understood that both parents had become critical to his conception of himself, of, as he put it, his "reassigning
myself as myself." He sees clearly that one motive for writing *The
Facts* lay in his desire to focus on the time in his life when both parents were alive and stabilized his universe. "I wonder," he writes to
his alter ego Zuckerman, "if I haven't drawn considerable consola-
tion from reassigning myself as myself to a point in life when the
grief that may issue from the death of parents needn't be contended
with, when it is unperceivable and unsuspected, and one's own departure is unconceivable because they are there like a blockade."[4]
Having lost his mother in 1981 and being destined to lose his father

in 1989, Roth begins in *Patrimony* to cope with the meaning of his father's legacy, the precise meaning of the gift implied in the title of the book. That meaning is itself connected as much to death as it is to life. Moreover, it may also once again be connected, as in *The Facts*, to his mother as much as to his father.

2

In *Patrimony*, Roth creates an elegy for the father, one that is almost classic in its linear structure and clear, direct, unaffected imagery. Roth exhibits both elegiac structure and imagery in his interpretation of a dream he had once had of his father's death. In his interpretation, by associating his father's death with a memory of the death of President Franklin Delano Roosevelt as well as with the dream's image of a silent warship emptied of people and "stripped of its armaments and wholly disabled, [floating] imperceptibly toward the shore,"[5] Roth makes the sort of linkages one finds in the traditional elegy. These linkages, in the terms of Jacques Lacan, connote the move from the everyday Imaginary to the transcendent Symbolic. That move is absolutely plain in the book's very last words. There, Roth suggests that his father transcends the finite, concrete father to become the Symbolic father, the one who, says Lacan, rules the domain of Law and of whom we speak as the Name of the Father. "The dream," says Roth, "was telling me that, if not in my books or in my life, at least in my dreams I would live perennially as his little son, with the conscience of a little son, just as he would remain alive there not only as my father but as *the* father, sitting in judgment on whatever I do."[6]

Interpreting his dream, Roth calls it a picture. There is a picture—a photograph—that Roth makes as central to *Patrimony* as the elegiac dream. The photograph is the one appearing on the cover of the book. Roth describes it in some detail in *Patrimony*'s last few pages.

> On the bureau across from the sofa was the enlargement of the fifty-two-year-old snapshot, taken with a box camera at the Jersey shore, that my brother and I also had framed and situated prominently in our houses. We are posing in our bathing suits, one Roth directly behind the other, in the yard outside the Bradley Beach rooming house where our family rented a bedroom and kitchen privileges for a month each sum-

mer. This is August of 1937. We are four, nine, and thirty-six. The three
of us rise upward to form a V, my two tiny sandals its pointed base, and
the width of my father's solid shoulders—between which Sandy's pixyish
bright face is exactly centered—the letter's two impressive serifs. Yes, V
for Victory is written all over that picture: for Victory, for Vacation, for
upright, unbent Verticality! There we are, the male line, unimpaired and
happy, ascending from nascency to maturity![7]

The picture on the book's cover bears out most of what Roth says of
it here. But two things are wrong with Roth's description. One is that
the year 1937 is a bit early for all the World War II trumpeting of
"Victory." The second is that in the description Roth effaces a figure
standing to our left, in the deep background, beyond a hedge and
next to a parked automobile. The figure is that of a woman. She
looks at the scene Roth describes, but from behind it and to the side.

In this woman's virtually absent-presence, as seen in her marginality vis-à-vis the center of the photograph, we may begin to find meanings that are, in both the literary and Lacanian senses, quite
symbolic. Although the woman is almost assuredly not Roth's
mother, who is most probably the one operating the box camera
that made the picture, the woman represents well enough the role
and figure of the mother in Roth's text. If, in Roth's words, his
mother is "subterraneanly" present in *The Facts*, she is similarly present in *Patrimony*. In the absent presence left by death, she is the focal
point in *Patrimony* of the first of two cognitive legacies Roth's father
conveys to him. In the first, Roth recounts his father's reaction to
Besse Roth's death. In his grief, the old man was almost manic in his
effort to get rid of his dead wife's belongings. At first Roth is puz-
zled. But he ultimately concludes that something primal was involved. "It was my father's primitivism that stunned me," says Roth.
That primitivism, Roth decides, goes beyond the palliative symbol-
ism of the sophisticated. There was, he says, "something almost admirable in this pitilessly realistic determination to acknowledge,
instantaneously, that he was now an old man living alone and that
symbolic relics were no substitute for the real companion of fifty-five
years. It seemed to me that it was not out of fear of her things and
their ghostlike power that he wanted to rid the apartment of them
without delay—to bury *them* now, too—but because he refused to
sidestep the most brutal of all facts."[8]

In the second cognitive legacy, it is the maternal, if not the
mother herself, that stands behind the gift to Roth. This legacy is

the one Roth explicitly calls the patrimony. It comes from the scene, perhaps destined to be the most famous in the book, in which Roth himself plays what can only be called a maternal role. Because of the infirmity resulting from the brain tumor, Roth's father had beshat himself in the bathroom and had made matters worse by trying to clean up the mess. Finding his father in the aftermath of a veritable Hurricane Andrew of a shitstorm that had left shit everywhere, on the floor, on the walls, on the shower curtains, all over the old man himself, Roth lovingly and patiently cleans him up first and then re-signedly addresses the bathroom. There, he finds the legacy of the realist or the ironist. It is more than the other paternal bequests mentioned earlier in the text—the old man's money, or his tefillin (the prayer boxes), or the shaving mug handed from father to son to son. Almost in astonishment, Roth exclaims, when he realizes the legacy, "So *that* was the patrimony. And not because cleaning it up was symbolic of something else but because it wasn't, because it was nothing less or more than the lived reality that it was. There was my patrimony: not the money, not the tefillin, not the shaving mug, but the shit."[9]

3

If, in *Patrimony*, Roth overtly focuses on the father's legacies and only subterraneanly includes the maternal ones, in *Sabbath's Theater*, he focuses directly on the legacy of the mother. In this novel, Roth suggests that a mother's legacy is a history of unresolved mourning that drives Mickey Sabbath away from the family and into a lifelong search for satisfaction of desire that suggests Mickey himself has not achieved the integration into the domain of the symbolic that comes with a successful resolution of the Oedipus complex. Roth makes the Oedipal element rather overt. Early in the first chapter, Roth tells us that, lately, when Sabbath, age sixty-four, suckles on the "ub-erous breasts" of his fifty-two-year-old lover Drenka Balich, "he was pierced by the sharpest of longings for his late little mother. Her primacy was nearly as absolute as it had been in their first incompa-rable decade together."[10] Roth makes of that "incomparable dec-ade" the paradise Freudians tell us it must have been. Of Mickey Sabbath at Drenka's breast, Roth says, "Emotions were stirred up in him that he had not felt since he was eight and nine years old and [Yetta Sabbath] had found the delight of delights in mothering her two boys. Yes, it had been the apex of her life, raising Morty and Mickey."[11] But Sabbath loses that paradise and falls into a troubled world of endless mourning when his brother, Morty, goes off to war as a pilot in the Pacific and is killed there. Not only does Sabbath lose the brother who has been his ego ideal, but he also loses his mother. She does not die from Morty's death in 1944, but she is never the same again. "For nearly a year," Roth tells us, "Sabbath's mother wouldn't get out of bed."[12] Having lost her elder son, in that year she simply forgets her younger. As soon as he gets out of high school, Sabbath leaves home, becomes a merchant seaman, and pursues his dream of sexual satisfaction in all the ports of the new world. But all his pursuit, Roth makes clear, devolves to the loss of the mother's love and attention that came with Mort's death, that very ironically tautological phrase—the death of death. Before, "They'd had endlessness. He'd grown up on endlessness and his mother—in the beginning they were the same thing. His mother, his mother, his mother, his mother, his mother."[13] After, they had betrayal. "Take your pick," Sabbath says, "Get betrayed by the fantasy of endlessness or by the fact of finitude."[14]

Sabbath feels his life has been marked by many such betrayals. His brother dies in the war. His mother effectively dies because his brother dies. His first wife, Nikki, a gifted actress and the star of his lower East Side theater troupe, simply disappears one day in 1964, never to return and never to be confirmed as dead. So Mickey Sabbath spends much of his waking life thereafter trying to find Nikki, spends it as much in mourning for her as his mother had spent hers mourning for Morty. Then dies Drenka, his lover of thirteen years, the one whose uberous breasts have returned him in memory to his mother. In a particularly emotional moment at the end of the first chapter, having just learned that Drenka is dying of cancer, Sabbath addresses his mother. "Mother, he thought, this can't be so. First Morty, then you, then Nikki, now Drenka." From these losses he concludes, "There's nothing on earth that keeps its promise."[15] But if Drenka in life had merely reminded him of his mother, Drenka in death actually returns Sabbath's mother to him—not as a person, but as a ghost. After Drenka dies, Sabbath feels his mother's presence and shares his thoughts with her. With a certain irony, Roth reports that Sabbath might have expected to talk to his dead father for, after all, his father had not "deserted [him] however much Morty's death had broken him too."[16] Instead, we are told, "now Sabbath talked to *her*. And this he had not expected."[17]

As in the observation Roth had made about his father's "primitive" response to Besse Roth's death in *Patrimony*, here he tells us that Sabbath is a "ferocious" realist who had never before seen evidence that "the dead were anything other than dead." Indeed, in *Patrimony* Roth offers a view that foreshadows events in *Sabbath's Theater*, but produces an entirely different theme about the dead. There, Roth writes, "If there's no one in the cemetery to observe you, you can do some pretty crazy things to make the dead seem something other than dead. But even if you succeed and get yourself worked up enough to *feel their presence*, you still walk away without them. What cemeteries prove, at least to people like me, is not that the dead are present but that they are gone. They are gone and, as yet, we aren't. This is fundamental and, however unacceptable, grasped easily enough."[18]

But, in *Sabbath's Theater*, after Drenka's death, Roth does indeed give us one who finds himself in the presence of the deceased. "His mother was there every day," Sabbath tells us, "and he was talking to her and she was communing with him."[19] Why? Why has she returned? Why now? His answer is that she has been "loosed" upon him by some force that wants him. "She had returned," he decides, "to take him to his death."[20] But, of course, Sabbath has it exactly wrong. As he eventually realizes, she returned to restore him to real, ordinary, meaningful life.

In this function, the mother's ghost serves a psychoanalytic purpose described by the Lacanian social critic Slavoj Žižek. "From within the symbolic order," says Žižek, "spectres, apparitions, the 'living dead,' and so on, signal . . . unsettled (symbolic) accounts; as such, they disappear the moment these accounts are settled by way of symbolization."[21] In Lacanian terms, the ghost of the mother is an irruption of the Real into the structure—itself, in the symbolic, essentially "fictional"—of ordinary existence. "This," says Žižek, "is what Lacan has in mind when he asserts that the truth has the structure of a fiction—one has to distinguish strictly between fiction and spectre: fiction is a symbolic formation that determines the structure of what we experience as reality, whereas spectres belong to the Real; their appearance is the price we pay for the gap that forever separates reality from the Real," the price we pay, that is, "for the fictional character of reality."[22] In terms of some simple emplotment, the ghost in *Sabbath's Theater*, like the ghost in Hamlet (bear in mind that Roth calls the second and final section of the book "To be or not to be"), must bring Sabbath to the symbolization of the grief that has driven his outrageously transgressive life. That symbolization appears in a carton containing his brother's things. These things—Mort's things, death's things, as it were—have been kept safe for almost fifty years, kept first by his mother and then by his father's century-old cousin "Fish," a man whom Sabbath visits in the old neighborhood on the last day the novel covers, the day that Sabbath had meant to be the day of his death as it was the day—April 13—of his brother's birth in 1924.

After finding Mort's things in a sideboard once belonging to his mother that somehow Fish had come to possess, Sabbath finally puts to rest his mother's ghost. Sabbath tells us that "inside that sideboard was everything [I] had come looking for. I knew this. Something is there that is not my mother's ghost: she's down in the grave with her ghost. Something is here as important and as palpable as the sun."[23] That something, perhaps, is grief itself: grief for his loss, grief for his loss of his brother, grief for his loss of himself because by such a close attachment he in effect was that brother. He was that brother because he too had died in his mother's eyes when Mort died in 1944. The "something" is a suffering brought on by the carton of Mort's things, a suffering such as he had never endured before. "The pure, monstrous purity of the suffering," Roth tells us, "was new to him." It "made any and all suffering he'd known previously seem like an imitation of suffering. This was the passionate, the violent stuff, the worst, invented to torment one species alone, the remembering animal, the animal with the long memory. And prompted merely by lifting out of the carton and holding in his hand what Yetta Sabbath had stored there of her older son's."[24]

While this moment in *Sabbath's Theater* feels like a conclusion, the novel's real conclusion occurs about fifty pages further on. The real one does, however, build on this moment. Sabbath makes of Mort's things, death's things, the mission that will keep him alive. "How could he kill himself," he asks, "now that he had Morty's things?" But Sabbath does not greet this mission with any particular gladness. He curses it for its contravening what he had taken as his other mission, to kill himself in some way. "Something," he rants, "always came along to make you keep living, goddammit."[25] With Mort's things in tow and looking for a home for them and himself, Sabbath returns to the town where his estranged, twelve-step devotee of a wife lives, at first expecting she will welcome him back. Instead, he finds her in their old house, there in bed with another—no, not another man, but another woman, one with whom Sabbath and

Drenka themselves had occasionally engaged in a ménage à trois. But though it throws him into a momentary funk, the spectacle of the others'—his wife's and the other woman's—enjoyment does not kill his spirit because he can relish the irony of his wife's defection and unintended revenge. Still, in a later moment, the climactic one in the novel, Sabbath thinks that although he cannot kill himself, he might allow himself to be murdered. What's more, the potential murderer, Drenka's son, a state patrolman who has read his mother's sex diary and knows Sabbath's role in her life, even appears with Sabbath at Drenka's grave, a site Sabbath has frequently consecrated with his urine and other precious penile fluids. But for his own reasons, Drenka's son releases Sabbath from arrest and, as representative of official public law, consigns him to life. As one might expect of Roth, he leaves Sabbath with "no one to kill him except himself." But, at last, Sabbath reaches his own strange, perverse, inverted truth: He "couldn't do it. He could not fucking die. How could he leave? How could he go? Everything he hated was here."[26] If love can't keep him alive, then perhaps the sheer animus of hatred can do the trick. In a novel by Roth, could it be otherwise? Did we really expect that Philip Roth would become a sentimentalist in his old age? All that we surely might expect is the Rothean irony that death's things, Mort's things, *les choses de Mort*, would also turn up as the things of life.

NOTES

Epigraph. Philip Roth, *The Facts: A Novelist's Autobiography* (New York: Farrar, Straus and Giroux, 1988), 8. Hereafter referred to as *Facts.*
  1. Ibid.
  2. Ibid., 8–9.
  3. Ibid., 9.
  4. Ibid.
  5. Philip Roth, *Patrimony: A True Story* (New York: Simon and Schuster, 1991), 235. Hereafter referred to as *Patrimony.*
  6. Ibid., 237–38.
  7. Ibid., 230.
  8. Ibid., 32.
  9. Ibid., 176.
  10. Philip Roth, *Sabbath's Theater* (Boston: Houghton Mifflin, 1995), 13. Hereafter referred to as *ST.*
  11. Ibid.
  12. Ibid., 15.
  13. Ibid., 31.

14. Ibid.

15. Ibid., 32.

16. Ibid., 16.

17. Ibid., 15.

18. *Patrimony*, 21.

19. *ST*, 16.

20. Ibid., 17.

21. Slavoj Žižek, *The Metastases of Enjoyment: Six Essays on Woman and Causality* (New York: Verso, 1994), 193.

22. Ibid., 194.

23. *ST*, 392.

24. Ibid., 403.

25. Ibid., 415.

26. Ibid., 451.

Philip Roth's American Tragedies

Bonnie Lyons

PHILIP ROTH IS STILL BEST KNOWN BY THE GENERAL READING PUBLIC AS A comic and satiric writer for his inventions of Portnoy and the sports-crazy Potamkins of *Goodbye, Columbus* (1959). He is hailed by postmodernists for his fictive propositions and counterlives. Yet three of Roth's most recent novels (*American Pastoral* [1997], *I Married a Communist* [1998], and *The Human Stain* [2000]) establish Roth as our most important author of significant American tragedies. Obviously I am not using the word "tragedy" to indicate a type of drama, but to assert that these are novels that share a deeply tragic vision or tragic version of reality. Like most dramatic tragedies, each novel focuses on a very different kind of tragic hero, but all three depict heroes whose fates are intricately enmeshed in their specifically American settings and times. Thus I argue that they are *American* tragedies.

The aptness of considering *The Human Stain* a tragedy is clear: its epigraph from Sophocles' *Oedipus the King,* the repeated references in the text to classical tragedy of the fifth century, and indeed the very profession of the protagonist, Coleman Silk, as a classics professor. But the earlier two novels also embody a tragic vision. In fact, in *American Pastoral,* the earliest of the three novels, Roth announces the theme of tragedy and the motif of the tragic fall. There, Nathan Zuckerman, the narrator, observes that "To embrace your hero in his destruction . . . to let your hero's life occur within you when everything is trying to diminish him, to imagine yourself into his bad luck, to implicate yourself not in his mindless ascendancy, when he is the fixed point of your adulation, but in the bewilderment of his tragic fall—well, that's worth thinking about."[1]

Each novel features a male protagonist of significant stature, and all three are men Zuckerman has admired or befriended. Unlike the earlier Zuckerman books (*The Ghost Writer* [1979], *Zuckerman Unbound* [1981], *The Anatomy Lesson* [1983], *The Prague Orgy* [1996], first published in *Zuckerman Bound* [1985], and *The Counterlife* [1986]), Zuckerman is not the fictional center: in these recent novels, Zuckerman plays the role of "a newer, novelistic version of the dramatic Chorus," as well as what Murray Krieger has called "a deconstructionist God, who saw chaos and said—not that it was good—but that it *was* and that he could *tell* it."[2] All three novels depict the hero in what Richard Sewall calls a boundary situation—man at the limits of his sovereignty, and all three also focus on the hero's will to "fight against his destiny, kick against the pricks, and state his case before God or his fellows"[3]—the crux of the tragic vision.

Although Zuckerman is ostensibly writing *American Pastoral* in 1995, the America he dramatizes is mostly the America from World War II through Vietnam and Watergate. The nation is then at the "greatest moment of collective inebriation in American history,"[4] America in "their exuberant heyday, at the peak of confidence, inflated with every illusion born of hope,"[5] but then descending into bleak disillusionment and self-disgust. We see the boundless hopes, optimism, and moral certainty of the World War II victory over the clear evil of fascism, coupled with the emergence of America as an overwhelming world power, followed less than thirty years later by a morally troubling and divisive war, political corruption, rage, and cynicism. The very title of the book, as opposed to titles with a protagonist's name like *Portnoy's Complaint* (1969), *Zuckerman Bound* (1985) and *Sabbath's Theater* (1995), underscores the centrality of America in the novel and suggests that a whole period of American history can be seen as a collective pastoral, a beautiful and fragile bubble bound to burst.

As the symbolic center of its America, *American Pastoral* focuses on the grotesque decline of Newark, New Jersey, from bustling center of industrial energy to a ravaged, crime-ridden city whose major industry is car theft. Newark's decline (complete with its disappearing industry, race riots, and uncontrolled crime) is the domestic parallel to the national and international decline of America epitomized by Watergate and Vietnam. The "well-meaning, well-behaved, well-ordered"[6] Seymour "Swede" Levov, living the American dream in Old Rimrock, is undone by his beloved daughter Merry, who throws a bomb into the local general store, killing an innocent bystander. But the story is told in such a way that the reader sees Swede not as the simple victim of his radicalized daughter, but more as the individual embodiment of a culture caught in a dream world; it is a shaken culture unable to provide adequate responses to the question Vietnam and Merry so insistently pose. Merry's bomb blows up Swede's pastoral dream—of Old Rimrock and a simple national American hero like Johnny Appleseed who is "just a happy American," along with the moral clarity of World War II.

In the penultimate scene of the novel, Seymour Levov discovers that his daughter had gone on to kill three other people, but that she is now so committed to nonviolence that she avoids killing even microorganisms. Later, in an almost apocalyptic dinner scene, he makes other awful discoveries: his beloved wife is having an affair with their architect friend, and another friend hid Merry after the first bombing and never told him. The architect's alcoholic wife, whom Swede's father is patiently trying to feed, responds by trying to poke out his eye with a fork. Meanwhile the female academic who witnesses this drunken apolitical violence laughs with delight at the "rampant disorder." American pastoral indeed.

Pastoral is, of course, also a theme in earlier Roth novels, especially *The Counterlife*. There Zuckerman defines the idea of pastoral as the *dream* of a unified, unconflicted world where each person is free to be himself. The repudiation of such a pastoral dream is based on the painful truth that it "cannot admit contradiction or conflict"[7] and is therefore no more than a dream of the return to the womb and a flight from history. In *American Pastoral,* however, Roth's tone is less intellectual and more emotional and more tragic. Roth prevents the reader from seeing Swede as a simpleminded, self-deluding escapist who needs and deserves to be awakened from a mindless dream. The sweetness and energy of the earlier America are also so densely evoked that it is impossible simply to dismiss and disdain that period. Thus the pastoral, which is wittily and ironically deflated in *The Counterlife*, is here, like Swede himself, mourned as tragic loss.

As is often his strategy, Roth in his next novel created a character precisely the opposite of the idealistic Swede. In Ira Ringold (a.k.a. "Iron Rinn"), Roth presents a protagonist most like the tragic hero ordinarily connected to Greek or Shakespearean tragedy—the strong individual with hamartia, a distinctive tragic flaw, such as Othello's jealousy. In *I Married a Communist* the flaw is the same as that of Achilles: Ira's violent anger—the "ire" suggested by his very name. Even his own brother, Murray, concludes that Ira's "whole life was an attempt to defuse the violent impulse."[8] As a seven-year-old, Ira "was too angry for tears"[9] at his mother's funeral and later broke his brother's nose when Murray laughed at a canary's funeral.

The defining act of Ira's life was when, as a young man, he deliberately killed an ugly, taunting anti-Semite in a brawl. Ira then spends years trying to channel his powerful impulses positively by supporting the Communist cause. But he is betrayed by his wife, who denounces him as a spy for the Soviet Union. Although an idealistic supporter of Communism, Ira is not involved in espionage; it is when his wife, Eve, discovers his sexual infidelity that she uses his Communist leanings to destroy him—thereby disguising her personal revenge as patriotism. Eve is like a 1950s politician "with a personal vendetta finding in the national obsession the means to settle a score."[10] Eve's revengeful slander enables Roth to expose the 1950s patriotism as a "pretext for self-seeking, for self-devotion, for self-adoration."[11] Murray tells Nathan Zuckerman that "Eve's behavior fell well within the routine informer practices of the era."[12]

Eve destroys Ira professionally with the help of politically ambitious friends, one of whom uses Eve's book about Ira "to ride his way into the House [of Representatives] on the issue of Communism in broadcasting."[13] One element, however, prevents the reader from interpreting Ira as a mere victim rather than as a tragic hero: Ira becomes once again violently angry after Eve's revenge. He plans to garrote Eve and her daughter. Luckily, he is prevented from enacting murderous violence again, but his response to Eve's natural death years later is the same "cackling crazy-kid laugh"[14] with which he responded to the murder he committed in his youth. Despite his idealism, genuine devotion to the common man, and his lifelong effort to change, he has succumbed to his "fate" and his hamartia.

Clearly, then, Roth used Swede Levov to explore the radical changes of the 1960s and Ira Ringold's unmaking to expose the betrayals and hypocrisies of the McCarthy era in America. His third American tragedy, *The Human Stain,* is a powerful denunciation of the hysterical Puritanism which resulted in President Clinton's impeachment in 1998. The very title of the book points in the direction of Monica Lewinsky's blue dress. But in Roth's novel the central issue is broader and more general than America's response to Clinton's sexual shenangians. *The Human Stain* is about the dangerous results of a national "purity binge" and the hypocrisies and sanctimoniousness of the politically righteous. These are people who refuse to acknowledge what the novel calls the "shameless impurity of life" and the "redeeming corruption that de-idealizes the species and keeps us everlastingly mindful of the matter we are."[15]

The tragic hero, Coleman Silk, is a man whose quest is for an individual or self-created life. A light-skinned black, he rejects the cozy, self-affirming solidarity of his family and all-black Howard University and insists instead on trying to determine his fate by his own resolve. He refuses to allow the ignorant, hate-filled intentions of a hostile society to define him. Sometimes he lets people's assumptions of his whiteness go uncorrected; sometimes he lies outright. Coleman is nonetheless presented by Nathan Zuckerman as a heroic individual attempting to create rather than passively accept his self-definition. What evolves into a lifelong lie is neither an act of racial shame nor of self-advancement; it is, according to Zuckerman's narrative, the *truth* of his psychological sense of himself as singular. Zuckerman presents Coleman's passing as white as his precious secret, a posture that ironically permits him to live an otherwise morally and socially compliant, even exemplary, life: dutiful husband, loving father, and committed academic. His one socially defiant act at once ensures his integrity and makes possible his acceptance of society's rules.

Referring to two students who never came to class as "spooks," however, brings Coleman vilification as a racist when it turns out that the absentees are black. Just as the word "communist" was a lethal weapon often used for concealed personal vendettas in the 1950s and in *I Married a Communist,* so is the word "racist" in the 1990s novel. Coleman Silk's peers knew from years of experience with him that he was not a racist, that he used the word "spooks" to mean "ghosts." A subsequent accusation that he is a misogynist, degrading and abusing his lover Faunia, who is a pathetic, illiterate young woman, is equally untrue; but it completes the destruction of what remains of his reputation. Coleman is subsequently killed by his lover's Vietnam war-crazed ex-husband, but he is first personally and professionally destroyed by a university colleague, Professor Delphine Roux. Delphine's lack of self-knowledge and political self-righteousness make her viciously misconstrue the nature of Coleman's relationship with Faunia. They also blind her to her own attraction to the man she is destroying. Yet, once again, however much Delphine Roux is depicted as a powerful negative antagonist or a kind of nemesis, Coleman—like Oedipus—is destroyed less by her than by the very force he aimed to escape. The man constructing a life of "I" meets the "we that is inescapable: the present moment, the common lot, the current mood, the mind of one's country, the stranglehold of history that is one's own time."[16]

In a sense that condition is true for all three tragic heroes; these

novels are about men whose selves and times are inextricably intertwined and together produce and nurture the tragic outcomes.

Philip Roth has published twenty-five books thus far. If only for
the sake of convenience, we need to group or discuss his works by
periods. My argument here has been that the three novels which appeared before the most recent work, *The Dying Animal* (2001), belong together. Other critics have called the three novels a trilogy
that depicts the ideological ethos of postwar America, and they have
praised Roth as a master chronicler of the American twentieth century. But my argument is that the novels are that and more—that
they are great American tragedies. Georg Lukács has stated that
"The deepest longing of human existence is the metaphysical root
of tragedy: the longing of man for selfhood, the longing to transform the narrow peak of his existence into a wide plain with the path
of his life winding across it, and his meaning into a daily reality."[17]
These three Roth novels embody that deepest longing and thus
their claim on our response is much deeper than that of mere
chronicles.

NOTES

1. Philip Roth, *American Pastoral* (Boston: Houghton Mifflin, 1997), 88. Hereafter cited as *AP*.

2. Murray Krieger, "The Tragic Vision Twenty Years After," in *Tragedy: Vision
and Form*, ed. Robert W. Corrigan (New York: Harper & Row, 1981), 44.

3. Richard B. Sewall, "The Vision of Tragedy," in Corrigan, *Tragedy: Vision and
Form*, 49.

4. *AP*, 40.

5. Ibid., 87.

6. Ibid., 93.

7. Philip Roth, *The Counterlife* (New York: Farrar, Straus & Giroux, 1986), 322.

8. Philip Roth, *I Married a Communist* (Boston: Houghton Mifflin, 1998), 292.

9. Ibid., 65.

10. Ibid., 9.

11. Ibid., 277.

12. Ibid., 264.

13. Ibid., 273.

14. Ibid., 313.

15. Philip Roth, *The Human Stain* (Boston: Houghton Mifflin, 2000), 37.

16. Ibid., 335–36.

17. Georg Lukács, "The Metaphysics of Tragedy," in Corrigan, *Tragedy: Vision
and Form*, 84.

The End of Identity: Philip Roth's Jewish
American Pastoral

Timothy L. Parrish

WHEN IRVING HOWE DISMISSED *PORTNOY'S COMPLAINT* (1969) BECAUSE IT betrayed "the thin personal culture" of its author, it seemed but another inevitable step in Philip Roth's quest to free himself from the aesthetic constraints of being perceived as a Jewish writer.[1] In the early 1960s Roth identified what would become his established position when he told an audience in Israel that "I am not a Jewish writer; I am a writer who is a Jew."[2] Against the perception—often abetted by Roth himself—that his fiction has compromised the integrity of Jewish-American cultural identity, Roth has consistently asserted his primacy as an artist by claiming and dramatizing what we might call the self's essential elusiveness. Near the conclusion of *The Counterlife* (1986) Roth's alter ego, Nathan Zuckerman, reflects that, should such an entity as "an irreducible self" exist, it "is rather small, I think, and may even be the root of all impersonation—the natural being may be the skill itself, the innate capacity to impersonate."[3] Roth's postmodern definition of self makes it difficult for his reader to assert with any confidence that his books endorse a particular point of view or cultural position, which is precisely why Roth disclaims the identity of "Jewish" writer. Nonetheless, with his work in the 1990s it has become obvious that Roth—in Cynthia Ozick's words—"is being catapulted along a fascinating trajectory" which is culminating in an expression of Jewish identity that no one—not Irving Howe or Philip Roth—could have imagined thirty years ago.[4] In his memoir *Patrimony* (1991), Roth stages his reconciliation with his father and his Jewish heritage by burying his father in the traditional burial shroud; in his magnum opus, *Operation Shylock* (1993), Roth stages the repossession of his identity as a Jewish writer by confronting his "other" in Israel.[5] *American Pastoral* (1997) completes Roth's trajectory in two remarkable ways. First, through Nathan

Zuckerman's identification with Swede Levov, "the blue-eyed blond born into our *tribe*," Roth explores the possibility of writing a kind of tribal narrative.[6] For the first time in his oeuvre Roth employs Zuckerman to imagine the type of story that might be told by a Jewish writer rather than by a writer who is a Jew. By framing the narrative through the perspective of Zuckerman, Roth also invokes the earlier Zuckerman canon to make sense of this story. Like his obvious model, Marcel Proust, who rewrites the life of "Marcel" until he has created *Remembrance of Things Past,* Roth rewrites Zuckerman's story as a way of rewriting all of his previous Zuckerman stories. In portraying Zuckerman's perspective on the meaning of the second half of the American twentieth century through his idolatry of Swede Levov, *American Pastoral* reframes Roth's entire oeuvre.

Zuckerman's reappearance in *American Pastoral* signals Roth's reevaluation of the fictional stance toward identity—whether understood as cultural identity or individual subjectivity—codified in *The Counterlife.* In *American Pastoral* it is as if Zuckerman is transformed into an earlier version of himself—the one that existed before he discovered the burden—and joy—of subjectivity. No longer his own subject, Zuckerman thus ostensibly removes himself from being the protagonist and displaces that role on to the character of Swede Levov. Where Zuckerman is the product of a culture "whose elders, largely undereducated and overburdened, venerated academic achievement above all else," Seymour "Swede" Levov is a stunning athlete, a master of "physical aggression," whose exploits on the field allow the community to indulge in "a fantasy about itself" that is "almost like Gentiles" in that they could make "athletic performance the repository of all their hopes."[7] Zuckerman's initial stance toward Levov is one of unadulterated hero worship. When he encounters Swede in 1985 at a Mets game, forty years since Swede was the Weequahic high school star, Zuckerman is as awestruck as he had been as a high school student. "You might as well have told us he was Zeus," a companion says to him.[8] Zuckerman reiterates, though, that the strength of Swede's appeal was not only his athletic greatness, but that he was a Jew who could compete with and defeat the Gentiles on their own field of dreams. Later, when Zuckerman is recreating Swede's life, he relates how Swede knocked the novel's arch-WASP, Joe Orcutt, and the history he represents "flat on its ass" for overstepping the established boundaries of the weekly touch football game.[9] Levov's nickname, Swede, like Zuckerman's description of his visage, "steep-jawed, insentient Viking mask of this blue-eyed blond born into our tribe," suggest that this character was born to make the transformation that Zuckerman has struggled so ardently for in his life and art: to become an American who happens to be a Jew.[10]

Zuckerman's awe for the athletic prowess of Swede masks his awe for the ease with which Swede appears to assimilate himself into mainstream American life. Where Zuckerman's fictional portrayal of Jews caused him to suffer the indignity of being called a traitor to the Jews, Swede's life affords Zuckerman the opportunity to dramatize how a Jew could receive as his due the promises of American success. Swede oversees a successful business, marries a Catholic former Miss New Jersey, fathers an attractive and gifted child, and owns a stunning country home built at the time of the American Revolution. If, in having all the accoutrements of a perfect American life, Swede is to Zuckerman emblematic of an "unconscious oneness with America," then the question that haunts Zuckerman and drives the narrative is a startling one, "where was the Jew in him?"[11] Before *American Pastoral,* Roth might have asked such a question in order to discover a role, a provisional identity. In this novel, however, Roth allows Zuckerman to raise this question precisely so he can explore the deleterious consequences of forsaking one's Jewish origins. Thus, when Zuckerman discovers in 1995 at his high school reunion that Swede Levov has just died having lived a life that did not fit the storybook plot Zuckerman had assumed, he finds himself inventing a narrative that locates Swede's fall in the loss of his Jewish identity. With *American Pastoral* Roth in a sense completes his assimilation story by rendering judgment upon its naïve hopefulness.

Of course Roth's judgment goes beyond saying that assimilation is bad or that Zuckerman and Swede were wrong to embrace the world outside of the one into which they were born. As Zuckerman notes, "the first postimmigrant generation of Newark's Jews had regrouped into a community that took its inspiration more from the mainstream of American life than the Polish shtetl their parents had re-created around Prince Street in the impoverished Third Ward." He adds that the "Keer Avenue Jews" such as the Levovs were "laying claim like audacious pioneers to the normalizing American amenities."[12] "At the vanguard of the vanguard," Swede was blazing a trail that was inevitable. Zuckerman writes this narrative as a way of looking back at what was to be. Appropriately, Zuckerman's mediation on Swede begins at their high school reunion. Most of the characters in the book are either dead or near death at the time of its writing. Zuckerman, like Swede, is a victim of prostate cancer that has rendered him impotent. In a very real sense, Zuckerman has been removed from the conflicts and desires that have enlivened his previous definitions of self and art. Given that Zuckerman's identity has been at times almost indistinguishable from the actions of his penis, it is almost as if Zuckerman's life has been completed.[13] He has no more stories to tell about himself except through others. Consequently, he can write about himself, not as an artist striving after the madness of art affronted by philistine Jews incapable of understanding his task, but as the almost anonymous member of a particular cultural enclave that acted out a particular cultural story. From this perspective, heretofore present but unemphasized in Roth's fiction, the protagonist's story matters to the extent that it reflects the transformation of the group of which he is a part.

Zuckerman's rapprochement with his past begins with his reinvention of the father. Zuckerman first begins to think about Swede as a subject for narrative at the suggestion of Swede himself. Swede writes Zuckerman to ask for his help in writing a tribute to his father, Lou Levov. Roth's assumed reader is of course well aware of Zuckerman's difficult relationship with his own father, whose trenchant analyses of how his son's fiction betrayed both their family life and American Jews generally became the primary subject of Zuckerman's work. Speaking of the ethos adopted by the generation of Jewish fathers that includes Swede's father and his own, Zuckerman observes that they were "men for whom the most serious thing in life is *to keep going despite everything.*"[14] Ironically, this motto describes Zuckerman's writing career as it does Swede's life. If in the end both Zuckerman and Swede betrayed their fathers' wisdom about maintaining the integrity of the clan, then their persistence in going on despite everything fulfills Zuckerman's assertion that "we were their sons. It was our job to love them."[15] Because Swede dies before Zuckerman can consider his collaboration seriously, the proposed story about Swede's father becomes Zuckerman's story of Swede. As a substitute father-story, Zuckerman's account of Swede's effortless immersion into America is concerned with the search for what might be called the father's wisdom. The story of Swede Levov also becomes the story of Lou Levov's judgment of Swede. Implicit within that story—indeed, motivating that story—is Zuckerman's desire to reach his own father as well.

As if uncomfortable with the prospect of writing a narrative that is not obviously about either himself or his father, Zuckerman begins by dramatizing how inappropriate Swede is as a subject for a Zuckerman narrative. If Zuckerman wants "to imbue Swede Levov with something like the tendentious meaning Tolstoy assigned to Ivan Ilych," then he is perhaps unaware of the extent to which Swede's story mirrors his own.[16] After asking himself "what did [the Swede] do for subjectivity?" Zuckerman decides to make Swede's seeming absence from identity conflict the point of the narrative.[17] To tell Swede's story, then, Zuckerman must transform himself into a character unafflicted by the call to transformation. Zuckerman says that he would "think about the Swede for six, eight, sometimes ten hours at a stretch, exchange my solitude for his, inhabit this person least like myself, disappear into him, day and night try to take the measure of a person of apparent blankness and innocence and simplicity, chart his collapse, make of him, as time wore on, the most important figure of my life."[18] In the guise of highlighting Swede's blankness, Zuckerman conceals from himself the nature of his identification with Swede. Both because Zuckerman idolized Swede as a child and because Zuckerman feels intellectually superior to him as an adult, he cannot quite admit to himself that he and Swede share the same story. As one whose interest in cultural identity has been refracted primarily through the question of what it means to be an artist, Zuckerman is unfamiliar with thinking about how identity choices might be made for reasons other than aesthetic experimentation. As Zuckerman writes, Swede does not become imbued with Zuckerman's sense of radical subjectivity; rather, Zuckerman's subjectivity is subsumed by Swede's narrative. Consequently, Zuckerman, almost despite himself, encases Swede's story within his own son-beset-by-father-and-Jews narrative.

Unlike Zuckerman, Swede is represented as one who is not obligated to choose either to be or not be a Jew. Zuckerman may ask where is the Jew in his protagonist, but the truth is that Swede's essential Jewishness is presumed. Presenting his narrative as if it were the music to Johnny Mercer's "Dream," Zuckerman orchestrates through Swede's destruction a reunion with the secure Jewish identity he and Swede and others like them forsook when they entered America:

I lifted onto my stage the boy we were all going to follow into America, our point man into the next immersion, at home here the way the Wasps were at home here, as American not by sheer striving, not by being a Jew who invents a famous vaccine or a Jew on the Supreme Court, not by

being the most brilliant or most eminent or the best. Instead—by virtue
of his isomorphism to the Wasp world—he does it the ordinary way, the
natural way, the regular American-guy way. To the honeysweet strains of
"Dream," I pulled away from myself, pulled away from the reunion, and
I dreamed . . . I dreamed a realistic chronicle."[19]

In the next sentence Zuckerman moves us from his reunion dance
to a seaside cottage in Deal, New Jersey where we encounter Swede
enjoying the fruits of his successful American life. Zuckerman provides no account of how Swede "made it" because his making it is
already assumed as his fate.

Zuckerman underscores how Swede thinks of himself as living "in
America the way he lived inside his own skin."[20] His choice of dwell-
ing, a glorious Revolutionary-era stone house set in the bucolic New
Jersey countryside, suggests how Swede feels himself to be inhabiting
his native land not so much as if he owned America but invented it.
This imaginary American Patriot tramps the Old Rimrock countryside as if he were Johnny Appleseed. The comparison is meant to
capitalize on the implication that Swede is as physically American as
he is psychologically American. Swede thinks how he "wasn't a Jew,
wasn't an Irish Catholic, wasn't a Protestant Christian—nope,
Johnny Appleseed was just a happy American. Big. Ruddy. Happy.
No brains probably, but didn't need 'em—a great walker was all
Johnny Appleseed needed to be. All physical joy. Had a big stride
and a bag of seeds and a huge, spontaneous affection for the land-
scape, and everywhere he went he scattered the seeds. What a story
that was. Going everywhere, walking everywhere. The Swede had
loved that story all his life."[21] As Johnny Appleseed, Swede can imagine himself the progenitor of the America he now inhabits: ancestor
and inheritor all at once.

Beneath Swede's idyllic vision, however, lies the reality of ethnic
strife and it is recognition of this conflict that eventually consumes
both Zuckerman's narrative and Swede's perfect life. Zuckerman introduces discord into this Garden of Eden through the presence of
Joe Orcutt, the image of WASP gentility and, as Swede painfully
learns, his wife's lover. Under Orcutt's supervision, Swede receives a
tour of Morris County—specifically the site that was George Washington's headquarters and a cemetery that dated back to the American Revolution. Orcutt of course is unaware of Swede's Johnny
Appleseed fantasy, but the effect of Orcutt's tour is to remind Swede
that his origins in the Revolution are pure fantasy. Put another way,

Orcutt takes Swede out to show him who really owns America and inhabits its mythology. Thus Swede reflects that "his family couldn't compete with Orcutt's when it came to ancestors. . . . Orcutt could spin out ancestors forever. Every rung into America for the Levovs there was another rung to attain; this guy was *there*."[22]

Swede's thwarted desire to possess America as his own is reinforced not only by Orcutt's possession of Swede's wife, but by Swede's own conception of his wife's meaning. To Swede, his wife is not a particular person, Dawn Levov (formerly Dwyer), but the means to and realization of a fantasy he first had as a young man. In this respect, Swede knows from the beginning the woman he would marry before he ever meets her, just as knows the house he would live in before he ever lives there. As an adolescent Swede envisions his life with the simplicity and the clarity of a character in a fairy tale: "At school he'd find himself thinking about which girl in each of his classes to marry and take to live with him in that house. After the ride with the team to Whippany, he had only to hear someone saying 'stone'—even saying 'west'—and he would imagine himself going home after work to that house back of the trees and see his daughter there, his little daughter high up in the air on the swing he'd built for her."[23] Swede's "ability to imagine himself completely" combined with his sense that he lives "in America the way that he lived inside his own skin" leads him to choose Miss New Jersey as his wife. More than comic extremism on the part of Roth, Swede's choice of a would-be Miss America for his wife raises a theme familiar to readers of Roth: the problem of the shiksa. In *Portnoy's Complaint* the protagonist subjects himself to the risks of indecent exposure on a city bus merely because he shares a seat with a shiksa. In *The Counterlife* a devout Israeli confronts Zuckerman about having had four wives, each a shiksa. When asked how he could do this as a Jew, Zuckerman responds "that's the sort of Jew I am, Mac."[24] In *American Pastoral*, however, Swede's desire to marry a shiksa becomes the engine of his dream's destruction. If marrying Miss Jersey seems to make Swede into Johnny Appleseed, then this marriage consummates every dire prophecy ever suffered by Zuckerman concerning the dangers of abandoning the tribe.

Through Swede, Roth both subjects Zuckerman to a systematic deconstruction of his assumptions about the making and unmaking of cultural identity and, at the same time, encourages the reader to confront the cultural consequences of Zuckerman's commitment to the infinite possibilities of self-transformation. Unlike Zuckerman,

though, Swede must confront more directly than Zuckerman the
cultural consequences of marrying outside the tribe since his union
with a shiksa actually produces a child.[25] Swede's brother, Jerry, is
quite succinct in helping Zuckerman to draw the conclusion that
Merry is the logical end to Swede's marriage: "[Swede] could have
married any beauty he wanted to. Instead he marries the bee-yoo-ti-
full Miss Dwyer. You should have seen them. Knockout couple. The
two of them all smiles on their outward trip into the USA. She's post-
Catholic, he's post-Jewish, together they're going to go out there to
Old Rimrock to raise little post-toasties."[26] Given Zuckerman's own
history, one might expect him to defend Swede's choice or at least
undermine the credibility of Jerry's position. Instead, Zuckerman
broadens Jerry's view in order to invest this union with its mythic
and tragic significance. For, as Jerry recognizes, Merry is the anar-
chic center of the novel. The daughter that Swede imagines tossing
in the air lands on his life with the literal force of a bomb. Merry
grows up to revile Swede's assimilated life and her place within it.
She equates her father's ideal of America with the imperial America
that wages war with a small distant country. Instead of being content
as Swede's precious daughter, she becomes the Rimrock bomber. Of
all the characters in the book, other than Jerry, Merry is most similar
to Zuckerman. They share as distinguishing character traits a relentless commitment to transformation and the desire to disrupt all pre-
tensions to complacency. Roth has said of his own protagonists that
"My hero has to be in a state of vivid transformation or radical displacement. 'I am not what I am—I am, if anything, what I am
not.'"[27] By that definition, Merry, and not Swede, should be the
hero of the novel. Her childhood is characterized by her desire to
make herself over into the image of some alternative self. In response to her mother's religious heritage, she goes through "a Catholic phase" during which she decorates her room with a picture of
the Sacred Heart of Jesus, a palm frond, and a plaster statue of the
Blessed Mother.[28]

This uneasy mixture of cultural identities paralyzes Swede even as
it echoes his own life. While her father wants to assure her that her
room is hers and "she had the right to hang anything there she
wanted," he also tells her that out of respect for her Jewish grandparents she should remove the Catholic icons before they visited.[29]
What her father might dismiss as adolescent role-playing is thus a
more extreme version of how he invents his life. Where Swede creates his self by imagining a single narrative future of Edenic bliss,

Merry extends and multiplies her father's logic of self-identification and fulfillment. Ultimately, Merry projects herself into the bombs she explodes as she explores the furthest boundaries of the self. Finally, passionately and cataclysmically, she identifies with those whom she perceives to be the victims of the American imperialist war with Vietnam. From being transfixed by the image of the Buddhist monk's self-immolation, she catapults herself along a journey during which she becomes first a revolutionary terrorist and then finally a Jain. An extreme version of her father's self-experimentation, Merry's innate curiosity to explore the outer limits of the self's possibilities aligns her with the novelistic sensibility of Zuckerman and Roth. As the daughter whose presence threatens to disrupt Zuckerman's familiar father-son narrative, Merry is perhaps the only character in Roth's fiction who succeeds in destroying the father.

Merry is *American Pastoral's* secret artist but she is given no acceptable form through which to create her self. Where Zuckerman writes stories, Merry throws bombs. Merry's inability to find an appropriate form for her rage is suggested by the fact that she stutters. When Swede encounters Merry for the first time after her Rimrock bombing, he is stunned to discover that her stuttering is gone, as if the act of detonating a bomb had cured her. To Swede and Dawn, Merry's stuttering had been like a potential bomb within the family threatening to blow apart its fragile unity. Countless efforts to solve Merry's problem are unsuccessful and her mother seems nearly unhinged by the entire phenomenon. Although Swede's patience with Merry is Job-like, he cannot comprehend the rage encapsulated in Merry's stutter and then later her bombs. If the bombs become a solution to Merry's stuttering, then that is only because they express the rage that the stutter concealed. As with Zuckerman's novels, Merry's chosen form of expression has the effect of destroying the family.

Why does Merry throw bombs? A plausible answer might be another question: Why does Zuckerman write? Although Roth often assigns possible motivations for the kinds of stories Zuckerman writes—psychological, sexual, cultural, etc.—the truth is that there is for Zuckerman no necessary justification other than the desire to create a persona and enact its possibilities. In the context of Roth's previous Zuckerman novels, Zuckerman and Merry are reverse images of one another: narrative doubles. In *American Pastoral*, however, Zuckerman presents Rita Cohen as Merry's double. That is, she is that part of Merry's self who speaks Merry's rage without stuttering. Acting as Merry's emissary while Merry is in hiding, Rita comes to Swede and makes a telling remark: "You have a shiksa wife, Swede, but you didn't get a shiksa daughter."[30] Rita's remark is made in the context of critiquing the emptiness—WASPish emptiness—of Merry's mother. According to Rita, "Lady Dawn of the Manor" is at the heart of Merry's identity crisis.[31] Cohen argues that this "is a mother who colonized her daughter's self-image" through her obsession for the blandishments of a conventionally idealized American womanhood.[32] To Rita, Dawn represents the empty promise to which Swede surrendered his life. This view is reinforced if one follows Rita's hint that Merry is no shiksa but a Jew conflicted by her inability to reconcile her Jewish identity with her Catholic heritage. "Don't you know what's made Merry Merry," she taunts Swede, "Sixteen years of living in a household where she was hated by that mother."[33] Or, more to the point, Merry has become Merry by virtue of Swede's indifference to the sort of cultural identity conflict his Johnny Appleseed vision has engendered.

At this point Merry's resemblance to Zuckerman becomes uncanny, even if the terms of their respective dramas of rebellion and identity have been transposed. Zuckerman shatters his family's self-image by seceding from their expectations about Jewish identity; Merry shatters her father's dream by calling him by the very name that he seemed fated to transcend: Jew. Because he has chosen to imagine—to place himself within—Swede's story, Zuckerman represses his identification with Merry. Indeed, being a Jew is what prevents Zuckerman from becoming the kind of postmodern horror Merry represents: someone who has ventured so far toward the outer edges of subjectivity that she finally chooses not to have a self at all. She becomes a Jain and renounces all acts that threaten the existence of any living creature. Of course this gesture could be interpreted as her way of atoning for her actions, but it also represents a degree of self-experimentation that even Zuckerman never approached. Declaring that she "is done with craving and selfhood," Merry enacts the reductio ad absurdum to Zuckerman's theory of the irreducible self as the impersonating self. Her ultimate act of impersonation and selfhood is to renounce identity altogether. This depiction of Merry as an extreme version of Zuckerman suggests that Roth in his late phase is distancing himself from the postmodern decentering of the self that has been one of the hallmarks of his fiction. Merry's critique of her father raises the possibility that a cultural identity, such as being Jewish, cannot be reduced to an arbitrary "subject position," but is the product of a history the claims of which cannot be written over with the adoption of a particular role.

In Roth's oeuvre, though, such a perspective is usually articulated by the father rather than the rebellious child. Invariably in Roth's fiction, the father's monomaniacal insistence on the claims of the clan is rendered by the son as well-meaning but myopic parochialism. In *The Ghost Writer*, Zuckerman's father challenges his son's representations of Jews by enlisting the aid of a Judge Wapter who asks Zuckerman questions such as "Do you practice Judaism? If so, how? If not, what credentials qualify you for writing about Jewish life for national magazines?"[34] As such the provincial literal-mindedness of the father is subjected to ridicule; the authority of the Jewish father is reconfigured and appropriated through the complexity of the son's art. In *Patrimony* Roth pursues this strategy by following his father's counsel that "You must not forget anything."[35] Roth's memoir of his father becomes the form in which the father's identity is entombed by the son. Against his father's wishes, Roth buries his father in a traditional shroud rather than a business suit in order to assert authorial control over his father's representation. While Herman Roth is not ridiculed as the fathers of Portnoy and Zuckerman often are, he is nonetheless subject to the son's unrelenting judgment of him.[36]

Rather than position Lou Levov as the lampooned father comically skewered by the traumatized son, Zuckerman gives Lou the final judgment, one that completes the critique of Swede's life that Merry initiates. The occasion for Lou's judgment is a 1973 dinner party hosted by Swede and Dawn. The centerpiece to the chapter is a discussion of the Watergate scandal and the cult porn movie, *Deep Throat*. To Lou Levov, a generation older than any of the other guests present, the lies and evasions of Richard Nixon are only a different version of the seductions performed for consumer pleasure in *Deep Throat* by Linda Lovelace.

To make his argument, Lou squares off with Marcia Umahoff, a professor of literature, an enlightened intellectual who, not unlike Zuckerman, has seen through the illusion of pretending to a stable moral order. Lou invidiously compares the stability that his life as a glove manufacturer gave to him and his family with the four divorces Swede's brother, Jerry, has inflicted on his multiple families. Similar to the speech Zuckerman writes in response to his high school reunion, Lou wonders if "more has changed since 1945 than in all the years of history there have ever been."[37] According to Swede's father, pornography, drugs, and violence have taken over American culture, and the popularity of *Deep Throat* is emblematic of that shift. When Lou confronts his audience as to why they permitted themselves to see *Deep Throat*, Marcia makes the case that *Deep Throat* reinforces a lesson as old as the Bible and the story of the Garden of Eden: "without transgression there isn't very much knowledge."[38] This familiar Rothian theme that has been the basis of all of the Zuckerman novels becomes the justification for the film and Lovelace's performance. If Lovelace's action is understood as a performance rather than something that is "really" happening on the screen, then she is merely enacting one of the self's many possibilities, a projection that obviously strikes a chord with a large audience. Where Lou says "she had made herself the scum of the earth," Marcia responds that "she has made herself into a superstar" and "is having the time of her life."[39]

Umahoff's defense of Lovelace is consistent with Zuckerman's critique of the irreducible self and is the sort of argument Zuckerman might have employed (particularly at the time of *Carnovsky*) to justify his star status as a notorious Jewish-American novelist. Lou cannot imagine that Lovelace might choose to adopt this persona except as a submission to a kind of personal degradation. Like Zuckerman's father, Lou is deaf to the call of art: the transformation of self into something other than its origins is always dangerous. Marcia Umahoff's command of wit and irony, not to mention her familiarity with postmodern ideas about the self, seems to give her the argument. At one point, after Lou's wife has prodded Lou to stop talking because he is "monopolizing the conversation," Marcia tells him to continue because "it's delightful to hear your delusions."[40] Lou professes not to know what that means but Marcia winningly answers, "It means social conditions may have altered in America since you were taking the kids to eat at the Chinks and Al Haberman was cutting gloves in a shirt and a tie."[41]

The final chapter, though, is framed so that Umahoff's superior intellect is inadequate to account for what happened to Merry Levov. At issue is how Umahoff's defense and Lou's attack on the ethic of performance relates to the absent Merry Levov. From Swede's afternoon encounter with his daughter, the reader knows where Merry's performance, her experiment in unfettered self-making, has taken her. She has killed four people, been raped twice, and now lives bereft of virtually all family connection. Perhaps, like Zuckerman, she would justify her actions as the only ones she could take and considers herself satisfied. However, because the narrative refuses to probe her motives except to the extent that they clarify the meaning of Swede's story, we cannot say for sure. In this respect, to the end, Merry stutters. While Marcia is undoubtedly right from the Swede-Zuckerman narrative perspective, only Lou's point of view can comprehend the tragedy that is Merry's life. Without a grounded sense of herself, rooted in a specific cultural identity, Merry is condemned to the performance of the self's loss, the self's absence.

Other than to defuse the tension the discussion creates, Swede is understandably removed from this conversation. With the day's many discoveries he has plenty to think about. Between seeing Merry and learning Sheila's true relation to his child, Swede tortures himself with how his story could have turned out differently. Convinced that had he known he could have at the very least saved Merry from the horrors she suffered (and continues to suffer) in exile, he lashes out at Sheila for not telling him she was keeping Merry in hiding. He calls Jerry to tell him he has found Merry and ask what he should do. Besides cursing Swede for his stupidity, his inability to break free from their father's assumptions, Jerry challenges Swede to go back to the wretched part of Newark where Merry has hidden herself and bring her back. Unaccountably, Swede refuses. Why? The answer may be that this is Zuckerman's "realistic chronicle," not Swede's. By refusing to interfere with his daughter's decision, Zuckerman imagines a father capable of accepting his child's every transformation—even its most extreme. Zuckerman would certainly agree with Jerry that Merry has made a mockery of Swede's cherished ideals. "All your fucking *norms*. Take a good look at what she did to your *norms*."[42] However, Swede's refusal to "rescue" Merry dramatizes the steadfast commitment from parent to child that Zuckerman never experienced from his father. "If you love me, Daddy, you'll let me be" are the last words that Zuckerman has Merry say to Swede.[43] Swede is one Jewish father who will never call his child "bastard" even though that may be the word that she has for all practical purposes already called herself. Through Swede, Zuckerman can raise for a moment the possibility of a parent coming to a child for forgiveness and acceptance. Although Merry is more successful than even Zuckerman was in confronting her Jewish father directly, Zuckerman ultimately chooses to identify with Merry to the extent that her critique of Swede joins Lou's. In the end, though, Zuckerman, who has always imagined himself the son who

has betrayed the father's best intentions, surrenders his story as
Swede does to the unrelenting father who alone can identify the
point at which the child strayed.

Thus, while Zuckerman in his past works portrayed his father's
forays into literary and cultural criticism as preposterous, he allows
Swede's father to deflate Umahoff's subtle arguments with blunt as-
sertions. Aesthetically speaking, Lou's logic bludgeons hers. When
she asks Lou to articulate his interpretation of the Garden of Eden,
Zuckerman allows him to assert the law of the father: "when God
above tells you not to do something, you damn well don't do it—
that's what. Do it and you pay the piper. Do it and you will suffer
from it for the rest of your days."[44] This not only describes Swede's
fate, but characterizes the poor choice he made as a father. Instead
of suffering Merry with an almost holy patience, Swede should have
laid down the law so that she would have had order and security in
her life. Married to Dawn Dwyer, the Catholic beauty queen, there
was no way for Swede to do this. Zuckerman reinforces this perspective by recalling the conference that Lou had with Dawn Dwyer years
earlier to set the ground rules for their "mixed" marriage at this
crucial juncture. Placed at the end of the novel and on this most
fateful day in Swede's life, the recollected scene hovers over Swede's
story as if it took place before the Oracle at Delphi. It underscores
the doomed nature of his union with the ironically-named Dawn.
Swede remembers how his father addressed his fiancée: "LET'S GET
DOWN TO BRASS TACKS, MARY DAWN. WHAT DO YOUR PARENTS SAY
ABOUT JEWS?"[45] Lou's assumption that Dawn's parents must make
anti-Semitic comments is rivaled only by Dawn's comic admission
that they do.

The comedy here hinges in part on Lou's feigned surprise that
anti-Semitism exists and that it is a part of Dawn's world. While the
comedy builds in the scene it also becomes clear that the point of
the narrative we have just read is that the conflict that creates the
comedy will also overwhelm it. The cultural difference between
Dawn and Swede is, finally, no laughing matter. After an extended
discussion that includes how and if Christmas and Easter will or will
not be celebrated, the issue turns on whether the child, should it be
a boy, will be baptized or bar mitzvahed. Dawn argues that the child
can choose; Lou says that the child must choose what the parents
have decided. Where Roth's previous work has been tilted toward
the child's right to make his life as he pleases, this time the father's
say is given more weight. The tragedy of the Levovs is not only that

they did not decide this question, but that they thought it was irrelevant. Trusting in the child's ability to choose denies history and culture. Zuckerman, who bears the responsibility for the curse his father heaped upon him, imagines that Swede relents to this logic: he admits that "he should have listened to his father and never married her. He had defied him, just that one time, but that was all it had taken—that did it."[46]

Swede here renders judgment on his life according to the logic of his father; moreover, he implicitly accedes to Merry's critique of him as well. Zuckerman constructs Swede's recognition in this way: "And the instrument of this unblinding is Merry." The scourge of Swede's misbegotten marriage, Merry is the fruit of his cultural transgression. "The daughter has made her father see. And perhaps this was all she ever wanted to do. She had given him sight, the sight to see clear through to that which will never be regularized."[47] While Swede does eventually remarry and has another child, a son this time, we do not learn if his wife is Jewish, or his son bar mitzvahed. Zuckerman does not allow us to see in what the second marriage reconciles the conflict of the first. However, by depicting Swede's acceptance of his father's critique of him, Zuckerman allows us to imagine Swede in a sense recuperating his relationship with Merry. Swede's Jewish family, torn asunder, is reconstituted through his acknowledgement of his error. In this way Swede, the one who "got caught in a war he didn't start," dies as a kind of war hero, a Jewish martyr to the American dream of assimilation.[48]

If *American Pastoral* continues Roth's interest in the transformation of Jewish identity in America, then it raises this subject to critique the American ideal of cultural transformation. Instead of subordinating claims to an authentic Jewish identity within the larger American identity, Roth evokes in *America Pastoral* the turbulent late sixties and early seventies to suggest how doomed the ideal of assimilation actually is. According to Zuckerman, Swede Levov is to experience the "American Pastoral" by being an American rather than a Jew who lives in America. Instead of the American Pastoral, Swede experiences "the counterpastoral," what Zuckerman calls the "American berserk" and which he personifies as the unrest of the sixties.[49] Thus, what seems to be a family narrative—the story of how descendants of immigrant Jews achieve the American dream—is also a national one. For instance, when Swede's daughter, Merry, watches in horror the now famous image of the Buddhist monk immolating himself to protest the Vietnam War, her rage is directed simultaneously at her father and her country. To Merry, her father embodies that mixture of American exceptionalism and cultural imperialism that made the war in Vietnam possible. Not only is Swede an example of the American dream that this generation will be better off than the previous one, but as the owner of glove factories in Newark and Puerto Rico his success story is the result of exploiting—specifically African Americans and Puerto Ricans. When Merry becomes a revolutionary and detonates a bomb in the local post office that kills an "innocent" bystander, she also explodes her father's happy success story into the American berserk. In this moment, national history becomes family narrative to the extent that the Vietnam War and the American unrest of the sixties is caused not by American foreign policy or Communist revolutionaries but by our American belief in cultural transformation as an inherent social good. In depicting how the American pastoral inevitably gives way to the American berserk, the novel ultimately mourns the inevitable disappearance of the Jewish identity experienced by Swede and Zuckerman and Philip Roth as boys when they were simply Jews among other Jews.

Significantly, Roth does not allow Zuckerman to imagine a scene in which Swede admits his error to his father or to Merry. Roth therefore intimates that Zuckerman and Swede are doppelgängers— Jewish sons who have violated their fathers' law without the opportunity to make amends. Second, by having Swede accede to Lou, he recuperates Merry's critique of her father and the America his dream of himself represents. Merry and Lou join voices in their condemnation of American life. Just as Merry rails against the war crimes of Lyndon Johnson, so does Lou damn the perfidy of Richard Nixon. "Nixon liberates him to say anything—as Johnson liberated Merry. It is as though in his uncensored hatred of Nixon, Lou Levov is merely mimicking his granddaughter's vituperous loathing of LBJ."[50] Merry and Lou blaspheme the President in order to deface the genteel/gentile image of American innocence that Swede has wished to uphold. The rage against authority that Merry and Lou enact is also a surrender to the American berserk, which engulfs these characters and obliterates the kind of secure cultural perspective that loyalty to a specific ethnic group can provide. Their descent into the American berserk carries with it the recognition that the transformation of identity promised by the American dream is finally a curse rather than a blessing. Thinking of Merry's rebellion in the context of other sixties' rebellions, Swede at one point wonders

"What happened to our smart Jewish kids? They *are* crazy. Something is driving them crazy. Something has set them against everything. Something is leading them into disaster."[51] Zuckerman's Swede sees Merry as the victim of the sixties. Had there not been a bomb to throw symbolically at her family, then she never would have gotten in so much trouble. Roth, by contrast, portrays the sixties as a bomb set not by so much by American imperialism as by the kinds of cross-ethnic identity conflicts experienced by the Levovs. Merry's critique of her father's unwitting complicity with imperialist and postcolonial American practices is a critique offered from within the family about the (American) family. Just as Swede's concession to his father derives from his recognition that he should have raised his daughter a Jew, so is Merry's disappearance "into the American berserk" the inevitable consequence of Swede Levov's dream of being Johnny Appleseed.

Roth ends the narrative with the 1974 dinner party rather than returning to the frame of Zuckerman's 1990s high school reunion as if to insulate Zuckerman from an irony almost too delicious to be swallowed by readers of Roth: Zuckerman surrenders to the Jewish father. Thus, Zuckerman is able to return Swede to his fallen family without having to confront how his version of Swede's story transforms his own oeuvre into the kind of story he has always avoided writing. I do not think the same critique can be made of Roth, since to his longtime readers the story Zuckerman fashions to tell the fall of Swede Levov must be seen as gesture of reconciliation as well. Whether it belongs to Roth or Zuckerman depends on the reader. It seems to me that *American Pastoral* portrays the cultural wisdom of the American Jewish fathers prior to Roth and as such is Roth's truer, more appropriate filial tribute than even *Patrimony* was. At one point Swede reflects that "what was astonishing to him was how people seemed to run out of their own being, run out of whatever the stuff was that made them who they were."[52] By the end of the narrative this seems to be Swede's fate, as if he has used up his identity, run out of self. Swede's meditation upon the end of self takes Zuckerman full circle from his previous position that the self resides solely in its various performances. After years of writing art that rebels against the father and the version of Jewish identity he represents, Zuckerman's narrative performances give way here to Swede's exhaustion of identity. While Swede remarries, Zuckerman's narrative is left stranded in 1974 at the moment his protagonist succumbs to the forces that Zuckerman once presumed to transcend. Possibly,

Roth invokes the end of identity as a way of summoning death and acknowledging that, despite endless resurrections, his Zuckerman must eventually disappear into silence. When Swede dies we understand that Zuckerman in a way has died too—yet only to symbolically raise the specter of Zuckerman's most surprising transformation of all. Zuckerman's performing American self inhabits Swede's corpse to identify the Jew who remains.

NOTES

1. Irving Howe, "Philip Roth Reconsidered," in *Philip Roth*, ed. Harold Bloom (New York: Chelsea House Publishers, 1986), 79. Reading the initial reactions to Roth thirty years later, one is struck by the enormous critical importance placed on Roth's subject matter, that is, the fact that he was writing about Jews. In response to *Goodbye, Columbus*, many prominent Jewish intellectuals helped to establish Roth's reputation as a serious writer (Philip Roth, *Goodbye, Columbus and Five Stories* [Boston: Houghton Mifflin, 1959]). In part, they meant to defend Roth from the accusations of readers whose sense of literature had not been refined by a healthy dose of modernism. Leslie Fiedler, Alfred Kazin, Irving Howe, and Saul Bellow each weighed in on Roth and in the process gave to Roth's work an early stamp of seriousness that it likely would not have received if he were not writing about Jews (Leslie Fiedler, "The Image of Newark and the Indignities of Love: Notes on Philip Roth," review of *Goodbye, Columbus*, by Philip Roth, *Midstream* 5 [Summer 1959]: 96–99, Alfred Kazin, "The Vanity of Human Wishes," *Reporter*, August 16, 1962, 54; Irving Howe, "The Suburbs of Babylon," *New Republic*, June 15, 1959, 17; Saul Bellow, "The Swamp of Prosperity," review of *Goodbye, Columbus*, by Philip Roth, *Commentary* 28 [July 1959]: 77). By contrast, Jeremy Larner, writing in the *Partisan Review*, took issue with the assessments of Bellow, Howe, and Kazin on the grounds that Roth's account of suburban Jewishness was "incorrect" ("The Conversion of the Jews," in *Critical Essays on Philip Roth*, ed. Sanford Pinsker [Boston: G.K. Hall, 1982], 27–32). Roth himself seemed uncomfortable that he could excite so much critical attention from this fact and his next two works, *Letting Go* (New York: Random House, 1962) and *When She Was Good* (New York: Random House, 1967), in different ways veered considerably from the cultural milieu of *Goodbye, Columbus* and the early stories. Roth's return to an aggressively "Jewish" subject matter with *Portnoy's Complaint* (New York: Random House, 1969) reignited a critical firestorm among his Jewish audience. Yet, after this reaction, which included Howe's famous critique, it was Roth, not his critics, who continued to make an issue of how American Jews read his work. In addition to the essays by Fiedler, Kazin, Howe, and Bellow, see Allen Guttmann, "Philip Roth and the Rabbis," in Bloom, *Philip Roth*, 53–62 and Theodore Soloratoff, "Philip Roth: A Personal View," in Bloom, *Philip Roth*, 35–51.

2. Quoted in Cynthia Ozick, *Art and Ardor* (New York: Knopf, 1983), 158.

3. Philip Roth, *The Counterlife* (New York: Farrar Giroux Straus, 1986), 320. Hereafter referred to as *Counterlife*.

4. Quoted in Elaine M. Kauvar, "An Interview with Cynthia Ozick," *Contemporary Literature* 34, no. 3 (1993): 373.

5. Philip Roth, *Operation Shylock: A Confession* (New York: Simon & Schuster, 1993); *Patrimony: A True Story* (New York: Simon & Schuster, 1991). For a discussion of how *Operation Shylock* re-enacts Roth's entire career, see Timothy L. Parrish, "Imagining Jews in Philip Roth's *Operation Shylock*," *Contemporary Literature* 40, no. 4 (Winter 1999): 577–604.

6. Philip Roth, *American Pastoral* (Boston: Houghton Mifflin, 1997), 3, emphasis mine. Hereafter referred to as *AP*. Roth's use of the word "tribe" to describe Zuckerman's Newark cultural milieu recalls Mark Shechner's remark twenty-five years ago that "Roth's Jews are not a *people*, a *culture, nation, tradition,* or any other noun of rabbinical piety. They are a *tribe*, which, after its own primitive fashion, observes arbitrary taboos and performs strange sundown rituals that look like obsessional symptoms" ("Philip Roth," in Pinsker, *Critical Essays*, 122–23).

7. *AP*, 3–4.

8. Ibid., 17.

9. Ibid., 381.

10. Ibid., 3.

11. Ibid., 20.

12. Ibid., 10.

13. Zuckerman for instance reflects in *The Ghost Writer* that "when I came upon Babel's description of the Jewish writer as man with autumn in his heart and spectacles on his nose, I had been inspired to add, 'and blood in his penis,' and then had recorded the words like a challenge—a flaming Dedalian formula to ignite *my* soul's smithy" (*The Ghost Writer* [New York: Farrar, 1979], reprinted in Roth, *Zuckerman Bound*, 49).

14. *AP*, 11.

15. Ibid.

16. Ibid., 30.

17. Ibid., 20.

18. Ibid., 74.

19. Ibid., 89.

20. Ibid., 213.

21. Ibid., 316.

22. Ibid., 306.

23. Ibid., 190.

24. *Counterlife*, 90.

25. In *The Counterlife*, Zuckerman argues with Maria on this point, admitting that he would want to have any son of his circumcised. *American Pastoral* draws out the implications of that imagined conversation.

26. *AP*, 73.

27. Philip Roth, *Reading Myself and Others: A New Expanded Edition* (New York: Penguin, 1985), 164.

28. *AP*, 93–94.

29. Ibid., 94.

30. Ibid., 138.

31. Ibid., 135.

32. Ibid., 136.

33. Ibid., 137.

34. Roth, *Ghost Writer,* 102–3.

35. Roth, *Patrimony,* 238.

36. For an excellent consideration of Roth's complicated burial of his father, see Jeffrey Rubin-Dorsky, "Honor Thy Father," review of *Patrimony,* by Philip Roth, *Raritan* 11, no. 2 (Spring 1992): 137–45.

37. *AP,* 365.

38. Ibid., 360.

39. Ibid., 361.

40. Ibid., 354.

41. Ibid.

42. Ibid., 275.

43. Ibid., 266.

44. Ibid., 360.

45. Ibid., 393.

46. Ibid., 385.

47. Ibid., 418.

48. Ibid., 65.

49. Ibid., 86.

50. Ibid., 299.

51. Ibid., 255.

52. Ibid., 329.

The Critique of Utopia in Philip Roth's *The Counterlife* and *American Pastoral*

Andrew Gordon

SOME *VERSIONS OF PASTORAL* IS THE TITLE OF A CRITICAL WORK BY WILLIAM Empson, and Philip Roth, in at least two novels, *The Counterlife* (1986) and *American Pastoral* (1997), has been concerned with deconstructing some contemporary versions of this pastoral. Roth's satiric, subversive bent makes him an anti-utopian and anti-pastoralist who questions utopian longings and validates perpetual struggle, complexity, and uncertainty in both life and art. Nevertheless, *The Counterlife* is the more consistent critique of various pastoral myths. In *American Pastoral*, despite his demolition of the American dream, Roth paradoxically ends up clinging to certain pastoral ideals, contrasting the wonderful lost America of his Newark childhood in the 1940s to the fallen America of the 1960s and 1970s.

The pastoral was originated by the Greek poet Theocritus and the Latin poet Virgil, who wrote poems about the lives of shepherds ("pastor" is Latin for "shepherd"). The traditional pastoral is "a elaborately conventional poem expressing an urban poet's nostalgic image of the peace and simplicity of the life of shepherds and other rural folk in an idealized natural settings."[1] Empson expands the definition of pastoral to include "any work which opposes simple and complicated life, to the advantage of the former."[2] In other words, any pastoral contains an element of utopian longing.

In *The Counterlife*, Nathan Zuckerman's lover Maria tells him: "The pastoral is not your genre. . . . Your chosen fate, as you see it, is to be innocent of innocence at all costs."[3] What she says of Zuckerman is equally true of Roth. Like Zuckerman, Roth constantly fights his own tendency to be attracted by pastoral illusions. As the repetitive structure of *The Counterlife* indicates, part of Roth's struggle is against the persistent appeal of pastoral fantasies of innocence: defeat one and another emerges in its place. As Maria tells Nathan, "I

151

think that you are embarrassed to find that even you were tempted
to have a dream of simplicity as foolish and naïve as anyone's."[4]

In *The Counterlife*, Roth sees us all as fiction makers and forces us
to reconsider the nature of the utopias we all script, the counterlives
we would prefer to live. Each section of the novel constitutes a critique of a utopia which is constructed only to be deconstructed.
Among the utopian concepts Roth critiques in the novel are the
myths of romantic love, of Zionism, and of "Christendom." He rejects all these as fantasies of innocence, retreats to the womb. In the
end of the novel, the only utopia Roth will allow is that of fiction
making itself: the power of the human mind endlessly to imagine
and to reimagine our lives.

The Counterlife constructs and then deconstructs a series of "pastoral myth,"[5] each represented by a place: Basel, Judea, Aloft, Gloucestershire, and Christendom. Each myth is a counterlife which
constitutes a utopian dream of innocence:

> what Judea means to . . . that belligerent . . . band of Jews . . . also what
> Basel meant to claustrophobic Henry lustlessly boxed-in back in Jersey
> . . . also . . . what you [Maria] and Gloucestershire once meant to me.
> . . . [A]t the core is the idyllic scenario of redemption through the recov-
> ery of a sanitized, confusionless life. In dead seriousness, we all create
> imagined worlds, often green and breastlike, where we may finally be
> "ourselves." Yet another of our mythological pursuits.[6]

The "green and breastlike" world alludes to "the fresh green
breast of a new world" evoked at the end of *The Great Gatsby*. Fitzgerald's hero too foundered on his utopian dream, his American pastoral. Gatsby was a perpetual adolescent, "borne back ceaselessly into
the past." "*Bring it all back,*" Nathan imagines Henry thinking, "*the
sixties, the fifties, the forties.*"[7] And Nathan also imagines Henry yearning for life as a prepubescent boy. The utopian dream is of a life
without confusion, a life of blissful innocence which can only be
found in the past, not in the present or future.

Even more, Roth's novel suggests that these "pastoral myths" represent a retreat not simply back to childhood but all the way back to
the womb: "the womb-dream of life in the beautiful state of innocent prehistory."[8] Only in the womb can we find a "sanitized, confu-
sionless life." The various fantasized locations of the novel—Basel,
Judea, Aloft, Gloucestershire, and Christendom—are all versions of
the yearning "to be taken off to the perfectly safe, charmingly sim-

ple and satisfying environment that is desire's homeland,"[9] the original utopia of the womb. Ironically, if the entire novel is Nathan's attempt to write his way out of his dilemma, to recover his potency, then he will not find it in the pastoral genre or in the utopian mode, for he perceives both to be puerile, infantile, and unmanly.

Nathan is Roth's fictional alter ego (Roth has called himself the ventriloquist and Nathan "my Charlie McCarthy . . . my dummy")[10] and Nathan's brother, Henry, and Nathan's lover, Maria, can be thought of as fictional subcreations of Nathan's stories within the story. Therefore, the dilemma is really Roth's as Jewish-American novelist as he searches for his masculine identity as Jew and as writer. That is why the novel opens with Henry confronting his impotence and ends with Nathan asserting to Maria the symbolic importance of the erect, circumcised Jewish penis.

Finally, the only utopia that the novel validates is the utopia of fiction making. If our identities are fictitious and we all live through fiction, then our goal should be to reject inferior fantasies and to imagine better fictions. For Roth, whose temperament is fundamentally oppositional, such fictions will be tense, unresolved, and even mutually contradictory, like those of *The Counterlife*.

In *American Pastoral,* Roth tackles the American dream as the ultimate American utopian fantasy. The critic Carol Iannone notes, in a review of *American Pastoral,* "To many a literary imagination, America represented from its inception a New World Eden where the American Adam faced boundless possibility and infinite, open-ended opportunity."[11] But against this Emersonian optimism, there has always been a tragic counterstrain in American literature, one represented by such authors as Melville, Hawthorne, Dreiser, or Mailer. "Now, in Roth's *American Pastoral,* the grain has darkened still further: the fruits of murder involve no less than the end of the American dream itself, destroyed, even as it comes most fully to fruition, by its own offspring."[12] Seymour Levov, the Swede, loses his innocence in the 1960s through the actions of his daughter, Merry. She sets off a bomb in their hometown post office to protest the Vietnam War, thereby killing a beloved local physician: "the daughter and the decade blasting to smithereens his particular form of utopian thinking, the plague America infiltrating the Swede's castle and there infecting everyone. The daughter who transports him out of the longed-for American pastoral and into everything that is its antithesis and its enemy, into the fury, the violence, and the desperation of the counterpastoral—into the indigenous American berserk."[13]

Michiko Kakutani observes that, in *American Pastoral*, Roth has split two sides of himself, "the optimistic strain of Emersonian self-reliance" versus "the darker side of American individualism . . . the American berserk" into Swede and his daughter.[14] Also, in *American Pastoral*, Roth once again critiques several versions of pastoral. The critic Elizabeth Powers cites two examples: "Dawn's cattle farm, re-calling the occupations of traditional literary herdsmen, but also the Newark Maid Glove Factory over which Seymour presides, which stands in for the pastoral economy, one based on transmission of generational skills."[15]

Another pastoral dream Swede Levov attempts to live out is the immigrant dream of becoming a totally assimilated American by moving to the small town. Swede, born Seymour Levov, a son of the Newark Jewish ghetto, moves in the 1950s into rural New Jersey. "What was Mars to his father was *America* to him—he was settling Revolutionary New Jersey as if for the first time. Out in Old Rimrock, all of America lay at their door. That was an idea he loved. Jewish resentment, Irish resentment—the hell with it."[16] He imagines that in post–WW II America, the younger generation has moved beyond all the old prejudices and resentments, so that now "people can live in harmony, all sorts of people side by side no matter what their origins."[17]

Zuckerman later explains that this American pastoral of peaceful coexistence can be sustained only momentarily, in brief rituals such as the all-American holiday of Thanksgiving. "A moratorium on all the grievances and resentments, and not only for the Dwyers and the Levovs but for everyone in America who is suspicious of everyone else. It is the American pastoral par excellence and it lasts twenty-four hours."[18] But the Swede glories in such ordinary, small-town American pastimes as being able to walk from his home into the small town to pick up the paper at "Hamlin's general store, with the post office inside, and outside the bulletin board and the flag-pole and the gas pump—that's what had served the old farming community as its meeting place since the days of Warren Gamaliel Harding."[19] Entering this Norman Rockwell scene gives the Swede the illusion of being all-American, of belonging in Old Rimrock. In fact, the Swede never truly belongs in "rock-ribbed Republican New Jersey." In the 1920s, in the Harding era, the Klan burned their crosses in Old Rimrock.[20]

In exploding the Jewish dream of assimilation to small-town America, Roth is in the tradition of Nathanael West. In *Miss Lonelyhearts*, the urban hero goes for a pastoral retreat, a weekend in the country. He "drove into Monkstown for some fresh fruit and the newspapers. He stopped for gas at the Aw-Kum-On Garage and told the attendant about the deer. The man said there was still plenty of deer at the pond because no yids ever went there. He said it wasn't the hunters who drove out the deer, but the yids."[21] It is not far from the rural Americana of "the Aw-Kum-On Garage" in Monkstown to Hamlin's general store in Old Rimrock. Ironically, it is this same general store that Swede's daughter Merry later blows up. In his assimilationist delusions, the Swede even imagines himself as Johnny Appleseed: "Johnny Appleseed, that's the man for me. Wasn't a Jew, wasn't an Irish Catholic, wasn't a Protestant American—nope, Johnny was just a happy American."[22]

Aside from the glove factory, the cattle farm, the small town, and Johnny Appleseed, the nexus of the pastoral dream, for Zuckerman if not for the Swede, lies in the Newark ghetto of his childhood in the late 1940s. Sylvia Fishman Barack writes, "the truly elegized and unsullied 'Paradise Lost' of the story turns out to be the earlier existence that Levov shared with Zuckerman and the other Jewish progeny of Weequahic, in their baseball-besotted youth."[23] According to the critic Erik Lundegaard, "The constricting social mores that have been used to such comic effect in previous Roth novels are seen here through the soft focus of nostalgia—whether Roth's or narrator Zuckerman's, we don't know."[24] If the 1960s and 1970s are hell in *American Pastoral*, then the 1940s are heaven. Just as in *The Counterlife*, childhood represents paradise for Zuckerman. In both novels, Roth mines a rich vein of nostalgia. In *The Counterlife*, Zuckerman imagines his brother Henry yearning to recover lost childhood innocence: "*He stood in that tunnel behind the museum bringing back all by himself the most innocent memories out of the most innocent months of his most innocent years, memories of no real consequence rapturously recalled— and bonded to him like the organic silt stopping up the arteries of his heart.*"[25] Even amid the pleasure of his reverie, that final image expresses the potential dangers of such an immersion in nostalgia. In the first book of *American Pastoral*, "Paradise Remembered," Zuckerman, now sixty-two, attends his forty-fifth high school reunion and becomes overwhelmed with nostalgia. The souvenir *rugelach* offered at the reunion remind him of the *rugelach* his mother used to bake: "By rapidly devouring mouthful after mouthful of these crumbs whose floury richness—blended of butter and sour cream and vanilla and cream cheese and egg yolk and sugar—I'd loved since childhood, perhaps I'd find vanishing from Nathan what, according to Proust, vanished from Marcel the instant he recognized 'the savour of the little *madeleine*': the apprehensiveness of death." In the end, though, Zuckerman cannot escape his aged self, "having nothing like Marcel's luck."[26]

American Pastoral is a death-haunted novel. As in *The Counterlife*, Zuckerman faces impotence and his own mortality. "Let's speak further of death and of the desire—understandably in the aging a desperate desire—to forestall death, to resist it, to resort to whatever means are necessary to see death with anything, anything, *anything* but clarity."[27] In both novels, there is a recognition that the nostalgic desire to return to the past is a way to avoid thinking about death. Childhood becomes the ultimate pastoral dream. In both novels, Zuckerman also narrates the story of a counterhero, his double who can suffer the fate he fears. This becomes another way to displace the fear of decline and fall, of aging and death. In *The Counterlife*, Zuckerman's double is his brother Henry, who, in one version of Zuckerman's shifting stories, becomes impotent and dies from the same heart disease which afflicts Zuckerman. And in *American Pastoral*, Zuckerman discovers in the Swede a double who will die from the same prostate cancer which has rendered Zuckerman incontinent and impotent.

The final utopia which *American Pastoral* deconstructs is "the utopia of a rational existence."[28] The Swede, who lived devoted to order and reason, "learned the worst lesson that life can teach—that it makes no sense."[29] "Yes, at the age of forty-six, in 1973, almost three-quarters of the way through the century that with no regard for the niceties of burial had strewn the corpses of mutilated children and their mutilated parents everywhere, the Swede found out that we are all in the power of something demented."[30] "It is not rational. It is chaos. It is chaos from start to finish."[31] "The old system that made order doesn't work anymore."[32]

From such a bleak novel, it is surprising that one critic decided that Roth "loves the right things. His parents, his relatives, his hometown. His baseball and his country."[33] And this is true. It is the decline and fall of all the things he holds dear that infuriates him. "Roth isn't merely saddened but maddened by what he sees happening to his country."[34]

In deconstructing various pastoral myths, however, *The Counterlife* offers us no retreat into a better past. In the conclusion, Zuckerman writes to Maria, "The pastoral stops here and it stops with circumcision. . . . Circumcision is everything that the pastoral is not and, to my mind, reinforces what the world is about, which isn't strifeless unity. Quite convincingly, circumcision gives the lie to the womb-dream of life in the beautiful state of innocent prehistory, the appealing idyll of living 'naturally,' unencumbered by man-made ritual. To be born is to lose all that. The heavy hand of human values falls upon you right at the start, marking your genitals as its own."[35]

Unlike *The Counterlife*, however, *American Pastoral* is structured as a tragedy, a story of decline and fall. Such a narrative trajectory implies that things were once better. According to Roth in *American Pastoral*, America has declined from the relative order, reason, and progress of the 1940s and 1950s, into the anarchy, irrationality, and lust for destruction of the 1960s and 1970s. In *The Counterlife*, there is no such decline and fall because there is no baseline reality. Writes Robert Boyers of *American Pastoral*, "The nostalgia for the 'country that used to be' is so palpable in this novel that it virtually immobilizes the imagination of reality. . . . Once, not long ago, according to this narrative, everybody had it good, or good enough. But many Americans suddenly went unaccountably crazy" and wrecked it all for no reason.[36] It is as if Roth has taken his own self-division—between the "paleface" and the "redskin," between the side that craves order and reason and the side that desires only to shock and outrage—and projected it onto America, playing it out in the division between the Swede and Merry, between parent and child, and between the past and the present.

If nostalgia in *The Counterlife* is viewed as dangerous, "like the organic silt stopping up the arteries of his heart," then nostalgia in *American Pastoral* is viewed relatively unironically. Starting in the 1960s, a disorder spread like a plague throughout the country, ruining the cities, decaying morality, and finally destroying the American family. If this is true, then it is not true, as the novel seems to imply, that life makes no sense and never did. Once upon a time, in America and in Weequahic in the 1940s, things were better and life made sense. But "the old system that made order doesn't work anymore."[37] Despite his apparently thorough and unrelenting critique of pastoral myths and utopian illusions, in *American Pastoral* Roth suffers from a blind spot. Like so many conservative social critics in America today, he wants to blame it on the sixties. Through his nostalgia for a vanished America, for the supposedly good old days of his youth, he ends up reinforcing yet another pastoral myth. Again, Roth, like Zuckerman, was "tempted to have a dream of simplicity as foolish and naïve as anyone's."[38]

NOTES

1. M. H. Abrams, *A Glossary of Literary Terms*, 5th ed. (New York : Holt, Rinehart and Winston, 1988), 127.

2. Ibid., 128.

3. Philip Roth, *The Counterlife* (New York: Farrar Straus Giroux, 1986), 317, 318. Hereafter referred to as *Counterlife*.

4. Ibid., 318.

5. Ibid., 322.

6. Ibid.

7. Ibid., 9.

8. Ibid., 323.

9. Ibid., 322.

10. Linda Matchan, "Philip Roth Faces 'The Facts,'" in *Conversations with Philip Roth*, ed. George J. Searles (Jackson: University Press of Mississippi, 1992), 240.

11. Carol Iannone, review of *American Pastoral*, by Philip Roth, *Commentary* (August 1997): 55.

12. Ibid.

13. Philip Roth, *American Pastoral* (Boston: Houghton Mifflin, 1997), 86. Hereafter referred to as *AP*.

14. Michiko Kakutani, "A Postwar Paradise Shattered From Within," *New York Times*, April 15, 1997, C11.

15. Elizabeth Powers, review of *American Pastoral*, by Philip Roth, *World Literature Today* 72, no. 1 (Winter 1998): 136.

16. *AP*, 310.

17. Ibid., 310–11.

18. Ibid., 402.

19. Ibid., 317.

20. Ibid., 309.

21. Nathanael West, *Miss Lonelyhearts* (1933; repr. New York: New Directions, 1969), 37–38.

22. *AP*, 316.

23. Sylvia Fishman Barack, review of *American Pastoral*, by Philip Roth, *America*, August 30, 1997, 25.

24. Erik Lundegaard, "Roth's Back, With More Complaints," *Seattle Times Book Section*, May 11, 1997, M3.

25. *Counterlife*, 9.

26. *AP*, 47.

27. Ibid.

28. Ibid., 123.

29. Ibid., 81.

30. Ibid., 256.

31. Ibid., 281.

32. Ibid., 422.

33. Mayer Schiller, review of *American Pastoral,* by Philip Roth, *National Review* (June 16, 1997): 54.

34. Peter Kemp, "Once Upon a Time in America," *Sunday Times,* June 1, 1997, n.p.

35. *Counterlife,* 323.

36. Robert Boyers, review of *American Pastoral,* by Philip Roth, *The New Republic* (July 7, 1977): 41.

37. *AP,* 422.

38. *Counterlife,* 318.

Newark Maid Feminism in Philip Roth's *American Pastoral*

Marshall Bruce Gentry

I HAVE BEEN INTERESTED FOR SOME TIME IN GENDER DIALOGUE IN twentieth-century fiction—in other words, the ways in which novels dramatize the differences of opinion among authors, narrators, and characters that result from gender differences. Especially interesting is the work of Philip Roth, often accused of misogyny, as he tries to figure out a way to be fair to his female characters and even learn from them. M. M. Bakhtin theorizes interestingly about the possibility of characters' winning battles with their own authors,[1] and Roth sometimes experiments with ways to leave women room to show him up. Roth occasionally tries too hard, playing metafictional games that presume to subvert the author while they actually overwhelm the reader with the author's cleverness.

For some examples of experiments in gender dialogue, consider the 1990 novel *Deception*, where Roth writes long sections in the form of dialogue between a man and woman without making it obvious which speaker is male and which female, presumably to insure a level playing field. There is also a passage in which a female character directly attacks Philip the novelist for his early female characters: "Why did you portray Mrs. Portnoy [of *Portnoy's Complaint*] as a hysteric? Why did you portray Lucy Nelson [of *When She Was Good*] as a psychopath? Why did you portray Maureen Tarnopol [of *My Life as a Man*] as a liar and a cheat?"[2] In addition, toward the end of *Deception*, a woman threatens to tell the truth about Philip by writing her own book, called *Kiss and Tell*.[3] These devices in *Deception* are mildly successful; however, one other device Roth tested for it inadvertently had a spectacular effect. In one nearly final draft of the novel, the character Philip says that he has been concealing all sorts of sexual affairs from his wife, who suspects not a thing, and that her name is Claire. Roth's novel clearly refers to Claire Bloom, the famous Jewish actress to whom Roth was married from 1990 to 1995. Mixing art and life this way is presumably a sort of admirable risk taking for a male novelist—a good gender dialogue—because the power of women in real life might overwhelm the male's control over his art. In real life, Claire Bloom reports in her tell-all autobiography *Leaving a Doll's House* (1996), when Roth showed her the draft of *Deception* in which she is the deceived lover, she threatened to sue him, and he removed her name from the character.[4] That *Deception* may have contributed in some way to Bloom's decision to write *Leaving a Doll's House*, that Roth may have caused Bloom to write the sort of *Kiss and Tell* book that *Deception* imagines, does not persuade me that Roth has succeeded in creating genuine dialogue.

Sabbath's Theater, Roth's 1995 novel composed while his marriage with Bloom was breaking up,[5] features Mickey Sabbath, a protagonist who, for all his rule breaking, appears determined to prove that he does not consider women his puppets. Alan Cooper is correct in writing, "This is a love story. Sabbath has known, outside marriage, a love whose depth, devotion, and selflessness the reader may well envy."[6] Sabbath and his ideal lover, the immigrant Drenka Balich, are such an equal match that, just as he helps her with her English, she can eventually put words into his mouth, causing him to "speak translated Croatian."[7] The equality of Sabbath and Drenka is also suggested by lovemaking so intensely satisfying that they seem to exchange genders.[8] Sabbath has so thoroughly learned the lesson of not treating women as puppets that he lectures his first wife, Nikki, when she refuses to give up her mother's dead body. Sabbath says, "Your mother is not a doll to play with."[9] In the novel's final pages, Sabbath learns that Drenka kept a secret diary about their relationship,[10] as if the reader needed a final reminder that Philip Roth is empowering his female characters.

Roth's women in *Sabbath's Theater* sometimes manage to seem as powerful as the male protagonist, certainly, but they seem to achieve this status primarily through Sabbath's and Roth's powers of imagination and idealization. All three of the most powerful women in this novel—Drenka, Nikki, and Sabbath's mother, who haunts him—are dead and/or gone. For all the joys to be found in this novel, it can also be read as part of Roth's battle with Bloom. Sabbath composes an obituary for himself in which the Countess du Plissitas is interviewed about her book in which she attacks Sabbath and defends Nikki, called *Nikki: The Destruction of an Actress by a Pig*.[11] If Nikki, the wife and actress who left, is to some extent Claire

Bloom, then the Sabbath-Drenka relationship can be read as Roth's proof that he can imagine an ideal love and be the ideal lover, even with a woman modeled "in stature and build" after Roth's infamous first wife, Maggie.[12]

Roth's novel *American Pastoral*, awarded the 1998 Pulitzer Prize for fiction, avoids literary experimentalism for what looks like good old-fashioned realism, and it is in my opinion a beautiful novel, in part because of its feminist subversion of male authority. That *American Pastoral* follows the publication of Bloom's *Leaving a Doll's House* makes Roth's accomplishment even more remarkable; Bloom describes Roth as at best temporarily insane during their marriage, at worst as horrible a misogynist as anyone suspected. *American Pastoral* is in part a response to Bloom's book, but it is also to some extent a confession, and it revises the gender politics in previous works by Roth. The women in this book seem to win a battle over the dominant male voices of its main character Swede Levov, the narrator Nathan Zuckerman, and even, to some extent, Philip Roth himself.

Of course there is reason to doubt such claims about *American Pastoral*. One problem is that no single female character can outtalk the novel's dominant males alone; Swede Levov is put in his place by his brother's attacks more than by the women's words. A more significant problem has to do with the prediction by Malcolm Jones, Jr., that Roth would get back at Bloom through his fiction.[13] If one wanted to, one could read *American Pastoral* as a spirited attack on the sort of passivity that Claire Bloom repeatedly admits to in the course of her marriage to Roth.

Another problem is that the reviewers of *American Pastoral* regard it as a novel about a good man punished for his virtues. Seymour ("Swede") Levov, a Jew for whom athletics was the pathway toward totally successful assimilation into American culture, marries his fantasy of a Catholic beauty queen who was once a Miss New Jersey, makes a great success with his father's business of manufacturing ladies' gloves, and buys a beautiful house out in the country—only to have all his hard-earned treasures spoiled by a terrorist daughter who, caught up in 1960s revolutionary non-thought, kills a man when she bombs the local post office. R. Z. Sheppard, at a loss to explain the disaster, suggests that the Levovs may be guilty of a *kina-hora*, but he seems more persuaded that the book simply says that "irrationality rules."[14] Steve Brzezinski concludes confidently that "Roth's message is clear: no one, even those seemingly graced with good looks, plenty of money, and exceptional talents, is immune from the pain, suffering, and sheer randomness of human events and human nature."[15] Michael Wood seems inclined to blame Swede's misfortunes on his "inexplicable" daughter, who is ironically nicknamed Merry.[16] Todd Gitlin assumes that if Swede is not done in by his daughter, he is a victim of 1960s revolution.[17] Louis Menand, writing for *The New Yorker* the most sensitive review of all, nevertheless reaches conclusions I consider mistaken. Menand emphasizes that Swede may be considered a Job figure and that the novel ends with a question mark, as if Swede's fall is totally mysterious; Menand also wonders—bizarrely, I think—whether the novel is "about the corruption of American life by the culture of liberal permissiveness," as if Roth were taking back *Portnoy's Complaint* and perhaps even turning toward "the cultural right."[18] Edward Alexander concludes, somewhat similarly, that Roth in *American Pastoral* has come finally to agree with Irving Howe, at least when it comes to the flaws of 1960s leftist politics.[19] Another *New Yorker* article about Seymour Masin, the real man who became the basis for Swede Levov—without giving permission, by the way—treats Roth's character as thoroughly sympathetic, and Masin sees himself being portrayed positively too.[20] Elizabeth Hardwick ends her review of *American Pastoral* by suggesting that Levov's tragedy may simply be caused by the obsolescence of ladies' gloves, the product that built the family's wealth.[21] Similarly, *The New York Times Magazine* ran an article about ladies' gloves in which the assumption is made that Roth wrote the novel to mourn the passing of this particular item of apparel.[22]

These conclusions are understandable but wrong-headed. They are understandable because the book speaks beautifully when it pretends to be a eulogy for the culture of assimilated American Jews before the 1960s. Nathan Zuckerman as narrator loves Swede Levov as the novel begins, and Nathan is consistently reluctant to notice Swede's faults. Roth allows us to assume that he agrees with Zuckerman and Swede but, as the female characters respond to Swede, we may also find room to see Roth as more aware than Zuckerman is of the limits of Swede's world. Roth has written a feminist novel about how Swede and the culture, the politics, and the economic system he represents, have at least indirectly produced the nightmares they suffer. The novel blames the tumult of the 1960s on the culture of twentieth-century America as the male protagonist embodies them, and the various female reactions to Swede, taken as a whole, refute his reputation as the world's nicest guy.

The simplest of the major charges against Swede is that he accepts the injustices of capitalism. This charge is complicated by the fact that capitalism helped Jews in America assimilate, as the book demonstrates thoroughly in its early pages, and to some people, assimilation is a very good thing. While many of the attacks on capitalism expressed by daughter Merry can be dismissed as superficial—even if we agree with them—Roth includes a layer of more serious critique. The 1967 riots in Newark, which nearly destroy the Levov glove factory, bring out the deeper issues. When Swede remembers trying to save the factory from rioters, he momentarily reveals to the reader that he has not sufficiently appreciated his workers—here in the person of a black worker named Vicky—and that Merry was correct in saying that, when her father exploited black workers all he could, he would move the factory out of Newark to increase profits:

> Vicky would not desert him. She told him, "This is mine too. You just own it." He . . . knew the way things worked between Vicky and his family, knew it was an old and lasting relationship, knew how close they all were, but he had never properly understood that her devotion to Newark Maid was no less than his. . . . [A]fter the riots, after living under siege with Vicky at his side, he was determined to stand alone and not leave Newark and abandon his black employees. . . . [However,] [h]e wouldn't have hesitated—and wouldn't still—to pick up and move were it not for his fear that, if he should join the exodus of businesses not yet burned down, Merry would at last have her airtight case against him.[23]

A bit later, Swede's father, Lou Levov, unthinkingly considers the question of his own ethics. Lou complains generally about his black workers. He seems to think that they produced good gloves for years only because he "kissed Vicky's ass for twenty-five years, bought all the girls a Thanksgiving turkey every goddamn Thanksgiving, came in every morning with [his] tongue hanging out of [his] mouth so [he] could lick their asses with it."[24] He concludes by asking, "Where is *their* conscience after working for me for twenty-five years?"[25] The irony increases when one returns to the beginning of the book to recall the supposed glory days of leather making in Newark. It seems a vision of hell:

> The tannery that stank of both the slaughterhouse and the chemical plant from the soaking of flesh and the cooking of flesh and the dehairing and pickling and degreasing of hides, where round the clock in the summertime the blowers drying the thousands and thousands of hang-

ing skins raised the temperature in the low-ceilinged dry room to a hundred and twenty degrees, where the vast vat rooms were dark as caves and flooded with swill, where brutish workingmen, heavily aproned, armed with hooks and staves, dragging and pushing overloaded wagons, wringing and hanging waterlogged skins, were driven like animals through the laborious storm that was a twelve-hour shift—a filthy, stinking place awash with water dyed red and black and blue and green, with hunks of skin all over the floor, everywhere pits of grease, hills of salt, barrels of solvent. . . .[26]

Swede of course tells himself that he disagrees with his father about how to run the business, but he has thoroughly learned and still practices the false show of niceness his father has later in life simply abandoned.

The next charge against Swede Levov is that, although he is famous with cheerleaders for a last name that "rhymes with . . . 'The Love'!"[27] he never genuinely loves women. While some female characters may appear to be products of Rothian misogyny (and while Roth has certainly earned readers' suspicion), I believe Roth's females here are products of a deeply American misogyny that they are desperate to battle, and from which Roth is distancing himself (even as he sometimes lures the reader toward sympathy with it). The name of the glove company is symbolic: Newark *Maid*. The glove is a girl, a maid to be molded by the glovemaker into the lady he wants her to be. Swede expects his wife, Dawn, as well as his daughter and probably all women, like his gloves, to be the perfect products of his own manufacturing process. Note the contrasting manner in which gloves are treated in *Sabbath's Theater*, so that they are more simply erotic: Sabbath can take off a glove very seductively during a puppet show,[28] and Drenka asks to be turned "inside out" during sex the way "somebody peels off a glove."[29]

I agree with Swede's brother, Jerry, who asserts that Swede does not truly love women, that he loved Merry "as a thing. The way [he] love[s] [his] wife."[30] While Swede considers marrying Catholic Dawn Dwyer to be an act of rebellion against his father for the sake of love, Swede subjects her to nine pages[31] of his father's obnoxious grilling, prior to their marriage, on the subject of the religious upbringing of children; Swede consistently expects the woman he supposedly loves to placate his father. Also, Swede never takes seriously his wife's complaints that she disliked being a beauty queen. Even when Dawn is hospitalized for depression and starts to express her complaints in "a tirade aimed at him" over beauty pageants, Swede dismisses what she says and simply tells her to breathe slowly.[32] If *American Pastoral* contains a character who voices Philip Roth's opinions about the Miss America Pageant, I believe that character is a female, the literature professor Marcia Umanoff. Roth's 1957 essay on the pageant, "Coronation on Channel Two,"[33] suggests that he shares Umanoff's view that the pageant borders on prostitution.[34]

Swede seems to have a more active fantasy life about the house he wants to put her in than he has about Dawn herself. He loves the house for its "irregularity regularized"[35] and wants the women in it to be similarly regularized. Swede's exclamation about the joys of living in their house—"Dawnie, we're free!"[36]—drips with irony unintended by Swede. It is also worth noting that the hobby Dawn picks up—raising and breeding cattle—fits into a pattern of requiring women to tame the animalistic, beastly side of life to fit Swede's requirements. Swede's dream house is so constricting that even he rejects it temporarily, fantasizing about a new house in Puerto Rico.[37]

When Dawn finally decides to have a facelift, Swede claims to be humoring her in letting her go through with it, but the stretching and molding of her facial skin is at least potentially a metaphor for his allowing her to make herself one of his gloves. His repeatedly referring to her as "Dawnie" and his desire to see her in her beauty crown[38] remind us of the confined space in which he wants to keep her. Of course, Dawn sees the facelift as an attractive feature to the architect she has hired to construct a new house, Bill Orcutt, with whom she has an affair. When Dawn blows up Swede's life by having her affair, we can hardly blame her for using the tricks Swede has taught her. It may not be a wise choice to have an affair, but the affair is one of the few ways in which she can free herself of Swede's control and make her own choices. Bill Orcutt is no great prize as a new partner, but he will at least let her negotiate the looks of her new house. Despite the glowing descriptions of lovemaking between Swede and Dawn, her statement about good sex, "it's strange not being alone,"[39] suggests how alone she usually feels with Swede. After we learn of Dawn's affair, we can more easily believe Dawn's claim that "she first went into cattle . . . to get out of that terrible house" of Swede's.[40] Swede saves a newspaper article that reports on Dawn's supposed love for "the house, as well as everything else about their lives," and he tells himself that the only reason she did not like the article was that the photo caption mentioned she was Miss New Jersey.[41]

While Swede regularly tells himself that he is overly loving toward his daughter, several revealing moments confirm his brother Jerry's suspicion that Swede's love for Merry is hollow. When she was young, Swede pulled away from a moment of sexual attraction for his daughter by making fun of her severe stuttering. "Daddy, kiss me the way you k-k-kiss umumumother"[42] is answered with "N-n-no."[43] The kiss that Swede then plants on Merry—a kiss he thinks carries taboo passion—could just as easily teach Merry that her father expresses love only to cover up the distaste for her that her father thinks he must not allow to show. While Swede claims to believe in his daughter's innocence when she disappears after the bombing, Roth creates for Swede a possibly fantastic character named Rita Cohen, onto whom Swede can project all of his worst thoughts about Merry. When Swede finally rediscovers Merry, back in Newark after she's been raped while traveling around the country as a revolutionary, he vomits on her and flees, then imagines himself as one of her rapists, rather than getting her out of the filthy pit where she lives. It finally occurs to Swede that he betrayed his daughter, on two occasions, by telling others her whereabouts and revealing the full extent of her crimes to them so that these others could turn her in to the police;[44] Swede manages to let others act out his aggression while he remains the apparently noble one. The most telling line in the description of Swede's relationship with Merry is his wishful thought, "if only she had become an animal,"[45] for then he would be sure how to tame and mold her.

Merry's political actions are not important in terms of politics so much as they are desperate attempts to create her own life outside the role her father creates for her. She is the first in the family to realize that Swede's dream house is to be escaped. In spite of her crimes, we can understand her complaint that Swede never acknowledges her as a person outside his dream of her. The teenager who says "I don't want to be understood—I want to be f-f-f-free!"[46] becomes the adult who resorts to preferring her father's hatred to his love if the hatred is a feeling for her real self rather than for his fantasy of her: she says to Swede, "I am the abomination. Abhor *me.*"[47] Swede's foolish response to such statements is to conclude that Merry knows "nothing" about her family or even "about the person you pretend to be."[48] When Merry becomes a Jain and tor-

ments her father from a passive position of moral rectitude, she is
giving her father his own medicine.

Another charge against Swede is that he does not think for himself. Again, I agree with Jerry (although Jerry is generally hateful
toward the novel's women), when he says to Swede, "What you are
is you're always trying to smooth everything over. What you are is
always trying to be moderate. What you are is never telling the truth
if you think it's going to hurt somebody's feelings. What you are is
you're always compromising. What you are is always complacent."[49]
Much of this behavior Swede learned from Lou, who leads the way
in pretending to agree with Merry about politics purely in order to
control her voicing of her opinions.[50] Swede's methods may not resemble his father's, but his motives do. Nathan Zuckerman as narrator generally avoids direct comment on the action he has imagined;
but after reporting Swede's belief early on that his daughter is simply going through "a bad-tempered phase she would outgrow,"[51]
Zuckerman responds by writing, "A phase, [Swede] thought, and
felt comforted, and never once considered that thinking 'a phase'
might not be a bad example of not thinking for yourself."[52]

One of the novel's epigraphs is from "Dream," Johnny Mercer's
song popular in the 1940s, and the epigraph spreads around, to
some extent, the responsibility I am inclined to attribute to Swede.

> Dream when the day is through,
> Dream and they might come true,
> Things never are as bad as they seem,
> So dream, dream, dream.

Dreaming is dangerous for all Americans, not just Swede, and Nathan Zuckerman admits to letting Johnny Mercer inspire the dream
that created this novel.[53] But Zuckerman's dream is never as superficial as Swede's. The ultimate, most-difficult-to-forgive dream is the
one that connects the beginning of the novel to its ending. The
novel ends with Swede's father being stabbed in the face with a fork
by Jessie Orcutt, another desperate woman who can no longer toler-
ate his condescending, controlling attempts to understand and
"help" her;[54] though it was horses rather than cattle that Jessie has
spent years managing, she stands in at the climax for Lou's granddaughter and daughter-in-law. When we first meet Swede in this
novel, he has lived through all of the novel's climactic events, and
his response has been to repress the past once again into a desire to

write a "tribute" to his father.[55] Roth may oppose thoughtless rebellion in this novel, but thoughtful rebellion is much better than the unthinking acceptance that is the essence of Swede Levov. Jerry Levov, for all his mean-spiritedness, is a good guide to Swede's limitations, and Nathan Zuckerman's early, confused speculation that Jerry is gay[56] may ultimately act as a critique of Zuckerman's (and even Roth's) ideas about manhood.

In creating ambiguity about where he stands in relation to Swede, Philip Roth may be admitting that he has built a house of fiction that causes women to become bombmakers. Roth knows he should pay for any excessive admiration he feels for Swede Levov, and there is space in the novel for the reader to laugh along with Marcia Umanoff over the attack on Lou Levov at the novel's end.[57] When *Time* magazine compares Roth to a "master leather cutter" and says the novel "fits like a glove,"[58] I hope Roth sees the unintended irony; Roth's women, like Swede's, do not want to be shaped to the leather cutter's pattern, artistic or not. Roth is also critiquing America, with its empty dream of a melting pot. The essence of what is wrong with the dream of easy assimilation into America is expressed in the part of the book in which Roth discusses Thanksgiving. He describes meetings between Swede's Jewish family and Dawn's Catholic one.

> [I]t was never but once a year that they were brought together anyway, and that was on the neutral, de-religionized ground of Thanksgiving, when everybody gets to eat the same thing, nobody sneaking off to eat funny stuff—no kugel, no gefilte fish, no bitter herbs, just one colossal turkey for two hundred and fifty million people—one colossal turkey feeds all. A moratorium on funny foods and funny ways and religious exclusivity, a moratorium on the three-thousand-year-old nostalgia of the Jews, a moratorium on Christ and the cross and the crucifixion for the Christians, when everyone in New Jersey and elsewhere can be more passive about their irrationalities than they are the rest of the year. A moratorium on all the grievances and resentments, and not only for the Dwyers and the Levovs but for everyone in America who is suspicious of everyone else. It is the American pastoral par excellence and it lasts twenty-four hours.[59]

Roth seems to be saying that we have to confront our various beastly impulses—as seen in our cultural differences, political differences, gender differences, and religious differences—and let our beastly impulses provoke fights among us. While some readers, like Michael Lerner, may regard *American Pastoral* as an argument against assimilation,[60] I believe it is still the case that assimilation is a worthwhile goal in this novel. The problem is that there are no polite shortcuts. The novel's second epigraph (William Carlos Williams's reference to "the rare occurrence of the expected") suggests that expectations of rational compromise are generally foolhardy.

NOTES

1. See M. M. Bakhtin's "Discourse in the Novel," in *The Dialogic Imagination: Four Essays*, trans. Caryl Emerson and Michael Holquist, ed. Michael Holquist (Austin: University of Texas Press, 1981), 259–422.

2. Philip Roth, *Deception* (New York: Simon and Schuster, 1990), 114. Hereafter cited as *D*.

3. Ibid., 205.

4. Claire Bloom, *Leaving a Doll's House: A Memoir* (Boston: Little Brown, 1996), 182–84.

5. Alan Cooper, *Philip Roth and the Jews* (Albany: State University of New York Press, 1996), 279.

6. Ibid, 282.

7. Roth, *Sabbath's Theater* (Boston: Houghton Mifflin, 1995), 426. Hereafter cited as *ST*.

8. Ibid., 226.

9. Ibid., 121.

10. Ibid., 446–47.

11. Ibid., 193.

12. Cooper, *Roth and the Jews*, 70.

13. Malcolm Jones, Jr., "A Tale of Exes and Ohs," review of *Leaving a Doll's House*, by Claire Bloom, *Newsweek* (September 30, 1996): 78.

14. R. Z. Sheppard, "When She Was Bad," review of *American Pastoral*, by Philip Roth, *Time* (April 28, 1997): 74.

15. Steve Brzezinski, review of *American Pastoral*, by Philip Roth, *Antioch Review* 56, no. 2 (Spring 1998): 232.

16. Michael Wood, "The Trouble with Swede Levov," review of *American Pastoral*, by Philip Roth, *New York Times Book Review*, April 20, 1997, 8.

17. Todd Gitlin, "Weather Girl," review of *American Pastoral*, by Philip Roth, *The Nation* (May 12, 1997): 63–64.

18. Louis Menand, "The Irony and the Ecstasy: Philip Roth and the Jewish Atlantis," review of *American Pastoral*, by Philip Roth, *The New Yorker* (May 19, 1997): 94.

19. Edward Alexander, "Philip Roth at Century's End," review of *American Pastoral*, by Philip Roth, *New England Review* 20, no. 2 (Spring 1999): 184.

20. Tad Friend, "Philip Roth's Newest Fictional Character Unmasks Himself," *The New Yorker* (May 26, 1997): 29–30.

21. Elizabeth Hardwick, "Paradise Lost," review of *American Pastoral*, by Philip Roth, *New York Review of Books*, June 12, 1997, 14.

22. Holly Brubach, "Advice to the Glovelorn," *The New York Times Magazine*, July 27, 1997, 35.

23. Philip Roth, *American Pastoral* (Boston: Houghton Mifflin, 1997), 162–63; hereafter *AP*.

24. Ibid., 164.

25. Ibid., 165.

26. Ibid., 11–12.

27. Ibid., 5.

28. *ST*, 122–23.

29. Ibid., 132.

30. *AP*, 274.

31. Ibid., 391–400.

32. Ibid., 177.

33. Philip Roth, "Coronation on Channel Two," *New Republic* (September 23, 1957): 21.

34. *AP*, 363.

35. Ibid., 190.

36. Ibid., 308.

37. Ibid., 356.

38. Ibid., 404.

39. Ibid., 319.

40. Ibid., 193.

41. Ibid., 204.

42. Ibid., 89.

43. Ibid., 90.

44. Ibid., 417.

45. Ibid., 238.

46. Ibid., 107.

47. Ibid., 248.

48. Ibid., 263.

49. Ibid., 274.

50. Ibid., 288.

51. Ibid., 241.

52. Ibid., 242.

53. Ibid., 89.

54. Ibid., 422.

55. Ibid., 17–18.

56. Ibid., 31.

57. Ibid., 423.

58. Sheppard, "When She Was Bad," 74.

59. *AP*, 402.

60. Michael Lerner, "The Jews and the 60s: Philip Roth Still Doesn't Get It," *Tikkun* 12.3 (1997): 14.

Reading Race and the Conundrums of Reconciliation in Philip Roth's *The Human Stain*

Brett Ashley Kaplan

WHEN ELLIE ASKS COLEMAN "WHAT ARE YOU ANYWAY?" HE REPLIES "PLAY it any way you like." The ambiguity of his appearance excites them both, driving an identity game in which rules evaporate fast and anyone can be anything, depending on how one plays. The main character in Philip Roth's *The Human Stain* (2000), Coleman Silk, an African-American Dean of Faculty at the fictional and aptly named "Athena College," has refashioned himself as Jewish in order to attain freedom as the "greatest of the great *pioneers* of the I."[1] Playing it any way one likes and the delicious mystery of not being able to be "read" initially entice Coleman, but the confusions of not maintaining a fixed identity eventually overcome him. They lead him to "pass" as Jewish, thereby illustrating that the identity politics Roth questions in this work cannot be ignored. In this sense, *The Human Stain* offers an extended and cranky plea for a return to a universal "I" decoupled from the identity politics many of Roth's characters see as creating the "we-think" of "political correctness" that they believe has hijacked academia.

Yet because Coleman has chosen to identify himself as Jewish, he cannot escape the "tyranny" of categorization; read as either black or Jewish, Coleman alternately suffers racism or anti-Semitism. Thus, *The Human Stain* argues against itself: while it glories in an "I" free from the cloying group-think of the "we," its characters continually prove that the external demands of the historically determined "we"—especially that of race—cannot be jettisoned by sheer acts of will. If only, Roth seems to be arguing, the indeterminacy of "playing it any way you like" could transcend the trenchant categorization that marks much contemporary discourse on race, if only we did not need to read race (here, for the moment, including reading

172

Jewishness), then racial reconciliation could be achieved. But no; *The Human Stain* finds that because we are still obsessed by reading race we cannot overcome racism and anti-Semitism in America.

Indeed, according to the logic of *The Human Stain*, racial reconciliation can only be achieved by eschewing identity politics. I borrow the term "racial reconciliation" from former President Bill Clinton, who functions as a character in Roth's novel and who, in 1997, created the "President's Initiative on Race." Through "racial reconciliation," Clinton's initiative imagined a means of overcoming racism in contemporary America. By arguing that racial reconciliation relies on jettisoning the group identity associated with "identity politics," many of Roth's characters take a neoconservative argument against "political correctness" (PC) and transform it into a classical liberal argument about the powers of self-fashioning. The genesis of PC is often understood as a neoconservative attack on radical professors. But Richard Feldstein locates the first uses of PC in the 1940s as a Jewish leftist critique of communist party hardliners who remained faithful to the party after the Hitler-Stalin pact of 1939. Feldstein contends that, through the 1970s and '80s, PC became an in-joke among lesbian feminists gently chiding their own desire to be non-offensive to all genders, races, classes, sexual orientations, and so on. It has only been since the late 1980s that PC became a term of abuse flung against the left by neoconservatives wishing to mock the opening up of the canon to "others."[2]

Roth positions many of his characters as critical of PC or as representatives of its hypocrisy, especially when they share the fantasy of the dissolution of the category of race in favor of an uncompromised and untethered selfhood.[3] Hence Coleman's sister, Ernestine, decries the "buffoonery" of having to "be so terribly frightened of every word one uses," lest one be accused of racism.[4] Racial reconciliation, Roth implies here, can never be achieved as long as the "reactionary authorities" of political correctness remain unchecked.[5] In short, in *The Human Stain's* paradoxically liberally-inflected neoconservative view, political correctness prevents racial reconciliation by insisting on stifling categorization.

While *The Human Stain* thus charts the conundrums of racial reconciliation, it also leaves open the possibility of what Roth, in discussing Kafka, calls "personal reconciliation." Kafka haunts Roth and, as Sanford Pinkser notes, "if ever a contemporary American writer imagined himself as Kafka's döppleganger, it is Roth."[6] For example, in "'I Always Wanted You to Admire My Fasting'; or, Looking at Kafka" (1973), Roth traces the difference between Kafka's angst-ridden earlier stories and a later piece written on the eve of his death. Here he seems to have found some form of peace due in part to his relationship with the much younger Dora, who nurses him on his deathbed. Roth notes of Kafka's later work:

> this fiction imagined in the last 'happy' months of his life is touched by a spirit of personal reconciliation and sardonic self-acceptance, by a tolerance of one's own brand of madness . . . The piercing masochistic irony of the earlier [stories] . . . has given way here to a critique of the self and its preoccupations that, though bordering on mockery, no longer seeks to resolve itself in images of the uttermost humiliation and defeat.[7]

While "bordering on mockery," *The Human Stain* is similarly "touched by a spirit of personal reconciliation." This Roth/Kafka version of reconciliation—a denuded form of the much more idealized model proposed by President Clinton's initiative on race—is a means of coming to terms with the defects of the self, not a means of overcoming them. In modeling himself on Kafka, in being Kafka's dopplegänger, then, Roth offers a work that chronicles the struggle for reconciliation at both personal and social (in this case, racial) levels.

If Roth imagines himself as Kafka's double, claiming that "Everyone was influenced by Kafka in those days," Anatole Broyard, on whom Roth based his enigmatic main character, Coleman Silk, imagined himself as the disseminator of Kafka in America and as a figure who, like Kafka, longed to be "transfigured."[8] Broyard, who "helped shape the contemporary literary canon," was a *New York Times* literary critic and Village *flâneur* who dominated the literary life of postwar New York.[9] Titling his posthumously published memoir *Kafka was the Rage* (1993) is only one indication of the importance of Kafka to Broyard. While similarities and differences between Coleman and Broyard abound, their common "passing" takes precedence over their divergent stories. But more importantly, both Coleman and Broyard exhibit a similar structure of simultaneously hiding and revealing their origins. Judith Butler locates this curious structure in one of the classic works on passing, Nella Larsen's novella *Passing* (1929), where Butler finds "hiding [is] in that very flaunting."[10]

This structure of simultaneous display and obfuscation not only marks Coleman but also inscribes many of the other characters in *The Human Stain*, whose secrets resist being read even while they are flaunted. Further, along with Butler, we may link the repression of desire with the repression of race: "The question of what can and cannot be spoken, what can and cannot be publicly exposed, is raised throughout the text [Larsen's *Passing*] and it is linked with the larger question of the dangers of public exposure of both color and desire."[11] While the text in Butler's statement is Larsen's *Passing*, the sentence applies equally well to *The Human Stain* where, as I discuss below, the exposure of both desire and race—the revelation of passing—poses dangers to both Coleman and Delphine Roux. When I discuss the secret that Coleman harbored, his concealment only has meaning in terms of his own construction of what constitutes racial dissimulation and what can be said to be authentic. As Amy Hungerford argues, "the idea of passing in *The Human Stain* in fact is imagined as working against racial essentialism."[12] Indeed, while Roth's novel is about passing, it is also about the possibilities of thinking of race outside of the constrictions and categorizations that enable racism.

Henry Louis Gates, Jr. discusses passing in an article he published about Broyard in *The New Yorker* in 1996. By entitling the article "White Like Me," Gates alluded to the 1964 film *Black Like Me* (based on John Howard Griffin's book and starring James Whitmore), which recounted the travels of a white journalist who passed as black in order to experience Southern racism first hand. The implication of Gates's ironic title, then, is that despite his passing, Broyard is no whiter than Gates himself. Gates notes about passing: "When those of mixed ancestry—and the majority of blacks are of mixed ancestry—disappear into the white majority, they are traditionally accused of running from their 'blackness.' Yet why isn't the alternative a matter of running from their 'whiteness'?"[13] Why indeed must Broyard's and Coleman's stories be construed as harboring the "secret" of their blackness when their whiteness is more visible than their blackness?

That he passed as Jewish instead of merely generically white, as Broyard had done, disrupts the race-as-continuum theory in the story of Coleman Silk because Jewishness as ethnicity has not always been considered a form of whiteness. Indeed, in *How Jews Became White Folks*, Karen Brodkin uses her own family history to chart the transformation of Jews into whites via a post-immigration boom phenomenon that firmly took root with the advancements offered by the G.I. Bill.[14] Thus, shortly before Coleman decided in 1946 to try to pass as Jewish, his passing would have been construed as one person of color becoming another, slightly less oppressed person of color. When Coleman decided to pass as Jewish, quotas for limiting Jewish entrance to colleges were still in place, and anti-Semitism was still an accepted part of much popular discourse. Nonetheless, he equated this version of whiteness with freedom.[15] Passing as Jewish, then, was an uncomfortable passing that did not, in 1946, unequivocally guarantee the privileges of whiteness.

THE "HARSHLY IRONIC FATE" OF *THE HUMAN STAIN*

The critical reception of *The Human Stain* was markedly mixed. The British novelist William Sutcliffe panned it, claiming that "the book is both overwritten and underwritten" and that it lacks the "mysterious alchemy that makes a novel work."[16] Galen Strawson agrees with Sutcliffe that the writing is sometimes "overwrought," but he nonetheless finds it a "highly successful novel."[17] Similarly, Peter Kemp finds that *"The Human Stain* pulses with the strengths that make Roth a prime contender for the status of most impressive novelist now writing in and about America."[18] And David Lodge claims that the trilogy of which *The Human Stain* is the final installment is "triumphantly successful."[19] Jay Parini notes that "the Roth book, despite its many virtues, drifts too easily into the realm of caricature. A satirist at heart, Roth uses the campus setting as a way to vent his rage against political correctness."[20] As Jay Halio puts it, "Not since David Mamet's *Oleanna* has there appeared so powerful an indictment of political correctness and a travesty of student rights and faculty vulnerability in higher education."[21] Elaine Safer notes that "The range of humor in *The Human Stain* constantly shifts from the grim tone of black humor to farce."[22] William Tierney situates *The Human Stain* as a novel of academe and agrees with Parini that Roth has drawn a "silly portrait," yet he also claims that in the novel, "academic identity intertwines with today's great challenges: how to reconcile race, class, and gender."[23] Exemplifying the critical disagreements, Lorrie Moore finds that *"The Human Stain* is an astonishing, uneven, and often very beautiful book."[24] Thus most readers agree that, because of an unevenness of tone besets the novel, it is by turns brilliant, compromised, silly, smart, and overdone. This kind of mixed critical reception has characterized the reviews of many of Roth's nearly thirty novels, hence making his relationships to his readers sometimes vexed, sometimes hortatory.

Preceded by *I Married a Communist* (1997) and *American Pastoral* (1998), *The Human Stain* is the third installment of Roth's trilogy of novels narrated by Nathan Zuckerman. The novel is set in a small New England college town where the Dean of Faculty of Athena College is the seemingly Jewish seventy-one-year-old spry and athletic Coleman Silk. But Coleman is unexpectedly disgraced by a charge of racism against which he does not adequately defend himself. The harsh irony driving the novel—to borrow from Roth's "harshly ironic fate"—is that Coleman's secret is that he was born and raised in an African-American family of educators and is not Jewish. This fact might have been the one thing that could have saved him from his downfall, yet it is the one thing he cannot reveal.[25] The central irony of the novel is thus fueled by the suppression of desired disclosure. Coleman's trouble begins with a bogus charge put forth by two absent students. While taking attendance, Coleman asked the class if two students, who had never yet attended but who remained enrolled, were "spooks." Coleman tells anyone who will listen that he meant "spooks" in the sense of specter or ghost; as it turns out, these two students are African-American and take the word "spooks" as a racial slur. Dean Silk loses his position at the university, takes early retirement, and retreats into a bitterness into which he tries to draw the Roth alter-ego, Nathan Zuckerman, by imploring him to write an account of his experiences, to be appropriately entitled "Spooks." Had the Dean come out as African-American, he could presumably have cleared himself of the charge of racism and saved himself the disgrace to which he keeps referring. Yet had he done this, the "unexploded bomb" that was his secret would have exploded the lives of his Jewish wife and four Jewish children.[26] Had his community read his race differently, they would have read his utterance of "spooks" accurately; Roth thus sets up a conundrum whereby misreadings multiply.

More than one critic has noted that Coleman is the true "spook" in this novel. John Leonard finds that "Silk himself will prove to be a 'spook,'" and Michael André Bernstein notes that, "in his ghostly Jewishness, Silk is the novel's only real 'spook.'"[27] Ross Posnock claims that "'spooks' describes with uncanny aptness what Coleman's purity of self-making engenders."[28] In these assessments, Coleman's acquired Jewishness lends him a spectral quality. Conversely, I find that Coleman's achieved identity as Jewish is solid, fit-

ting, and not in the least spectral. Indeed, the concreteness of
Coleman's Jewishness bolsters Roth's argument about the malleabil-
ity of racial categories. Roth takes great pains to describe the physi-
cality of his main character, and to describe his comfort in his own
skin. The vision of Coleman as spectral implies that his identity is
not grounded. However, Roth depicts his main character as quite at
ease with his adopted identity, even though he makes no attempt
to describe the possibly uncomfortable process of passing as Jewish.
Indeed, it is when Coleman decides to pass as Jewish instead of generically white that passing becomes comfortable for him.

The Athena town and college community, without knowing about
his passing, also disgrace Coleman for his affair with Faunia, a supposedly illiterate woman nearly half his age who is the ex-wife of a
crazed Vietnam veteran, Les Farley. Coleman divulges the secret of
his past and his passing to Faunia and "Faunia alone," thereby moving toward reconciling his past and present lives.[29] Perhaps it is a bit
unfortunate that in both Roth's novel and in his retelling of Kafka's
life, a young woman acts as muse and salvation—in Coleman's case
through viagra-fueled sex and in Kafka's case through a "chaste"
and almost familial relationship. In keeping with the rest of his
work, Roth gives female characters short shrift; nonetheless, Roth
partially exposes this male fantasy of regeneration through coupling
with a much younger woman when he imagines Faunia resisting
Coleman and Nathan's pastoral fantasies of her as at one with nature, milking cows and wishing to be a crow.[30] Thus, unlike other of
Roth's women, Faunia reveals an interiority and layering that allow
for the slow unveiling of her secrets.

The cultural background for Coleman's affair with a younger
woman is Bill Clinton's affair with Monica Lewinsky. In fact, the
novel opens with a sweeping historical panorama that places Clinton's troubles at the heart of the novel. It is 1998 and America ob-
sesses over the fipperies of a silly, get-rich-quick time in which the
country had nothing better to do than obsess over the unpolished
peccadilloes of a self-indulgent president. As Nathan notes: "It was
the summer in America when the nausea returned, when the joking
didn't stop . . . when the smallness of people was simply crushing."[31]
In contrast to the post-September 11 mood in America, Nathan's reminder of this late-twentieth-century "smallness" is striking. Frank
Rich, writing in the *New York Times* op-ed section a few days after September 11, catalogues a series of "summer ephemera" such as Lizzie
Grubman and Gary Condit. He observes that they were "typical of

an age in which we inflated troublesome but passing crises into ca-
tastrophes that provided the illusion of a national test of character."[32] Nathan captures Rich's tone exactly, yet Nathan recoils from
the inability of Americans to forgive the human failure of the president. Wishing to distance himself from the "piety binge" that beset
us in the wake of the Monica scandal, Nathan wants to drape a
Christo wrapping over the White House that reads "A HUMAN
BEING LIVES HERE."[33] This plea for forgiving (in Nathan's view)
the justifiable lapses of the president parallels his desire to see Coleman forgiven. Indeed, Nathan suggests that just as the Athena College community should have forgiven Coleman for his innocent
utterance of "spooks" and for his affair with Faunia, so Americans
should have forgiven their fallible president for his affair with
Monica.

This desire for forgiveness of duplicity resonates with the structure of concealment that marks this late Roth work. In the novel
everyone, including Clinton, bears a secret that masks his true identity, desires, or psychological state. Like the open secret of Coleman's affair with Faunia, Clinton's "secret emerged in every last
mortifying detail";[34] indeed, all the character's secrets will emerge
in all their mortifying details. For example, Delphine Roux, the
young, ambitious French academic whose secret crush on her nemesis, Dean Silk, will undo her, sends Coleman an anonymous note an-
nouncing "everyone knows." While we might imagine the note
refers to his passing, it rather refers to his affair with Faunia. Delphine inadvertently broadcasts the mortifying details of her secret
crush on Coleman by sending a personal ad to the entire faculty.[35]
Thus, whereas for Coleman the danger of exposure revolves around
race, the danger of exposure for Delphine revolves around desire.
Further, her desire for Coleman will presumably be complicated if
not doused completely by the revelation of his race. For Delphine,
the crusader for political correctness, secretly wants to affix an ad-
dendum to her personal ad that reads "Whites only need apply."[36]
Delphine wonders if, instead of such an obviously un-PC exclusion-
ary statement, she might ask potential suitors to send a photograph.
However, she rejects this option out of fear that the photograph
might be "designed to mislead *specifically* in the matter of race."[37]
Indeed, had she seen a photograph of Coleman, she would have
taken him for white. Thus, where Butler had located in *Passing* a
dual danger of the display of desire and race, in Roth's novel we
find that the revelation of Coleman's race would threaten the secret

desires of Delphine. Further, Roth's jab at the spectacle of the PC Delphine desiring only whites continues his attack on the hypocrisy of PC that preoccupies this novel.

In addition to Coleman and Delphine's secrets, Faunia, too, harbors a secret: while everyone thinks she is illiterate and working class, she in fact comes from a well-to-do Boston family and is literate, if not well educated. Because she had left her well-appointed home at the age of fourteen to escape a sexually abusive stepfather, her class status is severely diminished through successive escapades with ne'er-do-well men. Faunia and Coleman are haunted and tracked throughout their affair by Faunia's ex-husband, Les Farley, who suffers from post-traumatic stress disorder. His fury at his ex-wife stems from her having left him and from her accidentally killing their children by leaving them alone with a space heater that caught fire. Les must grapple with his PTSD by visiting the traveling version of Maya Lin's Vietnam memorial, by eating at Chinese restaurants, and by struggling with his anger. His anti-Semitism flares up against the aging Coleman when he asks himself: "Why is he [Les] suffering so much for what happened to him when she can go on giving blow jobs to old Jews?"[38] Eventually, Les's anger overcomes him and he kills Coleman and Faunia by a supposed auto accident. Les's secret is, therefore, that he has murdered his ex-wife and Coleman. Thus, while Clinton's open secret opens the novel, the revelation of every other major character's secrets sustains Roth's examination of disclosure and self-remaking.

When Roth wants to drive home the irony of Coleman's fate—that he cannot disclose the self he has made at the moment when this knowledge would save him—he compares him to Dr. Charles Drew, an African-American researcher who discovered how to bank blood so that it would not clot. Roth claims that Drew was injured in an automobile accident and the closest hospital refused to accept African-Americans, causing him to bleed to death at its gates. Historian Howard Zinn confirms Roth's story (including its irony) about Charles Drew, but does not mention his death: "It was, ironically, a black physician named Charles Drew who developed the blood bank system. He was put in charge of the wartime donations, and then fired when he tried to end blood segregation."[39] Nathan tells us that "the harshly ironic fate of Dr. Drew took on a significance—a seemingly special relevance to Coleman and *his* harshly ironic fate."[40] Both the irony of Coleman's secret being the one thing that could save him from disgrace and the irony that the scientist who developed an anticlot system was killed for lack of access to his own technology revolve around blood: in one case, Coleman's hidden bloodlines, and in the other Drew's literal blood loss.

The blood in the story of Charles Drew also continues the exploration of the "stain" in the title of the novel, and it does so in a manner that highlights the historical depth of the question of blood and its stain. The stain of this novel also refers to the infamous stain Clinton left on Monica Lewinsky's dress. Faunia most clearly explicates the title for us when she muses: "The human stain. . . . we leave a stain, we leave a trail, we leave our imprint. Impurity, cruelty, abuse error, excrement, semen—there's no other way to be here. Nothing to do with disobedience. Nothing to do with grace or salvation or redemption."[41] In this bleak vision, there is no hope for redemption or reconciliation. Roth thus demonstrates how we are all stained with the blood of our past and with the immobility of that past.

As Nathan narrates the story of Coleman's secret, his passing, he makes it clear that Coleman found it relatively easy to alter the way people read him. Coleman was barely eighteen when he joined the service in 1944, claiming to be a Jew; by the time he finished serving in '46 and used the G.I. bill to enroll at NYU, his passing was complete. Nathan describes Coleman's justification for his transformation from black to white in classically liberal terms that value freedom and social mobility:

> He had chosen to take the future into his own hands rather than to leave it to an unenlightened society to determine his fate—a society in which, more than eighty years after the Emancipation Proclamation, bigots happened to play too large a role to suit him . . . far from there being anything wrong with his decision to identify himself as white, it was the most natural thing for someone with his outlook and temperament and skin color to have done. All he'd ever wanted, from earliest childhood on, was to be free: not black, not even white—just on his own and free.[42]

This fantasy of an I "pioneered" sui generis from a sense of self, one divorced from sociocultural constructs, collapses when Coleman finds—and rather quickly—that one cannot be "free" from America's obsession with race. Thus, the irony of Dr. Charles Drew's fate is reflected in the irony of the "spooks" incident.

Coleman passes precisely because he cannot reconcile himself to the confines of a world in which race matters. His thinking on race derives from his idea of freedom from categories. His self-fashioning into a Jew reflects his rejection of the arbitrary nature of race and blood and his expertise as the "greatest of the great *pioneers* of the I."[43] Roth's concept of the self's ability to create and live by its own fictions combats the "tyranny of the we that is dying to suck you in, the coercive, inclusive, historical, inescapable moral *we* with its insidious *E pluribus unum*."[44] What Roth here terms the "tyranny of the we" might also be understood as identity politics, as the liberation of the oppressed self into the comforting culture of the "we."[45] In claiming that Roth's novel condemns the " 'tyranny of the we and its we-talk' propagated by political correctness," Ross Posnock explicitly links this "we-ness" with political correctness.[46] In this light, Roth demonstrates the absurdity of identity politics and political correctness by tracking Coleman's bitter, ironic fate after the needless "spooks" event.

The individualist vision to which Coleman adheres, where he imagines that he can pioneer or fashion an "I" free from the "prison" of his upbringing, comes crashing down around him during the "spooks" incident. Here, the extreme difference between 1946 and 1998 in terms of race relations is made manifest. In 1946, when Coleman considered how to chart his future, his options for college were limited to "colored" schools such as Howard, which Coleman attended for a brief, unhappy period. In Roth's caricatured vision of 1998 academic life, political correctness means that a ridiculous incident such as the one that turns Coleman's life topsy-turvy results from the tyranny of the "we." In her memoir, *Black, White, and Jewish*, Rebecca Walker resists this "tyranny" by refusing to be categorized by any of the identity markers in her title. She claims instead: "I do not have to define this body. I do not have to belong to one camp, school, or race, one fixed set of qualifiers, adjectives based on someone else's experience. . . . I am transitional space, form-shifting space."[47] This is exactly the kind of ambiguity that Coleman claims for his self-fashioned "I" before he discovers that the freedom of this transitional space evaporates when pushed against the societal limitations of postwar America.

After several years of passing and a two-year affair with the Icelandish-Danish-Minnesotan, Steena, Coleman invites Steena to his parents' house for Sunday dinner without telling her that his family is black. Steena balks and leaves him, whereupon Coleman renounces his family and marries a Jewish woman, Iris. One might imagine that Coleman should have had difficulty passing himself off as Jewish to a Jewish wife who would naturally have expected him to be circumcised. But Iris's "Yiddish-speaking father . . . was such a thoroughgoing heretical anarchist that he hadn't even had Iris's two older brothers circumcised."[48] Ironically, Coleman himself was circumcised, a fact which Roth explains by the following: "His mother, working as a nurse at a hospital staffed predominantly by Jewish doctors, was convinced by burgeoning medical opinion of the significant hygienic benefits of circumcision."[49] Indeed, while we do not know how many African-Americans were circumcised in America in 1926, there was a late nineteenth-century push towards circumcising Christians. Dr. Peter Remondino, for example, argued for circumcision in a widely read 1891 treatise where he claims that "The practice [of circumcision] is now much more prevalent than is supposed, as there are many Christian families where males are regularly circumcised soon after birth, who simply do so as a hygienic measure."[50] While there was a considerable backlash against the burgeoning practice of circumcision, it nonetheless—due in no small measure to Remondino's popular treatise—became standard practice for hospital-born Gentile infants. In his history of circumcision, David Gollaher argues that in the first decades of the twentieth century (i.e., when Coleman was born) circumcision became a middle-class marker.[51] In order to differentiate themselves from the teaming hordes of immigrants perceived as "dirty," "contaminated," or "polluted," middle-class whites opted for hospital births involving surgical circumcision as a symbol of cleanliness and as a shield against the onanism seen to be associated with retention of the foreskin. That Coleman's mother had her son circumcised in a hospital setting indicates her desire to assert her middle-class status. Ironically, circumcision as a social marker performed in sanitized hospitals was designed explicitly to set one apart from the Jewish ritual circumcision practiced privately, at a bris, by a mohel. Thus, while Coleman's circumcision was performed as a means of asserting a certain kind of black middle-class status, to distinguish him from the majority of uncircumcised African-Americans, it is taken as a marker of his Jewishness.

Apart from his circumcision, we know nothing about the contents of Coleman's adopted Jewishness. Perhaps because of Iris's secular Jewish upbringing, Coleman is never embarrassed by not understanding a Jewish reference and can therefore immerse himself quite comfortably in his role. After his transfiguration into a Jew, Coleman allows himself to sink into the postwar "Jewish self-infatuation" that was at its "pinnacle among the Washington Square intel-

lectual avant-garde."[52] Roth's description of this self-infatuation is
borne out by Arthur Goren, who, in reflecting on the postwar
"Golden Decade" of American Jewry, discusses the "new self-
consciousness American Jewry displayed after the conclusion of the
war."[53] Coleman's sui generis creation makes sense only when he
becomes Jewish, instead of merely white. As Nathan notes, becoming Jewish was the "secret to his secret," and "As a heretofore
unknown amalgam of the most unalike of America's historic undesirables, he now made sense."[54] Writing against the backdrop of the
supposed strife between African-Americans and Jews, Roth's novel
reflects on that strife by combining these two "undesirables" into
one category. And indeed, that Coleman indulges in "ravings about
black anti-Semitism"[55] indicates his acute awareness of the animosity
that developed between blacks and Jews in America after the civil
rights movement.

   In an emotional, polemical article about African-American and
Jewish relations, Norman Podhoretz asks: "How was it borne in upon
us so early, white and black alike, that we were enemies beyond any
possibility of reconciliation?"[56] Perhaps one of the most offensive
passages in this generally offensive essay is Podhoretz's comparison
of Jewish history to African-American history. Whereas, he argues,
the Jews have a "memory of past glory and a dream of imminent
redemption," African-Americans can merely lay claim to a stigmatic
past: "His past is a stigma, his color is a stigma, and his vision of the
future is the hope of erasing the stigma by making color irrelevant,
by making it disappear as a fact of consciousness."[57] This "stigma"
seems close to Roth's idea of the human stain—that part of ourselves that we cannot escape, change, or reconcile. In his descriptions of the reasons for Coleman's passing, Nathan makes it clear
that Coleman too wants to make "color irrelevant" and that he sees
his color as a stigma. Podhoretz's neoconservative claim that African-Americans desire the dissolution of identity politics—the disappearance of color—is not supported by other analyses of the
interactions among blacks and Jews.

   In a much more sober analysis of the supposed animosity between
blacks and Jews, Henry Louis Gates, Jr. discusses African-American
anti-Semitism and its uses. Gates argues that some African-American
leaders use anti-Semitism to bolster the isolationism essential to
their identity-driven platforms. These leaders use anti-Semitism because of—and not in spite of—the large numbers of Jews in the civil
rights movement. Gates finds that the "trans-ethnic, transracial co-

operation—epitomized by the historic partnership between blacks and Jews—is what poses the greatest threat to the isolationist movement."[58] In a curious sense, Gates's assessment agrees with the critique of political correctness that Roth voices throughout *The Human Stain*. For Gates, the "isolationist" goals of certain African-American groups rely upon what Roth would disdainfully term "we-think"—and transracial cooperation threatens such identitary thinking. Were Roth to have his way, we would all pioneer our "I"s and transfigure ourselves into complex beings incapable of being read into the unbearable constrictions of a binding "we."

WHAT DO YOU DO WITH A MAN WHO CAN'T BE READ?

Roth structures *The Human Stain* by revealing Coleman's secret to the reader long before Nathan Zuckerman discovers his past. While we imagine the narrative has switched to an omniscient narrator, we discover at the close of the novel that Nathan had been narrating in the third person throughout almost the entire text. Because Nathan only sometimes narrates in the first person, we do not share Nathan's surprise upon discovering, after Coleman's death, that his family had not been Jewish. Coleman's identity as white had been visible to Nathan, but it had not been "read." Indeed, even while Nathan reads him as Jewish, he simultaneously also reads him as black. Early on in their fast-blossoming friendship Nathan reflects that Coleman appeared as "the small-nosed Jewish type with the facial heft in the jaw, one of those crimped-haired Jews of a light yellowish skin pigmentation who possess something of the ambiguous aura of the pale blacks who are sometimes taken for white."[59] Thus Nathan simultaneously sees and refuses to see Coleman's secret. As with the rest of the characters in Roth's novel, Coleman wears his secret so openly that it can be read, purloined-letter style, while remaining invisible. Coleman plays this Janus-faced game of exposure and masquerade with his supposed Jewishness. By choosing to be Jewish rather than merely white, Coleman lays himself open to a whole series of readings, mis-readings, and oppressions. Indeed, Zuckerman sympathizes with Coleman for being (as he then thinks) *mistaken* for black, while bouncing back and forth between anti-Semitism and racism. Long before Nathan learns how to read Coleman correctly, he relays the following story: because his name didn't give him away as a Jew—because it could as easily have been a Ne-

gro's name—he'd once been identified, in a brothel, as a nigger trying to pass and been thrown out: "Thrown out of a Norfolk
whorehouse for being black, thrown out of Athena college for being
white."[60] Coleman was not born to a Jewish family and he did not
convert to Judaism, yet his community perceived him as Jewish and
Les Farley's murderous aims against him were fueled by his supposed Jewishness. As Zuckerman notes, "Buried as a Jew . . . and, if
I was speculating correctly, killed as a Jew. Another of the problems
of impersonation."[61] Being read as Jewish, in this case, contributed
to Coleman's downfall.

Indeed, one of the many themes of this novel is literacy and the
larger question of reading/knowing the other. Faunia pretends that
she cannot read when she is in fact literate (although no one ever
reads the "proof" of this—her posthumously discovered diary).
Also, Lisa, Coleman's once beloved and now estranged daughter,
teaches illiterate children how to read. Coleman thought of Carmen, a six-year-old who, despite twenty-five weeks of Lisa's dedicated
instruction, still cannot differentiate "couldn't" from "climbed,"
when he found that the underside of his "disgrace"—i.e., his relationship with Faunia—had been exposed to him by her loose and
rough behavior with a group of male janitors. In a surreal scene in
the chapter aptly entitled, "What Do You Do with the Kid Who Can't
Read?," Coleman imagines that an infantilized Faunia takes Carmen's remedial reading class, and his answer to the question that
titles the chapter is "what *he* did with the kid who couldn't read was
to make her his mistress."[62] The nexus of thinking of his daughter,
while thinking of his mistress (who is more or less his daughter's
age), while assimilating the mistress into the six-year-old student of
his do-gooder daughter leaves one in a tailspin of perverse speculation. But the reflection on reading and on the importance of reading the other remains a compelling part of this imaginary scene.
While the "Kid" in the chapter's title would seem to refer to Faunia
and Carmen, it also refers to Bill Clinton. As one of the unnamed
young male faculty members, whose discussion of the Monica affair
opens the chapter, notes: "He [Clinton] could read her. If he can't
read Monica Lewinsky, how can he read Saddam Hussein? If he
can't read and outfox Monica Lewinsky, the guy *shouldn't* be president. There's *genuine* grounds for impeachment."[63] According to
this commentator, inaccurate reading, rather than affairs in the
Oval Room, is grounds for impeachment.[64]

The tenuous nature of a good read also affects Delphine Roux's and Nelson Primus's relationships with Coleman. After her job interview, Delphine confesses that "It had been impossible to read his reading of her."[65] All of these struggles with getting an accurate read reflect on the characters' obsessions with reading race, gender, and desire, and the curious structure of their desiring exposure while shielding themselves from it. In the same way as Nathan simultaneously discovered and suppressed Coleman's secret, Roth structures Delphine's consciousness like a paradox of ill-fated discovery: "Afraid of being exposed, dying to be seen—there's a dilemma for you."[66] Or, in the context of Roux's guess that Faunia substitutes for her in Coleman's imagination, one "at once cleverly masquerade[s] and flagrantly disclose[s]."[67] In another sign that his masquerade was also flagrantly disclosed, Coleman insults a "waspy" lawyer, Nelson Primus, after Primus tells him to drop his affair with Faunia in order to protect him against Les Farley. Coleman insults him with: "I never again want to hear that self-admiring voice of yours or see your smug fucking lily-white face."[68] Primus ponders the slur, asking his wife repeatedly why Coleman chose whiteness as a means of derision. Primus, assuming Coleman is Jewish, also therefore assumes he is white and cannot read the racial categorizing of Coleman's slur. The term "lily-white" had been slung at Coleman by his elder brother, Walter, who was furious at Coleman for passing and renouncing his loving family. Walter tells Coleman: "Don't you dare ever show your lily-white face around that house again!"[69] By taking his brother's slur against him for passing and flinging it at this so-called waspy lawyer, Coleman might have given himself away, had Primus been able to read him differently. Thus Roth would appear to argue that racial reconciliation can be achieved only when the identity politics of the "we" are replaced by the originality of the self-fashioned individual. Yet each of the characters in the novel shows that racial reconciliation is always thwarted by the toxic power of unreconciled personal secrets.

The alternating series of racial designations that Coleman moves through suggest the troubles of misreading and the dangers of racism. Yet because of the academic mood in late twentieth-century America, Coleman's problems also highlight the trouble with political correctness. But Roth goes too far here. In linking the "piety binge" of late twentieth-century political correctness to the horrors of pre–civil rights racism, Roth vents his anger against what he sees—more in conspiratorial than historically accurate terms—as a new manifestation of the violence of "we-think." Yet despite this slippage from the "piety binge" to pre–civil rights racism, Roth is right to suggest that the desire to read people racially is at the heart of the American resistance to reconciling racism.

CONCLUSION

Bill Clinton's infidelities with Monica Lewinsky haunt *The Human Stain* and are explicitly compared with Coleman's supposedly secret affair with Faunia. Coleman rants against the smallness of people so interested in propriety that they can be discomfited by his and Clinton's affairs: "The luxury of these lives disquieted so by the inappropriate comportment of Clinton and Silk!"[70] Clinton appears throughout the novel as both an excuse for Nathan to vent his rage against the superficial "piety binge" that has beset the country in the wake of the Monica Lewinsky scandal, and as the focal point for the Vietnam veteran Les Farley's rage against those draft dodgers who have never faced the horrors of war and its attendant post-traumatic stress disorder. In discussing the Clinton scandals, Toni Morrison mused that "white skin notwithstanding, this is our first black President."[71] In this somewhat tongue-in-cheek assessment, Morrison nonetheless points towards another of the implicit connections between Coleman and Clinton. Not that Clinton passed as black, but he rather, in Morrison's words, "displays almost every trope of blackness."[72] Through his "President's Initiative on Race," Clinton tried to institute a national dialogue on race in order to "promote racial reconciliation."[73]

Roth mentions neither the Initiative nor its unachieved culmination in a presidential apology for slavery. Still, the echoes of these presidentially driven desires for reconciliation make themselves felt in Clinton's transformation, remarked upon in *The Human Stain*, from a figure who Americans seem unwilling to forgive to one who is finally not unseated and is forgiven. On June 14, 1997, the presidential advisory board on race met to discuss the possibilities of a national conversation on race and an apology for slavery.[74] The chairman of the advisory board, Dr. John Hope Franklin, claimed that "a national conversation about race and ethnicity has not occurred in our history;" Governor Kean added that Clinton "is the first president who's been willing to do this."[75] So the President to whom Roth compares Coleman, because they both share the secret of affairs with much younger women, is also the president who tried to initiate a national call for racial reconciliation. At the same time as the initiative on race, in the late nineties, Clinton also considered issuing a formal apology for slavery cut from the same cloth as his formal apology for the Tuskegee experiments. However, Newt Gingrich and other conservatives were opposed to the idea, and the apology never took place.

In conversations with Rob Seibert, the archivist for the Clinton Presidential Materials Project, I found a reticence to discuss why the apology did not take place. While the documents explaining why the apology failed to materialize will not be released under the freedom of information act until 2006, Seibert speculated that Clinton preferred to focus on the present rather than the past.[76] Elazar Barkan puts a darker spin on the absence of the apology by claiming that, "as the country indulged in Monicagate, the conversation on race fizzled."[77] Yet, as Joan Didion so powerfully argues, the national "indulgence" in Monicagate was engineered by conservatives who instigated the "piety binge" in order to "purge" the country of Clinton and all that he stood for. In Didion's words, the conservatives launched a "covert effort to advance a particular agenda by bringing down a president."[78] Perhaps the final irony in this ironic novel is that Roth blames the smoke of political correctness for the flame of conservative politicking. In comparing Coleman to Clinton, Roth comments on the failure of racial reconciliation to transcend the petty curiosity about sex that plagued late twentieth-century American popular discourse. By treading a thin political line between a neoconservative condemnation of so-called political correctness and a progressive idealization of a self free from the victimization of categorization, Roth's novel invites us to test our own reading practices and their attendant modes of conflating the rich complexity of the un-we'd.

Notes

1. Philip Roth, *The Human Stain* (New York: Vintage Books, 2000), 108. Hereafter referred to as *HS*.

2. Richard Feldstein, *Political Correctness: A Response from the Cultural Left* (Minneapolis: University of Minnesota Press, 1997), 4–6. See also Wendy Steiner, *The Scandal of Pleasure* (Chicago: University of Chicago Press, 1995). Steiner discusses the divergent views of the origins of political correctness in her chapter, "Caliban in the Ivory Tower." See also Cyril Levitt, Scott Davies, Neil McLaughlin, eds., *Mistaken Identities: The Second Wave of Controversy over "Political Correctness"* (New York: Peter

Lang, 1999). Indeed, the canon wars find their way into *The Human Stain* when Coleman rants against the paucity of classical readings of the classical texts he teaches. However, due to space considerations, I will not discuss this aspect of the novel here.

3. In a perhaps provocative question as part of a discussion of the relationship between the neoconservative position about multiculturalism and the fact that many neoconservatives are Jewish, Mitchell Cohen asks: "is neoconservatism a Jewish way of being gentile?" While the implication goes too far, it is interesting to note that the neoconservative view shared by many of Roth's characters denies the importance of Jewishness as a mode of ethnic identity. See Mitchell Cohen, "In Defense of Shaatnez: A Politics for Jews in a Multicultural America," in *Insider/Outsider: American Jews and Multiculturalism,* ed. David Biale, Michael Galchinsky, and Susan Heschel (Berkeley and Los Angeles: University of California Press, 1998), 48.

4. *HS,* 328–29.

5. Ibid., 329.

6. Sanford Pinsker, "Jewish-American Literature's Lost-and-Found Department: How Philip Roth and Cynthia Ozick Reimagine Their Significant Dead," *Modern Fiction Studies* 35, no. 2 (Summer 1989): 225.

7. Philip Roth, "'I Always Wanted You to Admire My Fasting'; or, Looking at Kafka," *Reading Myself and Others* (New York: Farrar, Straus and Giroux, 1975), 256.

8. Anatole Broyard, *Kafka was the Rage: A Greenwich Village Memoir* (New York: Carol Southern Books, 1990), 69.

9. Melissa A. Dobson, entry on Broyard in *The Scribner Encyclopedia of American Lives: Notable Americans who Died between 1986 and 1990,* vol. 2 (New York: Charles Scribner's Sons, 1999), 134–35.

10. Judith Butler, "Passing, Queering: Nella Larsen's Psychoanalytic Challenge," in *Female Subjects in Black and White: Race, Psychoanalysis, Feminism,* ed. Elizabeth Abel, Barbara Christian, Helene Moglen (Berkeley and Los Angeles: University of California Press, 1997), 268.

11. Ibid.

12. Amy Hungerford, *The Holocaust of Texts: Genocide, Literature, and Personification* (Chicago: University of Chicago Press, 2003), 143.

13. Henry Louis Gates, Jr., "White Like Me," *New Yorker* 72, no. 16 (June 17, 1996): 78.

14. Karen Brodkin, *How Jews Became White Folks and What that Says about Race in America* (New Brunswick, NJ: Rutgers University Press, 1994). See also the introduction to Biale, Galchinsky, and Heschel, *Insider/Outsider* (cited above).

15. See Lucy S. Dawidowicz, *On Equal Terms: Jews in America, 1881–1981* (New York: Holt, Rinehart and Winston, 1982); Debrorah Dash Moore, "At Home in America," in Jonathan Sarna, ed. *The American Jewish Experience* (New York: Holmes & Meier, 1986); and David Hollinger, *Science, Jews, and Secular Culture* (Princeton: Princeton University Press, 1996).

16. William Sutcliffe, "Monica and the Vacuum," *The Independent* (London), June 11, 2000, 47.

17. Galen Strawson, "Self-invention on an Epic Scale," *The Financial Times* (London), June 10, 2000, 4.

18. Peter Kemp, "American Booty," *Sunday Times* (London), May 14, 2000.

19. David Lodge, "Sick with Desire," *New York Review of Books,* July 5, 2001: 28–32, 28.

20. Jay Parini, "The Fictional Campus: Sex, Power, and Despair," *Chronicle of Higher Education*, September 22, 2000, B12–13, B13.

21. Jay Halio, "The Human Stain," *Shofar: An Interdisciplinary Journal of Jewish Studies* 20, no. 1 (2001): 173–75, 174.

22. Elaine B. Safer, "Tragedy and Farce in Roth's *The Human Stain*," *Critique* 43, no. 3 (Spring 2002): 211–27, 212.

23. William G. Tierney, "Interpreting Academic Identities: Reality and Fiction on Campus," *Journal of Higher Education* 73, no. 1 (January/February 2002): 168–69.

24. Lorrie Moore, "The Wrath of Athena," *New York Times*, May 7, 2000, 7. For other reviews see also: Bonnie Lyons, "Lies, Secrets, Truthtelling and Imagination in *The Human Stain*," *Studies in American Jewish Literature* 20 (2001): 89–94; Greg Changnon, "Roth Explores Identity, Perception, and Human Nature," *The Atlanta Journal-Constitution*, February 24, 2002, 5D; Jean-Louis Turlin, "Le 11 Septembre a entraîné un insupportable narcissime national," *Le Figaro* (interview), October 3, 2002; Ken Gordon, "The Zuckerman Books," *Salon.com*, March 26, 2002; Morris Williams, "Roth Saga Disdains Political Correctness," *The Daily Yomiuri* (Tokyo), November 25, 2001, 20; J. Bottum, "The Dying Novel: After Three Good Novels, Philip Roth Reverts to His Old Sex-Obsessions," *Weekly Standard*, July 2, 2001, 39; Nicholas Lezard, "Nicholas Lezard Relishes an Angry Indictment of Dumb America," *Guardian* (London), March 17, 2001, 11; Eric Neuhoff, "Le poison de l'hypocrisie," *Le Figaro*, September 19, 2002; Graham Higgin, "The Gripes of Roth," *Guardian* (London), May 27, 2000, 10; Charles McGrath, "Zuckerman's Alter Brain" (interview), *New York Times*, May 7, 2000, 8.

25. *HS*, 333.

26. Ibid., 320.

27. John Leonard, "A Child of the Age," *The New York Review of Books* 47, no. 10 (2000): 8; Michael André Bernstein, "Getting the American People Right," *Times Literary Supplement*, 5069 (2000): 21.

28. Ross Posnock, "Purity and Danger: On Philip Roth," *Raritan: A Quarterly Review* 21, no. 2 (2001): 85–101, 97.

29. *HS*, 213.

30. Ibid., 227.

31. Ibid., 3.

32. Frank Rich, "The Day Before Tuesday," *New York Times*, September 15, 2001, A23.

33. *HS*, 2–3.

34. Ibid., 2.

35. My colleague Bruce Rosenstock has pointed out that Delphine's inadvertent yet desired broadcasting of her crush on Coleman uncannily resembles the ending of Euripides' *Hippolytus*. Indeed, Coleman is a classics professor and classical references abound; one could write an entirely separate article about the use of classical references in *The Human Stain*.

36. *HS*, 262.

37. Ibid., 263.

38. Ibid., 259.

39. Howard Zinn, *A People's History of the United States* (New York: Harper & Row, 1980), 406.

40. *HS*, 333.

41. Ibid., 242.

42. Ibid., 120.

43. Ibid., 108.

44. Ibid.

45. Paul Gilroy discusses the power of the "we" by laying claim to its inherent political nature: "Identity helps us to comprehend the formation of that perilous pronoun 'we' and to reckon with the patterns of inclusion and exclusion that it cannot help creating. . . . Calculating the relationship between identity and difference, sameness and otherness is an intrinsically political operation." (*Against Race: Imagining Political Culture Beyond the Color Line* [Cambridge, MA: Harvard University Press, 2000], 99).

46. Posnock, "Purity and Danger," 86.

47. Rebecca Walker, *Black, White, and Jewish: Autobiography of a Shifting Self* (New York: Riverhead Books, 2001), 4.

48. *HS*, 127.

49. Ibid., 130.

50. P. C. Remondino, *History of Circumcision from the Earliest Times to the Present* (Philadelphia: F. A. Davis, 1891), iv. For a history that treats the mythical origins of circumcision, see Bruno Bettleheim, *Symbolic Wounds: Puberty Rites and the Envious Male* (Glencoe, IL: Free Press, 1954).

51. David Gollaher, *Circumcision: A History of the World's Most Controversial Surgery* (New York: Basic Books, 2000).

52. *HS*, 131.

53. Arthur Goren, "A 'Golden Decade' for American Jews: 1954–1965," in *American Jewish Life, 1920–1990,* ed. Jeffrey S. Gurock (New York: Routledge, 1998), 13.

54. *HS*, 132.

55. Ibid., 16.

56. Norman Podhoretz, "My Negro Problem—and Ours," in *Blacks and Jews: Alliances and Arguments,* ed. Paul Berman (New York: Delacorte Press, 1994), 83. See also Hedda Garza, *African Americans & Jewish Americans: A History of Struggle* (New York: Franklin Watts, 1995); and Cheryl Greenberg, "Pluralism and its Discontents: The Case of Blacks and Jews" in Biale, Galchinsky, and Heschel, *Insider/Outsider* (cited above).

57. Podhoretz, "My Negro Problem," 91.

58. Henry Louis Gates, Jr., "The Uses of Anti-Semitism, with Memoirs of an Anti-Anti-Semite," in *Blacks and Jews: Alliances and Arguments,* ed. Paul Berman (New York: Delacorte Press, 1994), 222.

59. *HS*, 15–16.

60. Ibid., 16.

61. Ibid., 325.

62. Ibid., 161.

63. Ibid., 147–48.

64. If space permitted, here might be a place to examine the largely unexamined Jewishness of Monica Lewinsky and what that says about her readability. In "Moniker," Margorie Garber argues that Lewinsky's Jewishness was remarked upon frequently abroad but almost not at all in America. *Our Monica, Ourselves: The Clinton Affair and the National Interest,* ed. Lauren Berlant and Lisa Duggan (New York: New York University Press, 2001).

65. *HS*, 185.

66. Ibid.

67. Ibid., 195.

68. Ibid., 81.

69. Ibid., 145.

70. Ibid., 154.

71. Toni Morrison, *The New Yorker*, October 5, 1998, 32. For commentary on Morrison's claim, where Micki McElya argues that Morrison mistakes race for class, see "Trashing the Presidency: Race, Class, and the Clinton/Lewinsky Affair," in Berlant and Duggan, *Our Monica, Ourselves*.

72. Ibid.

73. U.S. National Archives and Records Administration, "Pathways to One America In The 21st Century: Promising Practices for Racial Reconciliation," http://clinton3.nara.gov/Initiatives/OneAmerica/pirsummary.html

74. *One America in the 21st Century: Forging a New Future* (Washington, DC: U.S. Government Printing Office, 1998).

75. U.S. Department of Education, "Press Briefing by Presidential Advisory Board on Race," Press Release, June 14, 1997, http://www.ed.gov/PressReleases/06–1997/970614a.html

76. Phone conversation with Rob Seibert, January 28, 2003.

77. Elazar Barkan, *The Guilt of Nations: Restitution and Negotiating Historical Injustices* (New York: W. W. Norton, 2000), 288.

78. Joan Didion, *Political Fictions* (New York: Alfred A. Knopf, 2001), 254, 281.

The Dying Animal: The Art of Obsessing or Obsessing about Art?

Ellen L. Gerstle

PHILIP ROTH'S *THE DYING ANIMAL* (2001) CALLS UP QUESTIONS ABOUT obscenity and art, subjects that often have drawn him into conflict with his readers. Not surprisingly, a number of critics found the novella as slender intellectually as it is physically. Although Roth is surely no stranger to criticism, some complaints had a disturbingly familiar ring, echoing earlier rebukes of misogyny and sexual perversion. Other objections claimed Roth was overworking past themes. I agree that Roth was looking at an old theme: the nature of obsession. But he was doing so in a way that created a rich subtext to the obvious plot line of a May-December love affair.

Zoe Heller, for example, in *The New Republic* argued that despite Roth's caveat not to equate the writer with his work, "one of the areas in which a writer most nakedly asserts himself or herself is in the choice of subject."[1] She asked what we should think about a man who chooses over and over to write about "rutting and fretting. Fretting and rutting"? He must feel, she concluded, that an old professor obsessed with a twenty-four-year-old voluptuous student is somehow representative of the human dilemma. Disavowing any prescription for political correctness, she insisted that a writer of Roth's talents could surely move beyond "the realm of Freudian phantasm or adolescent cartoon" in his depiction of his female characters. Louis Begley, in the *New York Observer*, called Roth's sexual obsessions "circus animals" that he parades before us.[2] Sanford Pinsker, in *The Forward*, dismissed the book as a mere repetition of "Roth's ongoing sense that puritanical America pits unbridled sexual freedom against the forces of restraint."[3] Clearly all the Kepesh books do explore the boundaries of sexual freedom, and that connection partially accounts for Pinsker's complaint that he's read it all before. However, he also finds that the Kepesh novels strive for greatness, but fall far short of their mark: Roth is no Kafka in *The Breast* (1972), no Chekhov in *The Professor of Desire* (1977) and, without his distinct brand of humor, not even equal to himself in *Portnoy's Complaint* (1969).

To its reviewers, the primary offense of the book basically seems to be about Roth's treatment of sex. Even Charles Taylor, in his generally positive online review in Salon.com, admits that Roth's descriptions of sexual acts are so graphic that they might offend women[4] (and, I would ask Mr. Taylor, why not men?). It's safe to say that certain passages equal or go beyond the no-holds-barred discussions about exchanging bodily fluids aired on HBO's "Sex and the City." Of course, cable is hardly the only venue to publicize such private topics. In newspapers around the country, and in other forms of the media, the American people were told about acts of fellatio between the President of the United States and a woman young enough to be his daughter. So Roth's readers cannot claim to be strangers to detailed accounts of sexual behavior once considered too vulgar for polite conversation. Roth himself has made audiences squirm or raise their eyebrows many times since he wrote about Alex Portnoy masturbating into the family's prospective dinner. Why should readers be totally shocked when Roth writes about David Kepesh's licking of Consuela Castillo's menstrual blood?

The answer seems to be that readers do not find that this extraordinary passage and other sexually detailed ones serve a literary purpose. Like members of the Supreme Court assessing pornography, readers are looking for some type of aesthetic redemption. Their apparent failure to locate Roth's artistic intention is ironic, since Roth believes that writing should involve no more accidental sentences than a Cubist painting does any randomly placed shapes. And in *The Dying Animal*, Roth includes a number of paintings to highlight his idea that painters, like writers, transform materials that might otherwise be considered vulgar, obscene, perhaps pornographic, into aesthetic statements about life.

Many of Roth's ideas about writing have already been documented in his collection of essays *Reading Myself and Others* (1975).[5] In piece after piece, Roth explained his writing style, especially his rationale for including what some people had labeled "obscene" and others simply called "tasteless." Logic suggests that a writer who devotes as much time to his craft as Roth does (he's a self-confessed literary monk) is undoubtedly quite deliberate about the construction of each narrative. Thus, it seems reasonable to assume that the sexual language and sexual acts described in *The Dying Animal* exist to satisfy a number of Roth's literary purposes. But what are they?

My first clue to Roth's intent was the cover of the novella. Book jackets are designed primarily to attract the reader's attention, but I suspect that the reproduction of the Modigliani nude on the hardcover edition has an additional purpose: to call attention to Roth's subject—art as a medium to deal with our obsessions. Roth has been obsessed with the nature of art, particularly his art—writing—from the beginning of his career. Hence his subjects have often been man's obsessions—primarily sex, death, and free will. *The Dying Animal* focuses on the intermingling of art and obsession.

As a country, America finds the confluence of sexual and artistic freedom to be divisive, while advertising constantly challenges the limits of what might be called "polite nudity." Yet, Rudoph Guiliani, then Mayor of New York, went "American berserk," as Roth might say, over the decision in 1999, by the Brooklyn Museum of Fine Arts, to stage an exhibition of Chris Ofili's work featuring, among other things, a painting of the Virgin Mary with elephant dung as part of its mixed media. For Guiliani, the painting was not "art" but "outrage," an intolerable offense to the religious sensibilities of Christians. However, I personally observed that a similar painting by Ofili, hanging beside photographs of homoerotic art in Istanbul, Turkey, did not generate similar excitement there. American judicial history is filled with censorship suits: the U.S. Supreme Court tried many times in efforts to define the limits of artistic expression, to determine what constitutes pornography or obscenity. The sexual language and images in Roth's book belong to his ongoing exploration of that topic.

On the book jacket is a portion of an oil painting "Le Grand Nu," in which a voluptuous young woman, "the trademark Modigliani nude," is erotically resting with a "cylindrical stalk of a waist, the wide pelvic span, the gently curving thighs,"[6] and flaming pubic hair. Amedeo Modigliani, a controversial Jewish artist, refused to tailor his art to contemporary ideas about displaying the human body. In 1917, an exhibition of his work in Paris brought the police, who removed his nudes as affronts to decency and modesty. One nude in particular, displaying pubic hair, was considered especially egregious. In the novel, Consuela sends a postcard reproduction to Kepesh of "Le Grand Nu," an oil currently hanging in the Guggenheim Museum. The beauty and seductive power of the woman are undeniable. We are not affronted by this sexually provocative display either as the cover for the novel or as a postcard from a museum's collection. The nude can even pass through the United States mail without the government officials involved considering it a crime. We do not consider it pornographic; we call it art. In fact, when Kepesh likens the seductive power of Consuela to this fairly well-known painting, Consuela becomes more visible to the reader; in some measure, Kepesh's obsession with her erotic powers seems more understandable.

Roth reminds us that nude bodies can also be vulgar or visually repulsive—and either representation is still art, not pornography. For example, the British painter Stanley Spencer's double nude portrait of himself and his wife in their mid-forties makes the viewer feel like a person looking at them through a butcher shop window. Spencer, with his limp penis dangling, squats beside his reclining wife. He inspects her sagging breasts and slackened flesh through his wire-rimmed glasses. Close to their mattress, at the edge of a nearby table, is a large leg of lamb and a single small chop. The meticulously detailed pieces of meat no longer resembling a living lamb are a postmodern memento mori. Positioned in such close proximity to the husband and wife, the butchered flesh reminds us that we are all doomed to die one way or another just as the couple's passionless portrait of marriage reflects the predictable ravages of age and time on sexual attraction. Roth leaves the reader to draw his or her own inferences from Kepesh's obsession with this image once Consuela tells him about her breast cancer. Those inferences aside, one conclusion seems pertinent to Roth's exploration of the difference between pornography and art: context is all. Roth believes that an artist is capable of transforming sex as a subject from something pornographic to something aesthetic.

That Roth is deeply committed to illuminating the difference between pornography and art is suggested early in the narrative. Pornography, Kepesh informs us, does not have a simple definition. Ordinary pornography is a "fallen art form. It's not just make-believe, it's patently insincere."[7] The man having sex with the girl in the porno film is not a source for jealousy. He's simply a surrogate. But in real life, if a younger man usurps an older man's sexual place, Kepesh declares that picture is "the pornography of jealousy." The older man is still enthralled with a younger woman, but he's helplessly "outside the frame."[8]

Perhaps the passage that is most memorable (think of Portnoy's masturbation scene) and, at the same time, the most questionable (think obscene) is the following:

> Then came the night that Consuela pulled out her tampon and stood there . . . like Mantegna's Saint Sebastian, bleeding in a trickle down her thighs while I watched. Was it thrilling? Was I delighted? . . . I had set out to demand the most of her, and when she shamelessly obliged, I wound up again intimidating myself. There seemed nothing to be done . . . except to fall to my knees and lick her clean.[9]

The graphic depiction of this rare sexual moment tests our standards of good taste and challenges us to locate the aesthetic reason for including this description. Among the recently published letters of the famous conductor, Arturo Toscanini, is one written to a woman thirty years his junior; it contains a similarly questionable passage about drinking menstrual blood. This "fact" does not obviate any questions about Roth's reason for describing such behavior.

The excerpt is akin to another seemingly depraved moment in *Sabbath's Theater.*[10] Drenka Balich recalls the time that she and her lover, Mickey Sabbath, urinated into each other's mouths. What saves that picture and this one of Kepesh and Consuela is the context in which the reader is meant to understand their respective actions. Drenka identified that exchange as a defining moment in their relationship, because it signified their trust in one another. Each one was willing to do the forbidden in order to please the other person. But Kepesh recognizes his action with Consuela as the unavoidable consequence of satisfying one's obsession. To demonstrate to Consuela that he, at his age, was no less capable of worshiping her than Carlos, her fifteen-year-old companion from childhood, he performed this otherwise unimaginable act. For Roth, the context redeems these acts from being pornographic and also challenges Justice Stewart's simplistic standard of identifying pornography: "I know it when I see it."

Roth does not want literature judged differently than other artistic mediums when it comes to pornography. His inclusion of the Modigliani painting, the Spencer portrait, and the allusion to Mantegna's Saint Sebastian provide analogous situations to encourage less superficial thinking about what constitutes pornography and what constitutes art. Roth wants us to remember that sex is a driving force in our lives, whether we acknowledge that fact or not. This Freudian attitude, although currently out of fashion, explains fairly well what motivates Kepesh's behavior.

Freud warned there are distinct downsides to letting our sexual desires drive our actions. In pursuit of libidinal happiness, man may find himself exposed to suffering if rejected by his love-object, or if he should lose the object of his desire through unfaithfulness or death. His unquenchable need ironically evolves into the reason for his suffering when he loses her. And Kepesh loses Consuela twice as a sexual object—first through his own thoughtlessness, then through cancer that symbolically and physically strips her of her breast, an icon of femaleness and a basis for her sensual beauty. Her breasts, once a source of his lust, become a symbol of mortality. Perhaps, Roth is suggesting that man is in thrall to his obsessions and to his unavoidable fate; ultimately, man must accept that there is no such thing as unlimited freedom.

As the title states, Roth's novel is as much about dying—how we deal with it in youth and in our advanced years—as it is also about sexual desire, the boundaries on individual freedom, and artistic expression. All these topics are signature Rothian themes: all are clearly his obsessions. In the final analysis, it is difficult to say with certainty whether *The Dying Animal* represents Roth's discourse on the art of obsessing or Roth obsessing about art.

NOTES

1. Zoe Heller, "The Ghost Rutter," *The New Republic* (May 21, 2001): 41.

2. Louis Begley, "Roth Roars Again, Pitiless, Raging Against Age, Illness," *New York Observer* (May 14, 2001): 19.

3. Sanford Pinsker, "Roth Feels Bad About Being Bad: So What Else Is New?" review of *The Dying Animal*, by Philip Roth, *The Forward*, May 25, 2001, http://www.forward.com/issues/2001/01.05.25/arts3.html.

4. Charles Taylor, "Powells.com Book Review-a-Day," review of *The Dying Animal*, by Philip Roth, from Salon.com, June 1, 2001, http://www.powells.com/review/2001_06_01.html.

5. Philip Roth, *Reading Myself and Others* (New York: Farrar, Straus and Giroux, 1975).

6. Philip Roth, *The Dying Animal* (Boston: Houghton Mifflin, 2001), 98.

7. Ibid., 41.

8. Ibid.

9. Ibid., 71–72.

10. Philip Roth, *Sabbath's Theater* (Boston: Houghton Mifflin, 1995), 425–28.

Eros and Death in Roth's Later Fiction

Jay L. Halio

Erotics have always been a part of Philip Roth's fiction, but until recently death has scarcely entered as a major subject, certainly not in the context of eros, except tangentially in *The Anatomy Lesson* (1983). In *Sabbath's Theater* (1995) and *The Dying Animal* (2001), however, both eros and thanatos figure prominently. Whether this reflects Roth's current preoccupations, a result perhaps of his own advancing age and past serious illnesses, I cannot say, though it would hardly surprise me if that were true. We have learned, though, not to make too close a connection between fiction and autobiography. Roth has been emphatic about that issue. For instance, as his surrogate, "Philip," says in *Deception*, referring to his critics: "I write fiction and I'm told it's autobiography, I write autobiography and I'm told it's fiction, so if I'm so dim and they're so smart, let *them* decide what it is or it isn't."[1]

It's not likely that, in *The Dying Animal*, David Kepesh, who is resurrected from *The Breast* (1972) and *The Professor of Desire* (1977), serves as Roth's surrogate, any more than Mickey Sabbath does in *Sabbath's Theater*. Their ages are close enough—Sabbath is about Roth's age at the time he wrote the novel; Kepesh is three years older—but almost everything else is not. Sabbath is a puppeteer with crippled arthritic hands. Kepesh is a radio and television celebrity, a critic of culture, and a part-time professor at a college in New York. Roth has never been a puppeteer, has long since given up teaching, and was never a media star.

Both Sabbath and Kepesh have devoted their later years to various forms of hedonism—in Sabbath's case, to a totally uninhibited indulgence in sexual pleasure. Kepesh likes to bring students from his senior seminar in "Practical Criticism" to his apartment after their final exam, and it is then that he chooses the one he will sleep with. Long divorced from his (unnamed) wife and estranged from their only child, Kepesh for years has denounced bourgeois marriage. In-

200

stead, he has forthrightly given himself over to an unconstrained life of pleasure, especially sexual pleasure, though not in as many depraved, or at least unconventional, forms as Sabbath. But as both approach old age, the pleasures they seek take on greater significance than mere hedonistic enjoyment.

The collocation of sex and death is something that psychologists have long known and discussed, sexual activity being a means of defying death and asserting life. In both *Sabbath's Theater* and *The Dying Animal* this theme has the same importance, though in each novel it is developed in quite different ways. Significantly, *Sabbath's Theater* takes as its epigraph a line from Prospero's speech in Shakespeare's *The Tempest*: "Every third thought shall be my grave." The dedication, moreover, is to two recently deceased friends: Janet Hobhouse, 1948–1991, and Melvin Tumin, 1919–1994. Although the novel proper does not begin that way, the narrative is drenched in death, and many episodes take place in a cemetery.

Mickey Sabbath, no longer a practicing puppeteer and now living in the mountains of New Hampshire, receives from his lover, Drenka Balich, an ultimatum: "Either foreswear fucking others or the affair is over." These are the novel's opening words, and the following paragraph describes the dilemma into which Sabbath is accordingly hurled:

> This was the ultimatum, the maddeningly improbable, wholly unforeseen ultimatum, that the mistress of fifty-two delivered in tears to her lover of sixty-four on the anniversary of an attachment that had persisted with an amazing licentiousness—and that, no less amazingly, had stayed their secret—for thirteen years. But now with hormonal infusions ebbing, with the prostate enlarging, with probably no more than another few years of semi-dependable potency still his—with perhaps not that much more of life remaining—here at the approach of the end of everything, he was being charged, on pain of losing her, to turn himself inside out.[2]

Mickey Sabbath does lose her, not because he rejects or violates her ultimatum, but because she has cancer and dies. The event plunges Sabbath into a long quest for the meaning of life and death, and his decision is to commit suicide. It is not the first time he has lost a loved one; he recalls the death of his brother, Morty, a bomber pilot shot down in World War II; his mother's consequent breakdown; and the disappearance of his wife Nikki, for whom he has long searched in vain. His second wife's battles with alcoholism are cause enough, also, to plunge Mickey into despair, though his innate energy—his *élan vital*, if you will—keeps him going, thanks also in large measure to his longstanding affair with Drenka. Their lust, wild and extreme in every way, and up to now unobstructed by any vows of chastity to their spouses or to each other, testifies to their vibrant middle life. That is why Drenka's ultimatum and then her death are so devastating to Sabbath. In addition, his mother's ghost seems to hover over him relentlessly, and then an old friend from his New York days, Lincoln Gelman, following years of depression, commits suicide.

After Drenka's death and a final break with his wife, Roseanne, Sabbath determines to follow Lincoln's example of a few days earlier and commit suicide, too. Informed by their mutual friend Norman Cowan of the impending funeral, Sabbath drives to New York. En route, he is haunted by his mother's ghost "at his side, in his mouth, ringing his skull, reminding him to extinguish his nonsensical life. . . . Nothing but death, death, and the dead, for three and a half hours."[3] In this frame of mind he drives on and contemplates suicide: "And this was the first time that he realized or admitted what he had to do. The problem that was his life was never to be solved. His wasn't the kind of life where there are aims that are clear and means that are clear and where it is possible to say, 'This is essential and that is not essential, this I will not do because I cannot endure it, and that I will do because I can endure it.' There was no unsnarling an existence whose waywardness constituted its only authority and provided its primary amusement."[4]

When Mickey arrives in New York, he stays with Norman and his wife, Michelle. He quickly engages in several spectacular sexual exploits and in other outrageous behavior. After Norman throws him out, Sabbath heads for the Jersey shore to arrange for his interment in the cemetery where several family members lie buried. He decides to walk into the Atlantic and drown. Finding the cemetery at last, he purchases a plot and a tombstone and orders his own appropriate, if outlandish, epitaph:

> Morris Sabbath
> "Mickey"
> Beloved Whoremonger, Seducer,
> Sodomist, Abuser of Women,
> Destroyer of Morals, Ensnarer of Youth,
> Uxoricide,
> Suicide,
> 1929–1994

Sabbath then heads for the ocean. On the way he finds the board-walk he knew as a kid, and then the house where his cousin Fischel Sabas ("Fish") once lived. Much to Sabbath's astonishment, one hundred year-old Fish still lives there. While reminiscing with Fish and listening to him say that "being alive is better than being dead,"[5] Sabbath discovers a box holding the remnants of his brother Morty's belongings. Among the items are the flag that draped his coffin, a red-white-and-blue yarmulka, and other items that cause an unsettling rush of memories. Placing the box in his car, Sabbath finds it impossible to commit suicide, now that he has made himself custodian of Morty's things. "I cannot walk into the waves and leave this stuff behind," he muses.[6] More to the point, perhaps, his musings prompt recollections of Drenka's last hours in the hospital and her recalling one of their most astounding sexual escapades: urinating on each other in a wild ecstacy of delight, in what Drenka conceived as their *rite de passage*. Their forbidden act made them feel that they had become truly one.[7]

Sabbath then returns to Drenka's grave site, not to masturbate this time but to commemorate their former ecstatic encounter and to urinate on her grave stone. There Drenka's son, Matthew, a police officer, discovers him in the act. Sabbath is certain that he will now be killed by the outraged young man or by his sidekick, who arrests him moments later. He is astonished, however, to find that they let him go. Frantically, he cries after the departing police cruiser: "But I'm going free! I've reveled in the revolting thing one time too many! And I'm going free! I'm a ghoul! I'm a ghoul! After causing all this pain, the ghoul is running free! *Matthew!*"[8] The police car drives off, leaving no one to kill Sabbath but himself: "And he couldn't do it. He could not fucking die. How could he leave? How could he go? Everything he hated was here."[9] Left thus, if Sabbath cannot "fucking die," will he instead die fucking—defying death in this way as long as he can? The reader will have to decide, for this is where the novel ends.

"A rake among scholars, a scholar among rakes" is what David Kepesh calls himself as he recounts his story to an unspecified listener. It is probably a woman, his current mistress, but certainly not Dr. Spielvogel imported from *Portnoy's Complaint* or any other psychotherapist. His story focuses mainly upon a Cuban-American beauty, Consuela Castillo, she of the beautiful breasts who was once his student and later his lover. Kepesh digresses from time to time to recount his affairs with others, such as another former student,

Carolyn Lyons, who later entered his life again during his affair with Consuela—and with almost disastrous results. This digression and others put the story of his obsession with Consuela into perspective. Throughout, Kepesh details and defends his hedonism, which has been abetted by his friend, the Irish poet George O'Hearn. Though still married and a father of grown children, O'Hearn not only eggs David on to ever greater sexual triumphs, but also almost rivals him in his own numerous amours. Their code seems to be summed up in the idea that "only when you fuck is everything that you dislike in life and everything by which you are defeated in life, purely, if momentarily, revenged. Only then are you most cleanly alive and most cleanly yourself."[10]

But immediately after articulating this idea in both its negative and positive aspects, Kepesh remembers death: "Sex is also the revenge on death." Death is important to remember, and in its context he recognizes that even sex is limited in its power. "But tell me," he asks his listener, "what power is greater?" For David Kepesh, nothing else seems to be. When his friend George suffers a severe stroke and dies soon after Kepesh visits him, David, witnessing his friend's last erotic gestures, begins to realize more fully than ever death's primacy. It further confronts him when, after a lapse of six years, he receives a desperate call from Consuela, who now is afflicted from what she fears may be a fatal cancer of the breast.

In some deaths "A terrible beauty is born," as Yeats wrote, but David Kepesh has no such thoughts. For him, it is the supreme terror, however different it was for Mickey Sabbath. Roth writes an exquisite, non-salacious pornography of sex, as in his description of the way Consuela has an orgasm,[11] but he is equally adept in the pornography of death. His account of George O'Hearn's dying is full testimony to his ability to do so. But in *The Dying Animal*, unlike *Sabbath's Theater*, the confident assertiveness of life, the *élan vital* that keeps Mickey Sabbath finally from his planned suicide, is altogether absent. Whereas Mickey finds in becoming the caretaker of his brother's remains a reason to go on living, Kepesh decides that in spite of everything, he must go to Consuela in her anguish over her impending mastectomy, even as his interlocutor warns that "if you go, you're finished."

His interlocutor may be reflecting, wittingly or not, O'Hearn's earlier advice to Kepesh not to get entangled again in any way whatsoever with Consuela. "George was right of course," Kepesh admits, "and only repeating to me what I know. He who forms a tie *is* lost, attachment *is* my enemy."[12] Realizing that, and in the face of his interlocutor's warning, why does Kepesh nevertheless feel compelled to go to Consuela? From Consuela's last anguished visit, he knows that sex is no longer an option where she is concerned. Is he then, by going to her in her extremis, acknowledging the power of death and, in a way, capitulating to it at last? Is he "finished," as his interlocutor warns, and if so, how?

Kepesh may well be finished, done for in some way or other, though the novel ends in ambiguity. Clearly, Roth is not. He presents two contrasting attitudes towards eros and death through the characters of Mickey Sabbath and David Kepesh. While Sabbath at first wants to die to end his nonsensical life—as he briefly regards it—he finds he ultimately cannot commit suicide. His life force, his undiminished sexual drive—however influenced or qualified by what he hates—is too strong. Kepesh, on the other hand, has only his tawdry motivations to keep him going, and at the end of *The Dying Animal*, as the title suggests, they are not enough. There is an important distinction to be made, therefore, between the sexual encounters Kepesh seeks just for their own sake, and the drive that impels Sabbath. One character is a decadent pleasure seeker; the other proves to be a vital human being who disdains everything that Kepesh and others of his class, such as Norman Cowan, regard as important, including a position in the New York society of culture. Sabbath is by no means culturally deprived: he knows his *King Lear*, for example, and can speak the moving lines from the reconciliation scene in act 4—even as he panhandles his way through the subway with an envelope full of stolen hundred dollar bills in his coat pocket. He is one of Roth's most outlandish characters in almost every respect. But he has the redeeming attribute of energy fueled by eroticism, which defies death, against which Kepesh's hedonism pales in comparison and appears futile against the specter of death. Both characters must confront the death of a beloved paramour. But whereas Drenka's death, and the deaths of other loved ones, may plunge Sabbath into despair, he is able to recover and go on. Consuela's imminent demise threatens to finish off Kepesh, and it probably will. Unlike Sabbath, he lacks the vital energy to keep going, certainly as he has gone up to that moment. Eros successfully defies death in *Sabbath's Theater*, but it remains still the overwhelming threat in *The Dying Animal*.

Notes

1. Philip Roth, *Deception: A Novel* (New York: Simon and Schuster, 1990), 190.
2. Philip Roth, *Sabbath's Theater* (Boston: Houghton Mifflin, 1995), 3.
3. Ibid., 106.
4. Ibid., 108–9.
5. Ibid., 395.
6. Ibid., 415.
7. Ibid., 428.
8. Ibid., 451.
9. Ibid.
10. Philip Roth, *The Dying Animal* (Boston: Houghton Mifflin Company, 2001), 69.
11. Ibid., 103.
12. Ibid., 100.

Bibliography

Abrams, M. H. *A Glossary of Literary Terms.* 5th edition. New York: Holt, Rinehart and Winston, 1988.

Alexander, Edward. "Philip Roth at Century's End." Review of *American Pastoral,* by Philip Roth. *New England Review* 20, no. 2 (Spring 1999): 183–90.

Alter, Robert. "The Spritzer." Review of *Operation Shylock: A Confession,* by Philip Roth. *New Republic,* April 5, 1993, 32–33.

Bakhtin, M. M. "Discourse in the Novel." In *The Dialogic Imagination: Four Essays,* translated by Caryl Emerson and Michael Holquist, edited by Michael Holquist, 259–422. Austin: University of Texas Press, 1981.

Barack, Sylvia Fishman. Review of *American Pastoral,* by Philip Roth. *America,* August 30, 1997, 23–25.

Barkan, Elazar. *The Guilt of Nations: Restitution and Negotiating Historical Injustices.* New York: W. W. Norton, 2000.

Begley, Louis. "Roth Roars Again, Pitiless, Raging Against Age, Illness." *New York Observer,* May 14, 2001, 19.

Bellow, Saul. *The Adventures of Augie March.* New York: Viking, 1953.

———. *The Bellarosa Connection.* New York: Penguin Books, 1989.

———. *Ravelstein.* New York: Viking, 2000.

———. *Mr. Sammler's Planet.* New York: Viking, 1970.

———. "The Swamp of Prosperity." Review of *Goodbye, Columbus,* by Philip Roth. *Commentary* 28 (July 1959): 77.

Bernstein, André Michael. "Getting the American People Right." *Times Literary Supplement* 5069 (2000): 21.

Bettleheim, Bruno. *Symbolic Wounds: Puberty Rites and the Envious Male.* Glencoe, IL: Free Press, 1954.

Bignardi, Irene. "Che vergogna L'America." Translated by Jeffrey Wainwright. *La Republica,* June 25, 2000, 37.

Bloom, Claire. *Leaving a Doll's House: A Memoir.* Boston: Little, Brown, 1996.

Bloom, Harold. "Operation Roth." Review of *Operation Shylock: A Confession,* by Philip Roth. *New York Review of Books,* April 22, 1993, 45.

Booth, Wayne. *The Rhetoric of Fiction.* Chicago: University of Chicago Press, 1961.

Bottum, J. "The Dying Novel: After Three Good Novels, Philip Roth Reverts to His Old Sex-Obsessions." *The Weekly Standard,* July 2, 2001, 39.

Boyers, Robert. Review of *American Pastoral,* by Philip Roth. *The New Republic,* July 7, 1977, 36–42.

Brodkin, Karen. *How Jews Became White Folks and What that Says about Race in America.* New Brunswick, NJ: Rutgers University Press, 1994.

Broyard, Anatole. *Kafka Was the Rage: A Greenwich Village Memoir.* New York: Carol Southern Books, 1990.

Brubach, Holly. "Advice to the Glovelorn." *The New York Times Magazine,* July 27, 1997, 35.

Brzezinski, Steve. Review of *American Pastoral,* by Philip Roth. *Antioch Review* 56, no. 2 (Spring 1998): 232.

Butler, Judith. "Passing, Queering: Nella Larsen's Psychoanalytic Challenge." In *Female Subjects in Black and White: Race, Psychoanalysis, Feminism,* edited by Elizabeth Abel, Barbara Christian, and Helene Moglen, 266–84. Berkeley and Los Angeles: University of California Press, 1997.

Chambers, Andrea. "Philip Roth: Portnoy's Creator Would Like It Known: His Books Are Novels not Confessionals." *People Weekly,* December 19, 1983, 98.

Changnon, Greg. "Roth Explores Identity, Perception, and Human Nature." *Atlanta Journal-Constitution,* February 24, 2002, 5D.

Cohen, Mitchell. "In Defense of Shaatnez: A Politics for Jews in a Multicultural America." In *Insider/Outsider: American Jews and Multiculturalism,* ed. David Biale, Michael Galchinsky, and Susan Heschel. Berkeley and Los Angeles: University of California Press, 1998.

Cooper, Alan. *Philip Roth and the Jews.* Albany: State University of New York Press, 1996.

Cooper, Peter. *Philip Roth.* Scribner's Writers Series. New York: Charles Scribner's Sons, 1991.

Dawidowicz, Lucy S. *On Equal Terms: Jews in America, 1881–1981.* New York: Holt, Rinehart and Winston, 1982.

Denby, David. "The Gripes of Roth." Review of *The Facts: A Novelist's Autobiography,* by Philip Roth. *The New Republic,* November 21, 1988, 37.

Derrida, Jacques. *Of Grammatology.* Translated by Gayatri Spivak. Baltimore: Johns Hopkins University Press, 1976.

Didion, Joan. *Political Fictions.* New York: Alfred A. Knopf, 2001.

Dobson, Melissa A. "Broyard." In *The Scribner Encyclopedia of American Lives: Notable Americans who Died between 1986 and 1990,* Vol. 2., 134–35. New York: Charles Scribner's Sons, 1999.

Doctorow, E. L. *City of God.* New York: Random House, 2000.

———. *Lives of the Poets: Six Stories and a Novella.* New York: Random House, 1984.

———. *Ragtime.* New York: Random House, 1975.

———. *World's Fair.* New York: Random House, 1985.

Dodd, Philip. "History or Fiction: Balancing Contemporary Autobiography's Claims." *Mosaic* 20 (1987): 65.

Eakin, Paul John. *Fictions in Autobiography: Studies in the Art of Self-Invention.* Princeton: Princeton University Press, 1985.

———. *How Our Lives Become Stories: Making Selves.* Ithaca: Cornell University Press, 1999.

Eiland, Howard. "Philip Roth: The Ambiguities of Desire." In *Critical Essays on Philip Roth*, edited by Sanford Pinsker, 255–65. Boston: G. K. Hall, 1982.

Fein, Esther B. "'Believe Me,' Says Roth with a Straight Face." *New York Times*, March 9, 1993, B1–B2.

Feldstein, Richard. *Political Correctness: A Response from the Cultural Left*. Minneapolis: University of Minnesota Press, 1997.

Fiedler, Leslie. "The Image of Newark and the Indignities of Love: Notes on Philip Roth." Review of *Goodbye, Columbus*, by Philip Roth. *Midstream* 5 (Summer 1959): 96–99.

Finkielkraut, Alan. "The Ghosts of Roth." *Esquire* (September 1981): 94. Reprinted in *Conversations with Philip Roth*, edited by George Searles, 121–22. Jackson: University of Mississippi Press, 1992.

Finney, Brian. "Roth's Counterlife: Destabilizing *The Facts*." *Biography* 16 (1993): 372, 378.

Fleishman, Avrom. *Figures of Autobiography: The Language of Self-Writing in Victorian and Modern England*. Berkeley and Los Angeles: University of California Press, 1983.

Friend, Tad. "Philip Roth's Newest Fictional Character Unmasks Himself." *The New Yorker*, May 26, 1997, 29–30.

Furman, Andrew. *Israel Through the Jewish-American Imagination*. New York: State University of New York Press, 1997.

Garber, Marjorie. "Moniker." In *Our Monica, Ourselves: The Clinton Affair and the National Interest*, edited by Lauren Berlant and Lisa Duggan, 175–202. New York: New York University Press, 2001.

Garza, Hedda. *African Americans & Jewish Americans: A History of Struggle*. New York: Franklin Watts, 1995.

Gates, Henry Louis, Jr. "The Uses of Anti-Semitism, with Memoirs of an Anti-Anti-Semite." In *Blacks and Jews: Alliances and Arguments*, edited by Paul Berman, 217–28. New York: Delacorte Press, 1994.

———. "White Like Me." *New Yorker*, June 17, 1996, 66–81.

Gilroy, Paul. *Against Race: Imagining Political Culture Beyond the Color Line*. Cambridge, MA: Harvard University Press, 2000.

Gitlin, Todd. "Weather Girl." Review of *American Pastoral*, by Philip Roth. *The Nation*, May 12, 1997, 63–64.

Gollaher, David. *Circumcision: A History of the World's Most Controversial Surgery*. New York: Basic Books, 2000.

Gordon, Ken. "The Zuckerman Books." *Salon.com*, March 26, 2002, http://archive.salon.com/ent/masterpiece/2002/03/26/zuckerman/.

Goren, Arthur. "A 'Golden Decade' for American Jews: 1954–1965." In *American Jewish Life, 1920–1990*, edited by Jeffrey S. Gurock, 17–35. New York: Routledge, 1998.

Gray, Paul. "Philip Roth: Novelist." *Time*, July 9, 2001, 50.

Greenberg, Cheryl. "Pluralism and its Discontents: The Case of Blacks and Jews." In *Insider/Outsider: American Jews and Multiculturalism*, ed. David Biale, Michael

Galchinsky, and Susan Heschel. Berkeley and Los Angeles: University of California Press, 1998.

Greenstein, Michael. "Ozick, Roth, and Postmodernism." *Studies in American Jewish Literature* 10 (1991): 60–62.

Guttmann, Allen. "Philip Roth and the Rabbis." In *Philip Roth*, edited by Harold Bloom, 53–62. New York: Chelsea House Publishers, 1986.

Halio, Jay. "The Human Stain." *Shofar: An Interdisciplinary Journal of Jewish Studies* 20, no. 1 (2001): 173–75.

———. *Philip Roth Revisited*. New York: Twayne, 1992.

Halkin, Hillel. "How to Read Philip Roth." *Commentary* (February 1994): 43–48.

Hardwick, Elizabeth. "Paradise Lost." Review of *American Pastoral*, by Philip Roth. *New York Review of Books*, June 12, 1997, 12–14.

Harris, Martyn. "Damsels in Distress." Review of *Deception*, by Philip Roth. *New Statesman and Society* 3, no. 7 (September 7, 1990): 42.

Heller, Zoe. "The Ghost Rutter." *The New Republic*, May 21, 2001, 39–42.

Higgin, Graham. "The Gripes of Roth." *Guardian* (London), May 27, 2000, 10.

Hollinger, David. *Science, Jews, and Secular Culture*. Princeton: Princeton University Press, 1996.

Howe, Irving. "Philip Roth Reconsidered." *Commentary* (December 1972): 69–77. Reprinted in *Critical Essays on Philip Roth*, edited by Sanford Pinsker, 229–44. Boston: G. K. Hall, 1982. Also reprinted in *Philip Roth*, edited by Harold Bloom. New York: Chelsea House Publishers, 1986.

———. "The Suburbs of Babylon." *New Republic*, June 15, 1959, 17.

Hungerford, Amy. *The Holocaust of Texts: Genocide, Literature, and Personification*. Chicago: University of Chicago Press, 2003.

Iannone, Carol. Review of *American Pastoral*, by Philip Roth. *Commentary* (August 1997): 55–59.

Iser, Wolfgang. "The Reading Process: A Phenomenological Approach." In *Reader-Response Criticism: From Formalism to Post-Structuralism*, edited by Jane Tompkins, 50–69. Baltimore: Johns Hopkins University Press, 1980.

Jay, Paul. *Being in the Text: Self-Representation from Wordsworth to Roland Barthes*. Ithaca: Cornell University Press, 1984.

Johnson, Brian D. "Intimate Affairs." Review of *Deception*, by Philip Roth. *Maclean's*, April 30, 1990, 66–67. Reprinted in Searles, *Conversations with Philip Roth*, 254. Jackson: University of Mississippi Press, 1992.

Jones, Judith Paterson, and Guinevera A. Nance. *Philip Roth*. New York: Frederick Ungar, 1981.

Jones, Malcolm, Jr. "A Tale of Exes and Ohs." Review of *Leaving a Doll's House*, by Claire Bloom. *Newsweek*, September 30, 1996, 78.

Kakutani, Michiko. "A Postwar Paradise Shattered From Within." *New York Times*, April 15, 1997, C11.

———. "Roth within a Roth within a Roth: Where's Roth?" Review of *Operation Shylock: A Confession*, by Philip Roth. *New York Times*, March 4, 1993, 4C.

Kamenetz, Rodger. "'The Hocker, Misnomer . . . Love/Dad': Philip Roth's *Patrimony*." *Southern Review* 27 (1991): 942.

Kaplan, Brett Ashley. Phone conversation with Rob Seibert, January 28, 2003.

Kauvar, Elaine M. "An Interview with Cynthia Ozick." *Contemporary Literature* 34, no. 3 (1993): 373.

———. "This Doubly Reflected Communication: Philip Roth's 'Authobiographies.'" *Contemporary Literature* 36 (1995): 412–46.

Kazin, Alfred. "The Jew as Modern Writer." *Commentary* (April 1966): 37–41.

———. "The Vanity of Human Wishes." *Reporter*, August 16, 1962, 54.

Kelly, Robert. "Are You Now or Have You Ever Been . . ." Review of *I Married a Communist*, by Philip Roth. *New York Times Book Review*, October 11, 1998, 6–7.

Kemp, Peter. "American Booty." *Sunday Times* (London), May 14, 2000.

———. "Once Upon a Time in America." *Sunday Times* (London), June 1, 1997.

Klinghoffer, David. "Roth for Roth's Sake." *National Review* 42 (August 20, 1990): 48–50.

Kremer, S. Lillian. "Post-alienation: Recent Directions in Jewish-American Literature." *Contemporary Literature* 34, no. 3 (Fall 1993): 571–91.

Krieger, Murray. "The Tragic Vision Twenty Years After." In *Tragedy: Vision and Form*, edited by Robert W. Corrigan, 42–46. New York: Harper & Row, 1981.

Larner, Jeremy. "The Conversion of the Jews." In *Critical Essays on Philip Roth*, edited by Sanford Pinsker, 27–32. Boston: G. K. Hall, 1982.

Leavitt, David. "Looking Back on the World of Tomorrow." Review of *World's Fair*, by E. L. Doctorow. *New York Times Book Review*, November 10, 1985, 3, 25.

Lee, Hermione. "The Art of Fiction LXXXIV: Philip Roth." *Conversations with Philip Roth*, ed. George J. Searles, 162–87. Jackson: University Press of Mississippi, 1992.

———. "Kiss and Tell." Review of *Deception*, by Philip Roth. *New Republic*, April 30, 1990, 39–42.

———. "Life *Is* and': Philip Roth in 1990." *The Independent*, 2 September 1990. Reprinted in *Conversations with Philip Roth*, ed. George J. Searles, 259–266. Jackson: University Press of Mississippi, 1992.

Leonard, John. "Bedtime for Bolsheviks." Review of *I Married a Communist*, by Philip Roth. *The Nation*, November 16, 1998, 28–29.

———. "A Child of the Age." *The New York Review of Books* 47, no. 10 (2000): 6–10.

Lerner, Michael. "The Jews and the 60s: Philip Roth Still Doesn't Get It." *Tikkun* 12, no. 3 (1997): 13–16.

Levitt, Cyril, Scott Davies, and Neil McLaughlin, eds. *Mistaken Identities: The Second Wave of Controversy over "Political Correctness."* New York: Peter Lang, 1999.

Levy, Ellen. "Is Zuckerman Dead? Countertexts in Philip Roth's *The Counterlife*." *Caliban* 29 (1992): 126–27.

Lezard, Nicholas, "Nicholas Lezard Relishes an Angry Indictment of Dumb America." *Guardian* (London), March 17, 2001, 11.

Lida, David. "Philip Roth Talks—a Little: 'I'm not Quite the Schmuck Zuckerman Is,'" *Vogue* (September 1988): 434.

Lodge, David. "Sick with Desire." *The New York Review of Books*, July 5, 2001: 28–32.

Lukács, Georg. "The Metaphysics of Tragedy." In *Tragedy: Vision and Form*, edited by Robert W. Corrigan, 76–93. New York: Harper & Row, 1981.

Lundegaard, Erik. "Roth's Back, With More Complaints." *The Seattle Times Book Section*, May 11, 1997, M3.

Lyons, Bonnie. "Lies, Secrets, Truthtelling and Imagination in *The Human Stain.*" *Studies in American Jewish Literature* 20 (2001): 89–94.

Matchan, Linda. "Philip Roth Faces 'The Facts.'" In *Conversations with Philip Roth*, edited by George J. Searles, 237–41. Jackson: University Press of Mississippi, 1992.

McElya, Micki. "Trashing the Presidency: Race, Class, and the Clinton/Lewinsky Affair." In *Our Monica, Ourselves: The Clinton Affair and the National Interest*, edited by Lauren Berlant and Lisa Duggan, 156–74. New York: New York University Press, 2001.

McHale, Brian. *Postmodernist Fiction.* New York: Routledge, 1987.

Medwick, Cathleen. "A Meeting of Hearts and Minds." In *Conversations with Philip Roth*, edited by George J. Searles, 131–38. Jackson: University Press of Mississippi, 1992.

Menand, Louis. "The Irony and the Ecstasy: Philip Roth and the Jewish Atlantis." Review of *American Pastoral* by Philip Roth. *The New Yorker*, May 19, 1997, 88, 90–94.

Mitgang, Herbert. "Finding the Right Voice." Review of *Lives of the Poets: Six Stories and a Novella*, by E. L. Doctorow. *New York Times Book Review*, November 11, 1984, 36.

Moore, Deborah Dash. "At Home in America." In *The American Jewish Experience*, edited by Jonathan Sarna, 260–68. New York: Holmes & Meier, 1986.

Moore, Lorrie. "The Wrath of Athena." *New York Times*, May 7, 2000, 7.

Morrison, Toni. *The New Yorker*, October 5, 1998, 32.

Neuhoff, Eric. "Le poison de l'hypocrisie." *Le Figaro*, September 19, 2002.

O'Donnell, Patrick. "'None other': The Subject of Roth's *My Life as a Man.*" In *Reading Philip Roth*, edited by Asher Z. Milbauer and Donald G. Watson, 144–59. New York: St. Martin's, 1988.

One America in the 21st Century: Forging a New Future. Washington, DC: U.S. Government Printing Office, 1998.

Ozick, Cynthia. *Art and Ardor.* New York: Knopf, 1983.

Parini, Jay. "The Fictional Campus: Sex, Power, and Despair." *The Chronicle of Higher Education*, September 22, 2000, B12–13, B13.

Parrish, Timothy L. "Imagining Jews in Philip Roth's *Operation Shylock.*" *Contemporary Literature* 40, no. 4 (Winter 1999): 577–604.

Pinsker, Sanford. *The Comedy That "Hoits": An Essay on the Fiction of Philip Roth.* Columbia: University of Missouri Press, 1975.

———, ed. *Critical Essays on Philip Roth.* Boston: G. K. Hall, 1982.

———. "Jewish-American Literature's Lost-and-Found Department: How Philip Roth and Cynthia Ozick Reimagine Their Significant Dead." *Modern Fiction Studies* 35, no. 2 (Summer 1989): 223–35.

———. "Roth Feels Bad About Being Bad: So What Else Is New?" http://www.forward.com/issues/2001/01/05.25/arts3.html.

Podhoretz, Norman. "My Negro Problem—and Ours." In *Blacks and Jews: Alliances and Arguments*, edited by Paul Berman, 76–96. New York: Delacorte Press, 1994.

Posnock, Ross. "Purity and Danger: On Philip Roth." *Raritan: A Quarterly Review* 21, no. 2 (2001): 85–101.

Poulet, Georges. "Phenomenology of Reading." *New Literary History* 1, no. 1 (October 1969), 53–68.

Powers, Elizabeth. Review of *American Pastoral,* by Philip Roth. *World Literature Today* 72, no. 1 (Winter 1998): 136.

Remondino, P. C. *History of Circumcision from the Earliest Times to the Present.* Philadelphia: F. A. Davis, 1891.

Rich, Frank. "The Day Before Tuesday." *New York Times,* September 15, 2001, A23.

Riffaterre, Michael. *Fictional Truth.* Baltimore: Johns Hopkins University Press, 1990.

Rosenfeld, Alvin. "Promised Land(s): Zion, America, and American Jewish Writers." *Jewish Social Studies* 3, no. 3 (Spring/Summer 1997): 111–31.

Roth, Philip. *The Anatomy Lesson.* New York: Farrar Straus Giroux, 1983.

———. *American Pastoral.* Boston: Houghton Mifflin, 1997.

———. "Author's Note." In *Reading Myself and Others,* ix–x. New York: Penguin, 1985.

———. "A Bit of Jewish Mischief." *New York Times Book Review* (March 7, 1993): 1.

———. *The Breast.* New York: Holt, Rinehart and Winston, 1972; New York: Vintage, 1994).

———. "Coronation on Channel Two." *New Republic* (September 23, 1957): 21.

———. *The Counterlife.* New York: Farrar Straus Giroux, 1986.

———. *Deception: A Novel.* New York: Simon and Schuster, 1990.

———. "Document Dated July 27, 1969." In *Reading Myself and Others.* expanded edition, 23–31. New York: Penguin, 1985.

———. *The Dying Animal.* Boston: Houghton Mifflin Company, 2001.

———. "Eli, the Fanatic." In *Goodbye, Columbus and Five Short Stories.* 1959. Reprint, Boston: Houghton Mifflin, 1989.

———. *The Facts: A Novelist's Autobiography.* New York: Farrar, Straus, and Giroux, 1988.

———. *The Ghost Writer.* New York: Farrar, Straus, and Giroux, 1979; Harmondsworth: Penguin, 1980.

———. "The Ghost Writer." In *Zuckerman Bound: A Trilogy and Epilogue,* 69. London: Penguin, 1980.

———. *Goodbye, Columbus and Five Short Stories.* Boston: Houghton Mifflin, 1959.

———. *The Human Stain.* Boston: Houghton Mifflin, 2000.

———. " 'I Always Wanted You to Admire My Fasting'; or, Looking at Kafka." In *Reading Myself and Others,* 247–70. New York: Farrar, Straus, and Giroux, 1975.

———. "Imagining Jews." In *Reading Myself and Others,* 274.

———. *I Married a Communist.* Boston: Houghton Mifflin, 1998.

———. "In Response to Those Who Have Asked Me: 'How Did You Come to Write That Book, Anyway?' " In *Reading Myself and Others,* 35.

———. "Interview with *Le Nouvel Observateur.*" 1981, with Alain Finkielkraut. In *Reading Myself and Others,* 117.

———. "Interview with *The London Sunday Times.*" 1984, with Ian Hamilton. In *Reading Myself and Others.*

———. "Interview with *The Paris Review.*" 1984, with Hermione Lee, *Reading Myself and Others.*

———. "Juice or Gravy?: How I Met My Fate in a Cafeteria." *New York Times Book Review,* September 18, 1994, 22.

———. "Le 11 Septembre a entrainé un insupportable narcissime national." Interview by Jean-Louis Turlin. *Le Figaro* (October 3, 2002): n.p.

———. *Letting Go.* New York: Random House, 1962.

———. *My Life as a Man.* New York: Holt, Rinehart and Winston, 1974.

———. *Operation Shylock: A Confession.* New York: Simon and Schuster, 1993.

———. *Patrimony: A True Story.* New York: Simon and Schuster, 1991.

———. *Portnoy's Complaint.* New York: Random House, 1969.

———. *The Professor of Desire.* New York: Farrar, Straus, and Giroux, 1977.

———. *Reading Myself and Others.* New York: Farrar, Straus, and Giroux, 1975; London: Vintage, 2001.

———. *Sabbath's Theater.* Boston: Houghton Mifflin, 1995.

———. "This Butcher, Imagination." *New York Times Book Review,* February 14, 1988, 2–3.

———. "Two-Faced (Early Draft of *Operation Shylock*)." March 25, 1990, marked as "Draft 1."86a.

———. *When She Was Good.* New York: Random House, 1967.

———. "Writing About Jews." In *Reading Myself and Others,* expanded edition, ix–x. New York: Penguin, 1985.

———. "Writing American Fiction." In *Reading Myself and Others,* expanded edition, ix–x. New York: Penguin, 1985.

———. *Zuckerman Bound: A Trilogy and Epilogue.* New York: Farrar, Straus, and Giroux, 1985.

———. "Zuckerman's Alter Brain." Interview by Charles McGrath. *New York Times,* May 7, 2000, 8.

Rothstein, Mervyn. "Philip Roth and the World of 'What If.'" In *Conversations with Philip Roth,* edited by George J. Searles, 198–201. Jackson: University Press of Mississippi, 1992.

Rubin-Dorsky, Jeffrey. "Honor Thy Father." Review of *Patrimony,* by Philip Roth. *Raritan* 11, no. 2 (Spring 1992): 137–45.

Rutten, Tim. "A Novel End to a Love Affair." *Los Angeles Times Calendar,* July 19, 2003, E1, E23.

Safer, Elaine B. "Tragedy and Farce in Roth's *The Human Stain.*" *Critique* 43, no. 3 (Spring 2002): 211–27, 212.

Schiller, Mayer. Review of *American Pastoral,* by Philip Roth. *National Review,* June 16, 1997, 53–54.

Searles, George J., ed. *Conversations with Philip Roth.* Jackson: University Press of Mississippi, 1992.

Sewall, Richard B. "The Vision of Tragedy." In *Tragedy: Vision and Form,* edited by Robert W. Corrigan, 47–51. New York: Harper & Row, 1981.

Shechner, Mark. *After the Revolution: Studies in the Contemporary Jewish American Imagination.* Bloomington: Indiana University Press, 1987.

———. "Philip Roth." In *Critical Essays on Philip Roth,* edited by Sanford Pinsker. Boston: G. K. Hall, 1982.

———. "Zuckerman's Travels." *American Literary History* 1, no. 1 (Spring 1989): 219–30.

Sheppard, R. Z. " 'This Obsessive Reinvention of the Real': Speculative Narrative in Philip Roth's *The Counterlife.*" *Modern Fiction Studies* 37 (1991): 197–215.

———. "When She Was Bad." Review of *American Pastoral,* by Philip Roth. *Time* (April 28, 1997): 74.

Shostak, Debra. "The Diaspora Jew and the 'Instinct for Impersonation': Philip Roth's *Operation Shylock.*" *Contemporary Literature* 38, no. 4 (1997): 726–54.

Siegel, Ben. Introduction to *Critical Essays on E. L. Doctorow,* edited by Ben Siegel, 1–51. New York: G. K. Hall, 2000.

Smith, Paul. *Discerning the Subject.* Minneapolis: University of Minnesota Press, 1988.

Solotaroff, Theodore. "Philip Roth: A Personal View." In *Philip Roth,* edited by Harold Bloom, 35–51. New York: Chelsea, 1986.

Stegner, Wallace. *On Teaching and Writing Fiction.* Edited by Lynn Stegner. New York: Penguin Books, 2000.

Steiner, Wendy. Review of *Deception,* by Philip Roth. *Times Literary Supplement,* August 31–September 6, 1990, 917.

———. *The Scandal of Pleasure.* Chicago: University of Chicago Press, 1995.

Stelzig, Eugene L. *Hermann Hesse's Fictions of the Self: Autobiography and the Confessional Imagination.* Princeton: Princeton University Press, 1988.

Strawson, Galen. "Self-invention on an Epic Scale." *Financial Times* (London), June 10, 2000, 4.

Sutcliffe, William. "Monica and the Vacuum." *Independent* (London), June 11, 2000, 47.

Taylor, Charles. "Powells.com Book Review-a-Day from Salon.com. http://www.Powells.com/review/2001_06_01.

Thomas, D. M. "Face to Face with His Double." Review of *Operation Shylock: A Confession,* by Philip Roth. *New York Times Book Review,* March 7, 1993, 1.

Tierney, William G. "Interpreting Academic Identities: Reality and Fiction on Campus." *Journal of Higher Education* 73, no. 1 (January/February 2002): 168–69.

U.S. Department of Education. "Press Briefing by Presidential Advisory Board on Race." Press Release, June 14, 1997, http://www.ed.gov/PressReleases/06-1997/970614a.html

U.S. National Archives and Records Administration. "Pathways to One America In The 21st Century: Promising Practices for Racial Reconciliation." http://clinton3.nara.gov/Initiatives/OneAmerica/pirsummary.html

Updike, John. "Recruiting Raw Nerves." Review of *Operation Shylock: A Confession,* by Philip Roth. *New Yorker,* March 15, 1993, 110.

Wade, Stephen. *The Imagination in Transit.* Sheffield, England: Sheffield Academic Press, 1996.

———. *Jewish American Literature Since 1945.* Edinburgh: Edinburgh University Press, 1999.

Walker, Rebecca. *Black, White, and Jewish: Autobiography of a Shifting Self.* New York: Riverhead Books, 2001.

Wallace, James D. "'This Nation of Narrators': Transgression, Revenge and Desire in *Zuckerman Bound.*" *Modern Language Studies* 21, no. 3 (1991): 17–34.

West, Nathanael. *Miss Lonelyhearts.* 1933. Reprint. New York: New Directions, 1969.

White, Edmund. "The Hearts of Men: Who Knows What Shadows Lurk. . . ." *Vogue,* January 1987, 94.

White, Hayden. "The Value of Narrativity in the Representation of Reality." In *On Narrative,* edited by W. J. T. Mitchell, 1–23. Chicago: University of Chicago Press, 1981.

Williams, Morris. "Roth Saga Disdains Political Correctness." *Daily Yomiuri* (Tokyo), November 25, 2001, 20.

Wood, Michael. "The Trouble with Swede Levov." Review of *American Pastoral,* by Philip Roth. *New York Times Book Review,* April 20, 1997, 8.

Zinn, Howard. *A People's History of the United States.* New York: Harper & Row, 1980.

Žižek, Slavoj. *The Metastases of Enjoyment: Six Essays on Woman and Causality.* New York: Verso, 1994.

Contributors

MARSHALL BRUCE GENTRY is Professor of English at Georgia College & State University, where he edits the *Flannery O'Connor Review*. He has published articles on Jewish-American literature in *The South Carolina Review, South Atlantic Review, Contemporary Literature,* and *Kansas Quarterly.* He is the author of *Flannery O'Connor's Religion of the Grotesque* and co-editor of *Conversations with Raymond Carver.*

ELLEN GERSTLE teaches in the Humanities Program at Fairleigh Dickinson University. She has conducted writing workshops for Holocaust survivors at Drew University's Center for Holocaust/Genocide Studies. Her dissertation was "Constructing Truth and Reality: An Examination of Philip Roth's Written and Unwritten Worlds." She has also written on Roth for the *New Jersey Encyclopedia, Profils Americain,* and *Studies in American Jewish Literature.*

ANDREW GORDON is Associate Professor of English and Director of the Institute for the Psychological Study of the Arts at the University of Florida. He teaches contemporary American fiction, Jewish-American fiction, science fiction, and film. He is the author of *An American Dreamer: A Psychoanalytic Study of the Fiction of Norman Mailer,* and co-author of *Screen Saviors: Hollywood Fictions of Whiteness.*

JAY L. HALIO is Professor Emeritus of English at the University of Delaware. He is the editor of the *Dictionary of Literary Biography: British Novelists Since 1960* and the author of *Philip Roth Revisited.* A noted Shakespearean scholar, he has edited *Shakespeare's "Romeo and Juliet": Texts, Contexts, and Interpretations* and new editions of, among others, *King Lear* and *The Merchant of Venice.* Together with Ben Siegel, he has edited two volumes of essays in honor of the late Melvin J. Friedman.

BRETT ASHLEY KAPLAN received her Ph.D. from the Rhetoric Department at Berkeley and is currently an Assistant Professor in the

Program in Comparative and World Literature at the University of Illinois, Urbana-Champaign. She is finishing a book, *Unwanted Beauty: Aesthetic Pleasure in Holocaust Representation,* which tackles the question of aesthetics in Holocaust art and literature. She has published articles in the *Journal of Modern Jewish Studies, Comparative Literature Studies, International Studies in Philosophy,* and *Comparative Literature.*

BONNIE LYONS is Professor of English at the University of Texas at San Antonio. She is the author of *Henry Roth: The Man and His Work,* and co-editor of *Passion and Craft: Conversations with Notable Writers.* She has also published two books of poetry, *Hineni* and *In Other Words* (which consists of forty monologues spoken by different women in the Jewish Scriptures). Her articles, book chapters, and interviews have appeared in such journals as *The Paris Review* and *Contemporary Literature.*

JAMES M. MELLARD is Presidential Professor Emeritus in English at Northern Illinois University. His most recent book is *Using Lacan, Reading Fiction,* and among his recent articles are "Oedipus Against Narcissus: Father, Mother, and the Dialectic of Desire in Fitzgerald's 'Winter Dreams'" (*Arizona Quarterly*) and "Lacan and the New Lacanians: Josephine Hart's *Damage,* Lacanian Tragedy, and the Ethics of *Jouissance*" (*PMLA*).

G. NEELAKANTAN is Professor of English at the Indian Institute of Technology, Kanpur. He is the author of *Saul Bellow and the Modern Waste Land* and has published a number of essays on Bellow, Roth, and other modern writers. He is currently at work on Jewish intertextualities.

TIMOTHY PARRISH is an Associate Professor of English at Texas Christian University. He is the author of *Walking Blues* and has published in such journals as *Texas Studies in Literature and Language, Contemporary Literature, Studies in American Jewish Fiction, Prospects, Shofar, Modern Fiction Studies, Clio,* and *Critique.* He is currently at work on a study of historiography and postmodern American fiction.

DEREK PARKER ROYAL is Assistant Professor of English at Texas A&M University-Commerce. He is currently completing a book on narrative and identity in Philip Roth's later fiction and editing a collection of new essays on Roth. He is founder and current president of the Philip Roth Society and the editor of its new journal, *Philip Roth Studies.*

DEBRA SHOSTAK is a Professor of English at the College of Wooster in Ohio, where she teaches American literature and film. She is the author of *Philip Roth: Countertexts, Counterlives* (2004). She has also published essays on Roth, Maxine Hong Kingston, and John Irving, as well as an interview with Tim O'Brien. Her work has appeared in such journals as *Contemporary Literature, Modern Fiction Studies, Twentieth Century Literature, Critique, Shofar,* and *Arizona Quarterly,* as well as in several edited collections.

BEN SIEGEL is Professor of English at California State Polytechnic University, Pomona. Among his previously published works (alone or in collaboration) are *Puritan Heritage: America's Roots in the Bible, Biography Past and Present, Isaac Bashevis Singer, The Controversial Sholem Asch, Traditions, Voices, and Dreams: The American Novel Since the 1960s,* and books on Nathanael West, E. L. Doctorow, and Saul Bellow. Together with Jay Halio, he has also edited *Daughters of Valor: Contemporary Jewish American Women Writers.*

MARGARET SMITH is an Associate Lecturer at Manchester Metropolitan University, in England, where she is completing her dissertation on "Double Talk, Counterlives: Jewish Identity in the Fiction of Philip Roth." She has published reviews in *American Literature Post 1945,* in the *Year's Work in English Studies* (2001 and 2002), and she is now at work on Roth essays for several other publications.

ALEXIS WILSON recently received her M.A. from the University of Maryland. Her areas of interest include twentieth-century American literature, contemporary Jewish writers, poetry, and gender studies. Her current research examines representations of Eastern Europe in the works of the newest generation of American Jewish writers

Index